Contents

Drafting Commercial Agreements

Stuart Cakebread

The Law Society

© The Law Society 2010

ISBN-13: 978-1-85328-604-9

Published in 2010 by the Law Society
113 Chancery Lane, London WC2A 1PL

Typeset by Columns Design Ltd, Reading
Printed by TJ International Ltd, Padstow, Cornwall

The paper used for the text pages of this book is FSC certified. FSC (the Forest Stewardship Council) is an international network to promote responsible management of the world's forests.

FSC
Mixed Sources
Product group from well-managed
forests and other controlled sources

Cert no. SGS-COC-2482
www.fsc.org
© 1996 Forest Stewardship Council

Preface

There are many comprehensive and august publications which provide the modern practitioner with a cornucopia of precedents and legal expositions. Moreover, large commercial firms will frequently have their own bank of tried and tested drafts and pro formas. It is not the intention of the author of this volume either to repeat or replace any of these. Rather it is my hope that the busy High Street, West End or provincial practitioner will find here a simple and straightforward source of material for his everyday work.

This is not a book on either commercial or contract law. Rather it is directed entirely at the draftsman, especially one who in a general commercial practice finds himself also having to find time to advise on disputes, see clients, instruct counsel and the myriad other day-to-day tasks which are the experience of those who form the backbone of our legal profession.

To assist the draftsman's task this volume endeavours first to provide some advice and tips on matters to bear in mind when drafting any commercial contract. Very often apparently arcane rules have about them more mystery than they deserve. The fact is that even the most experienced draftsman will sometimes fall prey to avoidable error and so **Chapter 1** will, I hope, provide a useful crib and check.

In drafting a contract it is sensible to have in mind how a court will approach the matter of construction if any dispute arises, and so in **Chapter 2** I have set out a brief overview of likely approaches.

Chapter 3 is intended to be a comprehensive guide to the important matter of limiting and avoiding liability for breach. This lies at the heart of the commercial draftsman's craft because the fact is that things do go wrong. Included in the chapter are model clauses which should be of broad application.

Chapter 4 addresses what, in many ways, is the most difficult of commercial clauses – the liquidated damages clause. I make no apology for the length of this chapter. There is no short cut to drafting an effective liquidated damages clause and a thorough understanding of how they must work is a prerequisite for success. I have included some model clauses but, as the text emphasises, any liquidated damages clause must be approached with great care and be moulded exactly to the context and factual matrix of the contract.

Chapter 5 is intended to provide a comprehensive guide to common commercial (or boilerplate) clauses, other than those of exclusion or limitation. Their purposes are explained where appropriate and the most important legal considerations noted. Model clauses are included, in some cases in several versions to reflect the variety of types of agreement for which they will be destined.

The remaining chapters set out precedents in a variety of specialist areas which, it is hoped, will reflect the most common needs of the readers of this volume. It would have been an impossible task to provide a comprehensive bank of precedents for every conceivable area of commercial practice. I have not included precedents for those areas of commercial activity which are either highly specialist and niche or which demand very high volumes of complex documentation. If the reader is involved in those areas there are excellent publications that will assist him. Rather, in selecting the areas to be covered in this manual I have tried to put myself in the shoes of the hard-pressed High Street, West End or provincial practitioner whose clients are no less demanding than those of his City counterparts, but whose needs are likely to be of a more everyday kind.

I have included a commentary for each chapter. It is to be emphasised that to provide an extensive exposition of the law in each case would have defeated the object of this volume to provide a readily usable and accessible handbook. The commentary is therefore no substitute for consulting a specialist volume on matters of complexity.

The precedents themselves are intended to be straightforward and easy to use. Most of them are complete contracts. My intention is that a usable draft can be produced readily and quickly without the need to wade through countless alternatives or options. To simplify matters, therefore, I have repeated much boilerplate in different precedents to avoid the need for too much cutting and pasting.

Most of the precedents are readily adaptable for a variety of purposes. In some cases I have included indicative examples of detailed schedules, usually drawn from true-life situations. In general I have followed a structure where as much detail as possible is put into schedules, thereby enabling the base contract to be flexible and readily adaptable. Commercial clauses may be added, subtracted or adapted as the draftsman considers appropriate.

Now, a note of caution. The use of a precedent is common practice these days. It has a great deal to commend it, as someone else will have remembered to include the boilerplate and avoid the obvious (or less obvious) non sequiturs, etc. However, every contract is unique and the draftsman who is charging for his work must accept ultimate responsibility for what he produces. The use of a precedent should not be mechanical but intelligent, and based upon a firm grasp of the underlying principles and law which may one day inform a court having to decide the competing merits of two parties who no longer see eye to eye (assuming they ever did).

It is customary and appropriate to express thanks to all those who have assisted and supported an author during his labours. First and foremost I would like to record the encouragement and patience (in equal measure) that I have been shown by my publishers, especially Simon Blackett. I have a suspicion that over the years he has become more than a little familiar with the unreliability of counsel's time estimates. I am indebted to David Parry of 3 Paper Buildings, my one-time 'phone-a-friend', whose pragmatic but precise approach to commercial contracts is, I hope, properly reflected in the advice proffered in chapters 1 and 2. I must also thank Camilla Chorfi of Selborne Chambers for permitting me to volunteer her to check everything for me with very good grace. Any errors that remain are most definitely mine and not hers.

Lastly, I would like to express a quiet word of thanks to all those colleagues, family and friends who have been there for me in what has been a difficult year. With, I hope, appropriate humility, and in the sure and certain knowledge that it is the last book he would ever have opened, I dedicate this book to the memory of my son Edward. *Requiscat in pace*.

Stuart Cakebread
Selborne Chambers
Summer 2010

Table of cases

Table of statutes

Table of statutory instruments

Table of European legislation

PART I

Basic rules, structure and construction of a commercial contract

1

Basic rules and structure

1.1 Introduction

The modern tendency in drafting contracts is a welcome trend towards simplicity, clarity of expression, brief clauses and sub-clauses, which are usually given numbers and sub-numbers.

Provided that simple language conveys concisely and precisely the intended meaning of the draftsman and the client, there is everything to be said for this. Too often, however, the language used is imprecise and sometimes sloppy and does not convey the intentions or purposes of the agreement or those of the client. Sometimes it has unintended effects which follow from poor grammar or poor law.

1.2 Using a precedent

Someone has probably spent hours checking and cross-checking the basics that are needed for a particular type of agreement. Avoid, if you can, archaic drafts. You should have your own checklist as well but on the whole a good precedent will have addressed this. However, the golden rule is that a precedent is not a draft of the agreement you are being called upon to record or create. It is a guide only.

1.3 Using the form of a deed as a template

Very often in the contemporary commercial world the draftsman's most frequent task is to be asked to produce 'terms and conditions' rather than a contract in conventional form.

Where a traditional contract is required, one drafted following the form of a deed does produce a document whose shape at least is readily recognisable and which can clarify the thought process so as to avoid confusion between, for example, defining and operative provisions. It should also ensure that the basic structure is correct. There is, of course, no need to use archaisms such as 'whereas' or 'witnesseth'.

1.4   The traditional parts of a deed or contract

Regardless of whether the Latin names are attributed to the various parts of a deed, a deed generally consists of five parts:

(a) the date;
(b) the parties;
(c) the recitals;
(d) the operative parts; and
(e) the signatures or seals.

1.5   The defining parts of the contract

1.5.1   Date of the agreement

First, an agreement and a deed 'speak' from the date appearing on them – the document is effective according to its terms from the date appearing in it, usually at the beginning.

Documents do *not* speak from the date upon which they were signed or any other date, if different, from the date appearing at their head or foot.

Second, this does not mean that an agreement cannot contain a date other than the date upon which it takes effect. For example, a leasing agreement may state that the lease term runs for three years from 1 January 2007 but the agreement is made on 31 March 2008. That does not affect the operation of the rule that a deed or agreement is operative from the date appearing at its head or foot. The date of commencement of a term as inserted in an agreement is simply part of the definition of the period of that term.

Third, an agreement should almost never be backdated as this can invalidate the whole agreement and can, in some circumstances, amount to an offence under the Theft or Forgery Acts or even a conspiracy to defraud. The basic point is that the date of the agreement is the date that the parties are stating it was made and from when either one or both of them owed obligations. If, in fact, it was made at a later time it is a clear untruth.

There are exceptions to this. First, where the agreement did not have to be in writing and was, in fact, made orally at an earlier date then it may be permissible to backdate it. However, this exception would only apply if the terms had all been precisely agreed at the earlier date and for some reason it was not possible to sign the agreement then. A second exception would be where the original had been lost and the parties signed a duplicate. In both cases the document is on its face telling the truth.

A deed, however, can never be backdated and nor can an agreement required to be in writing, e.g. for the disposition of an interest in land, for the simple reason that an oral agreement does not bind any of the parties. Where parties sign the agreement at different times the date of the agreement must be the date of the second signature (unless the exceptions apply).

1.5.2   The parties

The appropriate parties to a contract and their roles need to be considered carefully. It is helpful and sensible to include a definition of their role, i.e. 'guarantor', 'principal', 'beneficiary', etc. which can also be used as their identity in the agreement itself, although that is a stylistic rather than substantive choice. Addresses, company registration numbers, etc. should be included.

For terms and conditions, a generic name for the other party is a simple and straightforward way of proceeding with the first party using either its name (or a shortened version thereof) or a generic name, e.g. the Contractor, the Supplier, etc.

1.5.3   Recitals

Long ago, the recitals in a deed were extensive and sometimes very extensive, in effect reciting the history by which the parties had come to the point of agreement to which effect was to be given by the operative parts. Nowadays, recitals are much simpler, briefer and are sometimes dispensed with altogether. However, they can provide a useful service and may assist in construing an agreement if an unintentional ambiguity is found to be present in its operative parts.

The recitals should contain the facts which form the background to the agreement, possibly stating the services/products, etc. which are the subject matter of the agreement and/or what the respective parties do, e.g. the supplier is a manufacturer of widgets, the purchaser a widget retailer.

Another approach can be to state what the agreement is intended to do. It is not uncommon for commercial contracts involving corporate finance to stray into becoming agreements about the transfer of land rather than the true intention to transfer the beneficial and legal ownership of a corporate entity. And, it has to be said, vice versa.

However desirable recitals may be for the purposes of explaining or clarifying what the agreement is intended to achieve, the operative parts of a deed or agreement must deal completely and clearly with giving effect to what the parties agree and intend.

For the purposes of construing and enforcing an agreement, the general rule is that the operative parts prevail over the recitals and the operative parts must be looked to in order to establish what has been agreed and what is enforceable.

That – the primary rule – sometimes has to yield to the secondary rule, which is that if the operative parts are not clear as to their intention or meaning, then the recitals may be consulted in order to clarify what the meaning and effect of the operative parts are. Nonetheless, it is the operative parts which will be effective and enforceable and if the operative parts are insufficiently clear as to be given effect to, then the agreement may not be enforceable at all.

1.6   The operative parts

These are the engine room of the contract. It is usually good practice to precede them with a definitions section which will provide clarity and avoid the need for repetition or explanation.

The operative parts will contain both clauses specific to the contract and commercial clauses (boilerplate), the important clauses that define the extent of, limit or exclude the parties' obligations. The commercial clauses we shall consider in detail below. In **Parts II** and **III** of this book are precedents which may be helpful. Inevitably some of the clauses will have to be new creations specific to the agreement. In every case, however, there are important rules for the draftsman to have in mind. The most important of these are set out below.

1.6.1   *Headings are not part of the agreement*

It is quite astonishing how often solicitors, barristers and even judges forget that in construing an agreement (or indeed a statute), headings are not part of the agreement. In the language of the lecture theatre they are 'rubrics'.

A rubric will usually provide an indication, in summary, of the contents of the clauses or paragraphs which appear under it. It does not need a term in the agreement stating that – though for good measure a draftsman may include one. It must be borne in mind that the mischief is that sometimes the clauses under a heading may encompass wider issues than the heading would suggest.

1.6.2   *Choose words and use them carefully and correctly*

Very often the draftsman is given instructions reflecting discussions or agreements in principle which, not unnaturally, are couched in loose and imprecise language. It is very important that the draftsman uses only language he fully understands and which avoids unintended ambiguity (intended ambiguity is altogether something else and may be considered the mark of the very good draftsman).

Very common and innocuous words can change their meaning. For example, 'presently' used always to mean '*not* at present'. To some it still does but to others it means the opposite. 'Inflammable' means 'can catch fire' but much of the world thinks it means 'not flammable', where the latter artificial word is deemed to mean what inflammable used to mean to everyone. A billion has always meant 1,000,000,000 in the New World but used to mean 1,000,000,000,000 to the rest of the English-speaking world. This last example is, of course, one resulting from there being two countries divided by a common language.

Special meanings are not confined to words and phrases used in specialist commercial contracts such as shipping, insurance and banking contracts. They are used and problems arise from their use in the context of agricultural contracts, contracts for the sale of fresh produce and many other fields. If the draftsman is not already well-versed in special meanings that are encountered in the context of specialised contracts that he is asked to draft, he must learn the use and abuse of the particular special language of a particular trade or industry. Resort can sometimes be had to the definitions section of the contract where a term, e.g. 'intellectual property rights', may be defined more fully than would be possible or appropriate in the main body of text. The draftsman should be very careful in particular not to assume common knowledge and understanding across different business disciplines.

The risk of ignoring these rules is always that if clear meaning cannot be attributed to the words and phrases that are used in a contract then the courts may not be able to attribute any meaning to them at all – so as to give rise to the risk that the whole or at least part of the document that has been drafted will not do the job that it was intended to do and so may become unenforceable.

1.6.3 If Latin tags are going to be used it is important to get the meaning precisely right

If Latin tags and/or words and phrases are going to be deployed that are in more or less common usage as a form of shorthand it is important to ensure that they are being used in their proper sense – *pari passu, pro rata, genus, etc.* (itself a Latin abbreviation) and a host of similarly abbreviated phrases can convey meaning concisely but if they are used in other than their proper sense, they merely mislead.

1.6.4 Gender

The 'he/she' style of drafting is inelegant and otiose. Only one is necessary as the other is implied under the Interpretation Act 1978. However, in the days of the word processor a contract involving an individual should be addressed to a person of their gender.

1.6.5 Numbers

Special care is required where numbers are concerned. The law reports are littered with examples of cases where contracts went wrong because somebody copied in the numbers incorrectly. The problem can be that in some cases the mistake is not obvious. As a rule it is wise to write significant numbers in both numbers and letters, bearing in mind that sometimes the words can be ambiguous (e.g. billion as set out above).

1.6.6 A company is not an individual

A company is a legal person separate and apart from the personality of its corporators, so that a 'person' can include either or both of a company and an individual person but an individual does not include a company as it means a human being.

1.6.7   Being consistent

One of the greatest sins of the draftsman is inconsistency so he should always check that he has not committed the twin sins of inconsistency and repugnancy in a contract. All too often one sees two or more clauses in a contract that are inconsistent with each other and hence that effect cannot be given to both of them. That, of course, can be the danger when more than one precedent is farmed for a draft. All contracts are to be construed as a whole and, so far as possible, meaning and effect are to be given to every part of a contract. If one provision in a contract defeats the purpose or effect of another, that cannot have been the intention of the parties to the contract and such inconsistency can result in the contract as a whole becoming unenforceable.

A particular commercial situation where repugnancy can occur is when there is an overarching contract, e.g. a long-term supply agreement which is then coupled with, say, individual sale of goods contracts based upon the supplier's standard terms for each transaction. A safety net can be provided by ensuring that the overarching contract expressly states which contract will prevail if there is a conflict. It is generally better, however, as any trapeze artist will attest, to avoid the safety net by staying in control. So the efficient draftsman will check the main contract against the terms and conditions so as to identify any anomalies and then to make express provision to deal with them.

1.6.8   The dangers of mathematical formulae

Mathematical formulae can be prima facie very attractive as a concise way of explaining something complex. However, a warning should be sounded. Unless the draftsman is confident of his understanding of how the mathematical formula works, has explained it carefully to his lay client (unless the latter has provided it) and has checked, re-checked and double re-checked it he should avoid it. The use of a formula is an accident looking for somewhere to happen. And very often the mischief is in the definitions that have to lie behind it. And, of course, it is so easy in many cases to omit a crucial variable or constant – see the background to *George Wimpey UK Ltd* v. *V.I. Construction Ltd* [2005] EWCA Civ 77 where the housebuilder left a multiplier out of its own formula in its final draft – and it was the experienced party in this form of transaction.

1.6.9   The 'expressio unius' rule

This is set out and explained in **2.4**.

1.6.10   The 'eiusdem generis' rule

This is set out and explained at **2.5**.

1.6.11   Use of schedules

Simplicity, clarity and flexibility in a contract may be effected by the use of schedules to set out details of obligations, etc. Details, e.g. fees, prices, etc. often change in a long-term contract. The use of schedules enables the main body of the contract to remain undisturbed. It is good practice to require that amended schedules are signed by the parties to avoid ambiguity or dispute.

1.6.12   Stress testing

One of the weaknesses that can affect any commercial contract including terms and conditions is that the draftsman has not stress tested the terms of the agreement to see what effect they would have in possibly extreme or simply unusual circumstances. Absence of such consideration can either have the undesirable effect of leaving the parties to rely upon implied terms, or more disastrously, may lead to a consequence quite unintended and undesirable to at least one of the parties. It is therefore very important to consider precisely how events may turn out.

For example, a contract which provides for listed shares to be paid in satisfaction of monetary consideration, and which will therefore need to define the value of the shares to be provided, must take into account the fact that over a period of time their value may change dramatically. If there is to be a material delay in transferring the shares to the vendor does your client want the value fixed at the time of transfer or at the time of the agreement? The issue is a commercial one and so the prudent lawyer will make sure that his client has in mind the commercial effect of the draft.

1.7   Signing the agreement

Only deeds need to be witnessed. In general an agreement will not be valid as a deed if the signatures are not witnessed. In the case of a deed signed by a director or company secretary on behalf of a limited company however, no witness is necessary to his signature because the law considers that the company is executing the deed not the individual and therefore the director or secretary is witness himself.

It should be remembered that the date of any signature should not be later than the date of the agreement unless one of the exceptions set out above applies.

If the agreement does not need to be a deed then no witnesses are necessary to the signatures.

How a contract is construed – modern rules of construction

2.1   Introduction

This chapter is not intended to be an exhaustive study of the modern law of construction of contracts. However it is hoped that it will give the putative draftsman clear signposts as to how a court will go about gleaning and deeming the meaning of a contract.

It is probably true to say that the old rules of construction, which did anything but enliven the minds of those who had to sit through lectures about them, are now relied upon by the courts far less often, if at all. The seminal case and statement of the modern law of construction is that contained in the speech of Lord Hoffman in *Investors Compensation Scheme* v. *West Bromwich Building Society* [1998] 1 WLR 896. We shall return to this below.

2.2   Literal interpretation

The primary rule is that a contract will be construed literally – the words used must be carefully considered and given effect in their usual and literal meaning.

The intention of the parties to the contract must be gleaned from the words of the contract itself. Evidence of the intention of the parties from outside the contract and of negotiations between the parties leading up to the contract will, in general terms, be inadmissible (the parol evidence rule). It is not generally open to either party to say: 'I know that that is what the contract says but that is not what I meant when I made it.'

The courts can and will have regard to the circumstances in which the contract was made – the factual matrix. Evidence of those circumstances will be admissible – but still the primary rule applies.

The courts may, in limited circumstances, omit or treat as being omitted words to which no meaning can be attributed in the context of the contract as a whole, but the court will not make agreements for the parties. If the document does not show what the intentions of the parties were when they made it then they face the risk that the courts will say that effect cannot be given to the contract as a whole, or parts of it at least.

The literal approach for the construction and interpretation of contracts is a feature of all systems of law based on the common law – Australia, most of the provinces of Canada, New Zealand and some other former colonies – all of which have common law based systems.

So, if a contract is being drafted that will have effect and may have to be construed in any of those countries the primary rule – the 'literal construction' rule – will be applied.

2.3   *Contra proferentem*

The one rule which every lawyer remembers is that terms in a contract will generally be construed against the originator (the *proferens*) of the agreement if there is ambiguity (though this approach would have only limited application where the purposive rule is being applied). This remains the case but may be abrogated by the insertion of an appropriate 'fair interpretation or meaning' clause.

2.4   The *expressio unius* rule

The Latin maxim '*expressio unius est exclusio alterius*' translates as 'the expression of one thing excludes other things of the same or similar type'. If a particular person or thing or power is expressed in an agreement, it may be taken to exclude any other person or thing or power not specified.

So, if a particular person or thing is specified in an agreement, it may be intended that only that person or thing shall be affected but it may sometimes be that – unintentionally – other persons or things are excluded. If, for example, there is a reference to 'ordinary shares', it may have been intended to affect only ordinary shares and not, for instance, preference shares. On the other hand, if the term 'ordinary shares' was used because that is the description that is habitually given to shares without considering whether or not they are shares of a particular category, then the use of the phrase 'ordinary shares' may have unexpected consequences if shares other than ordinary shares, properly so called, may be affected by the document which has been drafted. So, when words of definition and description are used it should be remembered that the 'literal' rule of construction (on which see more at **2.2**) will be applied when construing what has been written. Putting it another way, avoiding using the word 'only' does not avoid the possibility of excluding things which were not intended to be excluded.

2.5   The *eiusdem generis* rule

The Latin phrase '*eiusdem generis*' means 'of the same class or category'. If particular things or classes of things are specified in a contract, general words that follow will be construed as meaning that the things generally detailed or referred to are intended to be of the same class or category as the particular things.

The *eiusdem generis* rule arises and applies in many contexts and it can be easily understood in the context of insurance contracts. For example, an insurance policy may contain a clause relating to abatement of rent:

if the demised premises should be destroyed or damaged by fire, flood, storm or tempest or other inevitable accident

Here particular perils or risks are specified, followed by the non-specific – *'other inevitable accident'*. The only perils or risks covered by the general words will be perils or risks of the same type as those particularised, i.e. other inevitable accident of a kind similar to fire, flood, storm or tempest and not, for instance, impact of vehicles, aircraft or explosions.

However, to apply the *'eiusdem generis'* rule you must have a 'genus' – a class or category. The rule does *not* apply *if only one thing or matter* is particularised. For instance 'flood' followed by or 'other inevitable accident' would include vehicle impact, because 'flood' does not constitute a class or category on its own.

2.6   Purposive

The primary rule of construction applied in civil law countries that do not derive their law from the common law (and this, of course, encompasses all of the member states of the European Union except England, Wales (not Scotland) and the whole of Ireland (and to an extent the Channel Islands)) is the 'purposive' rule – the courts will look at the purposes for which the contract was made and construe it so as to achieve those purposes.

The Articles, Regulations and Directives that are issued by the European Commission under the Rome Treaty and related Treaties are issued in order to apply uniform policies for social and economic affairs and trade throughout the European Union. That is their purpose and they are construed and applied purposively – in order to give effect to the purposes for which they were promulgated. Similarly, private documents, including contracts, are construed under the jurisprudence applying in Europe upon the basis of a purposive construction.

In England and Wales, even though the primary rule of construction is the 'literal' rule, it is not applied inevitably and invariably. Even before the Rome Treaty and its offspring became part of the day-to-day life of lawyers applying English law, the English courts, while still applying the primary – 'literal' – rule, always had regard, so far as necessary, to more than the mere words used in the contract. The courts always took into account the circumstances in which a contract was made and the type of contract in question – if a court is faced with a contract of guarantee or a contract of insurance or a shipping contract, it will have in mind the particular characteristics of those types of contract and their purposes when deciding what the parties meant by the words which they chose and used.

In *Investors Compensation Scheme v. West Bromwich Building Society* [1998] 1 WLR 896 at 912 Lord Hoffman summarised succinctly the approach that judges should adopt towards construing contracts, which is to:

> assimilate the way in which contractual documents are interpreted by judges to the common sense principles by which any serious utterance would be interpreted in ordinary life.

Lord Bingham, when he was Master of the Rolls in 1995, said:

> The current approach of the courts to the construction of contracts is neither uncompromisingly literal nor unswervingly purposive.

The prudent draftsman and adviser will therefore have in mind both approaches when writing or construing an agreement.

PART II

Commercial clauses

3

Commercial clauses relating to limitation or exclusion of liability

3.1 Introduction

The purpose of this chapter is to examine, from a practical perspective, how the draftsman may do his best to ensure that commercial (or boilerplate) clauses intending to limit or exclude liability in a contract will be effective by (a) achieving their objectives and (b) not being open to successful challenge. It is important always to bear in mind that a clause which may be entirely effective in one contract may fail in another because of different subject matter or a materially different factual matrix. Ensuring success is therefore not simply a matter of mechanically copying a model form of a clause but also analysing carefully whether the context in which it is to be used will render it ineffective.

3.2 Exclusion and limitation of liability clauses

Two of the principal tasks of any contract draftsman are:

(a) to limit the instances where possible where his client may be liable for any non-performance, mis-performance or misrepresentation in relation to the contract; and
(b) to limit the amount of damages which may be recovered if there is a proven breach or misrepresentation. Closely allied to the latter may be the deployment of a liquidated damages clause (which will be considered in **Chapter 4**).

The following are the considerations and factors which the draftsman will need to have in mind when drafting or deploying an exclusion or limitation clause. The first section relates to the application of the common law, the second to relevant statutory intervention.

3.3 Common law

3.3.1 The exclusion must be clearly included within the clause

The courts will construe an exclusion clause against the party which benefits from it (which will normally be the *proferens* – see **Chapter 2**). It follows that ambiguity will be construed in the same way. Exclusion of warranties may not include exclusion of conditions – *Lowe* v. *Lombank Ltd* [1960] 1 All ER 611, [1960] 1 WLR 196, CA; exclusion of liability for breach of implied terms may not include express terms – *Andrews Bros (Bournemouth) Ltd* v. *Singer & Co Ltd* [1934] 1 KB 17, CA.

An exclusion clause will not usually be construed as excluding what amounts to non-performance or fundamental breach unless the words are unambiguously to that effect. This is a question of construction, not a principle of law – *Suisse Atlantique Société d'Armement Maritime SA* v. *NV Rotterdamsche Kolen Centrale* [1967] 1 AC 361 at 397, [1966] 2 All ER 61 at 70, HL; *Photo Production Ltd* v. *Securicor Transport Ltd* [1980] AC 827 at 845, [1980] 1 All ER 556 at 564, HL.

3.3.2   Repugnancy

Even a tightly drawn exclusion clause may be ineffective if it directly negatives a positive contractual commitment so as to be considered inconsistent or repugnant to it. Exclusion clauses in general terms and conditions may be ineffective if they are inconsistent with terms specific to the parties – *The Brabant* [1967] 1 QB 588, [1966] 1 All ER 961.

3.3.3   Exclusion of liability for negligence

Liability for negligence must generally be specifically excluded – *Thomas Witter Ltd* v. *TBP Industries Ltd* [1996] 2 All ER 573. Where the only likely form of liability is that which would arise from negligent performance or non-performance of the contract then this principle may be relaxed – *Spriggs* v. *Southeby Parke Bernet & Co Ltd* [1986] 1 Lloyd's Rep. 487, CA.

However, the courts have in practice drawn a distinction between clauses which seek to exclude and clauses which seek to limit liability for negligence. In cases of exclusion rather than limitation the following points should inform the draftsman (see especially *Canada Steamship Lines Ltd* v. *R* [1952] AC 192 at 208, [1952] 1 All ER 305 at 310, PC, per Lord Morton):

1. Where the clause expressly exempts the *proferens* from liability for the negligence of his own employees, the clause will be effective. There should be a specific reference to negligence or a word or words of similar meaning.
2. Absent specific reference to negligence (or a synonym thereof) the court must construe the words used to decide whether they encompass negligence on the part of the *proferens'* employees. Words such as 'howsoever caused' – *White* v. *Blackmore* [1972] 2 QB 651, [1972] 3 All ER 158, CA, 'at owner's risk' – *Levison* v. *Patent Steam Carpet Cleaning Co Ltd* [1978] QB 69, [1977] 3 All ER 498, CA and 'under no circumstances' – *L Harris (Harella) Ltd* v. *Continental Express Ltd* [1961] 1 Lloyd's Rep. 251, have all been found on the particular facts of each case to be sufficient. Best practice, however, is expressly to include negligence.
3. Even if the words can be construed as applying to negligence the court should go on to consider whether in fact they were intended to apply to some other head of damage – *Canada Steamship Lines Ltd* v. *R* [1952] AC 192 at 208, [1952] 1 All ER 305 at 310, PC, per Lord Morton.

3.3.4   Exclusions cannot be inconsistent with the purpose of the contract

One of the most difficult matters to consider in drawing an exclusion clause in a commercial contract is whether the effect of the exclusion would be to remove any obligation on the part of the *proferens* to perform the contract or alternatively to render a performance which is consistent with the purpose of the contract. The draftsman needs to stand back and ask himself whether he is in effect attempting to put his client in a position where his client will escape liability for non- or mis-performance to such an extent that the purpose of the contract could be defeated with impunity. Is he, for example, endeavouring to create a situation in a service contract where his client need not deliver the service envisaged by the contract? The issue is one of construction, not law. A court will simply not construe an exclusion clause so as to give it the effect of defeating the purpose of the contract – *Tor Line AB* v. *Alltrans Group of Canada Ltd, The TFL Prosperity* [1984] 1 All ER 103 at 111, [1984] 1 WLR 48 at 58, HL, per Lord Roskill. This can have the effect of depriving the clause of any effect. For example, suppose a party agreed to provide a fleet of buses but instead delivered a fleet of lorries. It is unlikely that a court would construe any exclusion clause, however widely or tightly drawn, as enabling him to escape liability for in effect failing to render any performance envisaged by the contract. Comparison can be made with a clause which exempts the party from liability for late delivery or even for loss of the goods due to negligence (as opposed to deliberate action/inaction by the promisor).

In drafting an exclusion clause intended to be very wide in its application it is not sufficient simply to use a well-tried precedent. Regard has to be had to the context. For example, a clause excluding liability for late delivery might not be inconsistent with the purpose of a sale of goods contract but might be wholly inconsistent with a specific contract to ensure that a particular item is delivered by a certain date for which a high premium has been paid.

It is also difficult to exclude liability for deliberate breaches because a court will be reluctant to construe an exclusion clause so as to include a party's deliberate non- or mis-performance. It is not inconceivable that the parties could so decide but the court would need the most clear and explicit language to accept it and in reality it is improbable that any party would knowingly agree to such a term – see, for example, *Internet Broadcasting Corpn* v. *MAR LLC* (trading as MARHedge) [2009] 2 Lloyd's Rep. 295.

3.4   Statutory intervention

Given the scope of this publication statutory intervention in respect of consumer contracts is, strictly speaking, outside of its ambit. Much of the statutory intervention in non-consumer contracts is in respect of very specialist areas which, again, this volume does not claim to encompass. There are, however, various remaining interventions which are of more general application. Those which are most likely to be engaged are those emanating from the Unfair Contract Terms Act (UCTA) 1977.

3.4.1   The Unfair Contract Terms Act 1977

UCTA 1977 has limited application to commercial contracts.

(i)   International supply of goods contracts

UCTA 1977 does not apply to an international supply of goods contract, i.e. one which has the following characteristics (s.26(3)):

(a)   either it is a contract of sale of goods or it is one under or in pursuance of which the possession or ownership of goods passes; and

(b)   it is made by parties whose places of business (or, if they have none, habitual residences) are in the territories of different States (the Channel Islands and the Isle of Man being treated for this purpose as different States from the United Kingdom).

A contract falls within (a) and (b) above only if either (s.26(4)):

(a)   the goods in question are, at the time of the conclusion of the contract, in the course of carriage, or will be carried, from the territory of one State to the territory of another; or

(b)   the acts constituting the offer and acceptance have been done in the territories of different States; or

(c)   the contract provides for the goods to be delivered to the territory of a State other than that within whose territory those acts were done.

(ii)   Domestic commercial contracts or international ones not involving the supply of goods

UCTA 1977 has broader application in the case of domestic contracts.

Regarding exclusion or limitation of liability for negligence, UCTA 1977 is concerned only with acts or omissions in the course of business – s.1(3). There can be no exclusion or limitation of liability for death or personal injury. Any exclusion clause should therefore be expressly qualified by excepting those two possible outcomes – s.2(1).

There can be no exclusion for breach of the warranty as to title, etc. – ss.6 and 7.

UCTA 1977 requires that any clause excluding or limiting liability for negligence must satisfy a test of reasonableness – s.2(2).

Regarding exclusion of liability for non-performance or substantially different performance, UCTA 1977, s.3 provides that:

(1)   This section applies as between contracting parties where one of them deals as consumer or on the other's written standard terms of business.

(2)   As against that party, the other cannot by reference to any contract term –

(a)   when himself in breach of contract, exclude or restrict any liability of his in respect of the breach; or

(b)   claim to be entitled –

(i)   to render a contractual performance substantially different from that which was reasonably expected of him, or

(ii) in respect of the whole or any part of his contractual obligation, to render no performance at all,

except in so far as (in any of the cases mentioned above in this subsection) the contract term satisfies the requirement of reasonableness.

It follows that in the case of written commercial agreements s.3 is likely to be engaged.

There are special provisions dealing with hire purchase and sale contracts (and other contracts where title passes – ss.6 and 7).

In drafting exclusion clauses in domestic commercial contracts, therefore, it is essential that the draftsman has a good understanding of the safe parameters of reasonableness.

The test is defined in UCTA 1977, s.11:

(1) In relation to a contract term, the requirement of reasonableness for the purposes of this Part of this Act, section 3 of the Misrepresentation Act 1967 and section 3 of the Misrepresentation Act (Northern Ireland) 1967 is that the term shall have been a fair and reasonable one to be included having regard to the circumstances which were, or ought reasonably to have been, known to or in the contemplation of the parties when the contract was made.

(2) In determining for the purposes of section 6 or 7 above whether a contract term satisfies the requirement of reasonableness, regard shall be had in particular to the matters specified in Schedule 2 to this Act; but this subsection does not prevent the court or arbitrator from holding, in accordance with any rule of law, that a term which purports to exclude or restrict any relevant liability is not a term of the contract.

...

(4) Where by reference to a contract term or notice a person seeks to restrict liability to a specified sum of money, and the question arises (under this or any other Act) whether the term or notice satisfies the requirement of reasonableness, regard shall be had in particular (but without prejudice to subsection (2) above in the case of contract terms) to--

(a) the resources which he could expect to be available to him for the purpose of meeting the liability should it arise; and

(b) how far it was open to him to cover himself by insurance.

(5) It is for those claiming that a contract term or notice satisfies the requirement of reasonableness to show that it does.

Schedule 2 to UCTA 1977, which applies to hire purchase, sale of goods and other contracts where title to goods passes, sets out various factors to which particular regard must be had:

(a) the strength of the bargaining positions of the parties relative to each other, taking into account (among other things) alternative means by which the customer's requirements could have been met;

(b) whether the customer received an inducement to agree to the term, or in accepting it had an opportunity of entering into a similar contract with other persons, but without having to accept a similar term;

(c) whether the customer knew or ought reasonably to have known of the existence and extent of the term (having regard, among other things, to any custom of the trade and any previous course of dealing between the parties);

(d) where the term excludes or restricts any relevant liability if some condition is not complied with, whether it was reasonable at the time of the contract to expect that compliance with that condition would be practicable;

(e) whether the goods were manufactured, processed or adapted to the special order of the customer.

It is important to bear in mind that the list is not intended to be exhaustive. The test is heavily evidence based and so previous decisions will not always provide effective guidance.

In summary, there is a statutory requirement in contracts not involving the international supply of goods that:

(a) if the exclusion clause is in the *proferens'* written terms there is a requirement that any term restricting or excluding liability for negligence satisfies the test of reasonableness;

(b) clauses seeking to limit or exclude liability for substantial non- or mis-performance are subject to a test of reasonableness;

(c) in contracts involving hire purchase or the transfer of title in goods there is a requirement that any exclusion of liability relating to fitness for purpose, conformity with description, etc. under the Supply of Goods (Implied Terms) Act 1973 and the Sale of Goods Act 1979 be reasonable;

(d) no exclusion clause will be effective to avoid liability for breach of title, etc.

The draftsman should also bear in mind that UCTA 1977, s.13 precludes various devices which might otherwise be employed to prevent its full effect:

(1) To the extent that this Part of this Act prevents the exclusion or restriction of any liability it also prevents –

(a) making the liability or its enforcement subject to restrictive or onerous conditions;

(b) excluding or restricting any right or remedy in respect of the liability, or subjecting a person to any prejudice in consequence of his pursuing any such right or remedy;

(c) excluding or restricting rules of evidence or procedure;

and (to that extent) sections 2 and 5 to 7 also prevent excluding or restricting liability by reference to terms and notices which exclude or restrict the relevant obligation or duty.

(2) But an agreement in writing to submit present or future differences to arbitration is not to be treated under this Part of this Act as excluding or restricting any liability.

3.4.2   Other statutory interventions

The Misrepresentation Act 1967, s.3 requires any clause attempting to exclude or limit liability for misrepresentation to be subject to a test of reasonableness.

Contracts relating to the carriage of goods by sea and air are subject to specific legislation. Detailed consideration of these is beyond the scope of this publication.

3.5   *Force majeure*

Although not strictly an exclusion or limitation of liability clause a *force majeure* provision may be effective if performance of a contract is rendered impossible because of an unavoidable event such as enemy action, an act of state or an act of God. If the draftsman includes a notice provision then there must be strict adherence to it – *Bremer Handelsgesellschaft mbH* v. *Vanden Avenne-Izegem* PVBA [1978] 2 Lloyd's Rep. 109, HL.

CLAUSE 3A   Exclusion and limitation of liability

1.1. Neither Party shall be liable to the other for any economic, consequential or other losses including loss of reputation, profit or goodwill whether resulting from misrepresentation, misdescription, breach of contract, breach of duty or other act or omission (unless fraudulent) however caused.

1.2. Nothing in these Conditions shall limit the right of either Party to seek to recover damages for personal injury or death occasioned by breach of contract or breach of duty by the other Party, its employees or agents.

or

1.1. The liability of the X (and of any sub-contractor) under or in connection with this Agreement for the provision of the Services whether arising in contract, tort, negligence, breach of statutory duty or otherwise howsoever shall not exceed [the amount of professional negligence insurance cover carried by X which shall not be less than £[...] *or* a refund of that part of the Fee for the Services which has been paid by Y to X under this Agreement. The relevant Fee for the purpose of this Clause [...] will be that which relates to the particular Services in respect of which a successful claim is brought by Y].

1.2. X shall not be liable to Y for any indirect, consequential or economic loss including but not limited to damage, costs or expenses of any description, loss of profit, business, goodwill, turnover or any other loss arising from its performance or non-performance of its obligations in connection with this Agreement whether arising from breach of contract, tort, breach of duty, negligence or any other cause of action.

Nothing in this Clause [...] shall limit or remove X's liability for causing personal injury or death.

CLAUSE 3B   *Force majeure*

1.1. X shall not have any liability to Y for any delay, omission, failure or inadequate performance of this Agreement which is the result of circumstances beyond the reasonable control of X. Where so affected in its performance of this Agreement it will notify Y as soon as is reasonably possible.

1.2. In this Clause [...] *force majeure* includes but is not limited to civil commotion, war and terrorist action, state action, industrial action whether lawful or otherwise, non-availability of raw materials, components and labour at commercially viable prices, unavoidable accident, fire, flood, earthquake, subsidence, epidemic and other natural or physical disasters.

4

Liquidated damages

4.1   Introduction

There is unfortunately nothing simple in the drafting of liquidated damages clauses. It is not a mechanical process and it is essential to have a firm grasp of the principles before trying to do so. It is more scratch building than kit assembly, to use a modelling metaphor.

4.2   Definition of a liquidated damages clause

The seminal case is the House of Lords decision in *Dunlop Pneumatic Tyre Co* v. *New Garage and Motor Co* [1915] AC 79 ('the *Dunlop* case').

Where parties to a contract, as part of the agreement between them, fix the amount to be paid by way of damages in the event of a breach of the agreement, that amount will be classed as liquidated damages if and only if it is:

> a genuine pre-estimate of the damage which would probably arise from the breach of the contract.

(per Lord Dunedin in the Dunlop case at 86)

It becomes a penalty clause if the liquidated damages stipulated in the event of a breach are disproportionate to the likely damages actually suffered. It is not, therefore, either an exclusion or limitation clause. It cannot relate to any sums payable to a third party on breach – *Export Credits Guarantee Department* v. *Universal Oil Products Co* [1983] 1 WLR 399, HL.

4.3   Avoiding a clause being construed as imposing a penalty

In deciding whether a clause is a penalty or not its genuineness as a pre-estimate of likely loss will be tested as at the time of making the contract, not when the breach or loss occurs – see, for example, *Clydebank Engineering Co* v. *Don Jose, Ramos, Yzquierdo y Castaneda* [1905] AC 6.

The heart of the test laid down in the *Dunlop* case is contained in Lord Dunedin's fourth rule, which it is essential for the draftsman thoroughly to grasp:

To assist this task of construction various tests have been suggested, which if applicable to the case under consideration may prove helpful, or even conclusive. Such are:

(a) It will be held to be a penalty if the sum stipulated for is extravagant and unconscionable in amount in comparison with the greatest loss that could conceivably be proved to have followed from the breach ...

(b) It will be held to be a penalty if the breach consists only in not paying a sum of money, and the sum stipulated is a sum greater than the sum which ought to have been paid ... This though one of the most ancient instances is truly a corollary to the last test ...

(c) There is a presumption (but no more) that it is a penalty when 'a single lump sum is made payable by way of compensation, on the occurrence of one or more or all of several events, some of which may occasion serious and others but trifling damage' ...

On the other hand:

(d) It is no obstacle to the sum stipulated being a genuine pre-estimate of damage, that the consequences of the breach are such as to make precise pre-estimation almost an impossibility. On the contrary, that is just the situation when it is probable that pre-estimated damage was the true bargain between the parties ...

This is the most important test for assessing whether the sum stipulated is liquidated damages or a penalty. In applying it a fundamental distinction has to be drawn between a clause which provides for damages to become payable on the breach of:

(a) one single obligation; and
(b) several differing obligations.

In drafting a liquidated damages clause it is to this point that the draftsman's mind should principally be drawn.

4.4 Drafting considerations

4.4.1 Single obligation

The simplest solution is to ensure that the liquidated sum applies to breach of a single obligation, ideally where there can be only one breach. Provided the sum is not 'extravagant' (to use Lord Dunedin's phrase) there should be no problem. An example would be failing to deliver specific goods by a particular date.

However, in many cases, although the liquidated sum relates to a single obligation, there may be multiple ways of breaching it and it may happen more than once. For example, a covenant not to solicit orders from former customers is capable of repeated breaches of varying degrees of commercial importance.

In such cases the clause should be effective provided that the following conditions are satisfied:

(a) the amount is not obviously excessive for every possible or likely breach;
(b) the difference between the breaches is likely to be one of degree rather than type.

However, even if the difference between the breaches could arguably be one of type, e.g. a newly constructed building could be unfinished or unsatisfactory for a variety of reasons, the courts will not split up what the parties have considered or deemed to be a single obligation into a series of different obligations – see *Law v. Redditch Local Branch* [1892] 1 QB 626, CA; Lord Atkinson in the *Dunlop* case at 93.

4.4.2 Multiple obligations

In some cases the contracting party or parties may wish the liquidated damages to cover several different obligations (as in the *Dunlop* case itself).

Different sums could be fixed for breaches of different obligations. This may not always be practicable or desirable.

If the clause is to cover multiple obligations then the following should be avoided:

1. *One of the obligations is self-evidently trivial and the breach of it could not possibly sound in the level of damages represented by the liquidated sum.*

    For example, in *Ford Motor Co v. Armstrong* (1915) 31 TLR 267, CA a resale price maintenance agreement provided for a liquidated sum to be payable for breach of an obligation not to resell goods below a certain price, not to sell them to certain prohibited persons and not to exhibit them without C's permission. The clause was held to be a penalty because of the inclusion of the last of those obligations. The draftsman in such a situation should be careful to exclude or not include breach of such an obligation.

2. *The likely loss flowing from breach of one of the included obligations could be readily ascertained or calculated and the liquidated sum would be manifestly excessive.*

    The solution is the same as for (a). It is helpful in both instances for the draftsman to have in mind the words of Lord Dunedin: 'The strength of the chain must be taken at its weakest link' (at 89).

There remain those situations where there may be a variety of obligations and probable breaches which may result in a wide range of losses, none of which can be predicted with any degree of accuracy and none of which is obviously trivial or of manifestly less significance in its effect. The way to approach the drafting of a suitable clause may be to insert a provision that the parties have agreed that a mean or average figure to encompass the whole range of possible losses would be reasonable – see *English Hop Growers v. Dering* [1928] 2 KB 174, CA at 182 in which it was considered to be reasonable that 'damages of the same kind, but difficult to value exactly, may be averaged'. Lord Parker in the *Dunlop* case suggested at 99:

> Supposing it were recited in the agreement that the parties had estimated the probable damage from a breach of one stipulation at from 5l. to 15l., and the probable damage from a breach of another stipulation at from 2l. to 12l., and had agreed on a sum of 8l. as a reasonable sum to be paid on the breach of either stipulation, I cannot think that the Court would refuse to give effect to the bargain between the parties.

This approach was approved by Lord Woolf in *Philips Hong King v. Attorney-General of Hong Kong* (1993) 61 BLR 41, PC.

4.5   Liquidated and unliquidated damages

The claimant is confined to the stipulated sum in the liquidated damages clause and cannot recover more. He cannot ignore the liquidated damages clause and attempt to be compensated in the ordinary way by an action for unliquidated damages. Neither can he claim unliquidated damages in the ordinary way in addition to the liquidated damages.

However, if other breaches have occurred which do not fall within the ambit of the liquidated damages clause, the claimant is entitled to sue for unliquidated damages in relation to those breaches over and above his claim for liquidated damages. In addition, if it can be shown that only part of the loss arising from a single breach is covered by a liquidated damages clause the additional loss can be compensated for by way of unliquidated damages. An example is *Total Transport Corp* v. *Amoco Trading Co, The Altus* [1985] 1 Lloyd's Rep. 423.

4.6   Injunctions and liquidated damages

Generally, it has been held that a claimant cannot claim both an injunction and liquidated damages – see *General Accident Assurance Company* v. *Noel* [1902] 1 KB 377. However, if the injunction sought relates to a different breach from that for which liquidated damages are sought, the claimant may be entitled to both. The *General Accident* case concerned covenants of restraint of trade, breach of which gave rise to payment of a single stipulated sum. In those cases it was reasonable to regard the two remedies as mutually exclusive.

4.7   Effect of finding a clause to be a penalty

If a clause is found to impose a penalty then it will be unenforceable. This does not prevent the claimant from suing and recovering for loss he can prove in the ordinary way.

4.8   Modern authorities

In *Murray* v. *Leisureplay* [2005] EWCA Civ 963, CA, a case concerning a provision for payment of one year's salary in the event of breach of an employment contract, Lady Justice Arden laid down a 'practical step by step guide' to ascertaining whether a clause imposed a penalty:

    (i)   To what breaches of contract does the contractual damages provision apply?

    (ii) What amount is payable on breach under that clause in the parties' agreement?

    (iii) What amount would be payable if a claim for damages for breach of contract was brought under common law?

    (iv) What were the parties' reasons for agreeing for the relevant clause?

    (v) Has the party who seeks to establish that the clause is a penalty shown that the amount payable under the clause was imposed *in terrorem* [as a way of punishing him], or that it does not constitute a genuine pre-estimate of loss for the purposes of the *Dunlop* case, and, if he has shown the latter, is there some other reason which justifies the discrepancy between (i) and (ii) above?

Another recent case in which the law on penalties was reviewed is *Alfred McAlpine Capital Projects Ltd* v. *Tilebox Ltd* [2005] EWHC 281 (TCC), where Jackson J discerned the following principles from his review (at para.48):

1. There seem to be two strands in the authorities. In some cases judges consider whether there is an unconscionable or extravagant disproportion between the damages stipulated in the contract and the true amount of damages likely to be suffered. In other cases the courts consider whether the level of damages stipulated was reasonable. [The Court accepts] that these two strands can be reconciled. In my view, a pre-estimate of damages does not have to be right in order to be reasonable. There must be a substantial discrepancy between the level of damages stipulated in the contract and the level of damages which is likely to be suffered before it can be said that the agreed pre-estimate is unreasonable.

2. Although many authorities use or echo the phrase 'genuine pre-estimate', the test does not turn upon the genuineness or honesty of the party or parties who made the pre-estimate. The test is primarily an objective one, even though the court has some regard to the thought processes of the parties at the time of contracting.

3. Because the rule about penalties is an anomaly within the law of contract, the courts are predisposed, where possible, to uphold contractual terms which fix the level of damages for breach. This predisposition is even stronger in the case of commercial contracts freely entered into between parties of comparable bargaining power.

4. Looking at the bundle of authorities provided in this case, I note only four cases where the relevant clause has been struck down as a penalty. These are *Commissioner of Public Works* v. *Hills* [1906] AC 368, *Bridge* v. *Campbell Discount Co Limited* [1962] AC 600, *Workers Trust and Merchant Bank Limited* v. *Dojap Investments Limited* [1993] AC 573, and *Ariston SRL* v. *Charly Records* (Court of Appeal 13th March 1990). In each of these four cases there was, in fact, a very wide gulf between (a), the level of damages likely to be suffered, and (b), the level of damages stipulated in the contract.

CLAUSE 4A   Liquidated damages

1. The Parties have agreed that the following represents a genuine pre-estimate of loss in the circumstances set out.

1.1. In the event that X commits a breach of the time stipulation in Clause [...] then the daily cost of delay will be £[...].

1.2. In the event that X fails to complete delivery by the Due Date then the daily cost to Y will be £[...].

1.3. In the event that any of the items listed in Schedule [...] fails to conform to the Specification then the costs of replacement will be £[...] per item.

2. Accordingly in the event that X is in breach of this contract as envisaged in Clause 1 above the damages payable in respect of each such breach shall be calculated on the basis set out in Clause 1.

or

1. The Parties have agreed that the following represents a genuine pre-estimate of loss in the circumstances set out.

1.1. If X acts in breach of the restrictive covenant in Clause [...] then the likely loss of profit suffered by Y will be £[...] per unit sold by X.

1.2. If X advertises or promotes the products of a competitor company then the likely loss of profit suffered by Y over one calendar year is estimated at £[...] and it is agreed that Y is likely to suffer the loss for [...] years.

2. Accordingly in the event that X is in breach of this contract as envisaged in Clause 1 above the damages payable in respect of [each] such breach shall be calculated on the basis set out in Clause 1.

or

1. The Parties agree that the contract cost to be paid by Y to X was increased by £[...] in return for X's undertaking to complete the works by the Due Date. It is therefore agreed that the contract price will be reduced by £[...] per day as a genuine pre-estimate of the loss of the value to Y caused by failure to complete by the Due Date [to a maximum of ...].

or

1. The Parties have estimated the probable damage from a breach of certain obligations ('the Obligations') as follows:

1.1. In relation to Clause [...] at between £[...] and £[...].

1.2. In relation to Clause [...] at between £[...] and £[...].

1.3. In relation to Clause [...] at between £[...] and £[...].

2. They have therefore agreed that a reasonable sum to be paid on the breach of any of the Obligations will be £[...].

3. For the avoidance of doubt the sum set out in Clause 2 will be payable [for each breach of each Obligation *or* only once and in total in respect of all breaches of each separate Obligation *or* only once and in total in respect of all breaches of all of the Obligations].

5

Safety and miscellaneous commercial clauses

5.1 Introduction

In any commercial contract it is usually prudent in order to protect the interests of the relevant party to include a number of commercial (or boilerplate) provisions which provide safety nets either for unforeseen developments in the performance of the contract or in the event that other provisions fail for whatever reason. For example, a part of an exclusion clause may be found to be unreasonable, or a potential issue arises as to the applicable or proper law of the contract. This chapter provides an overview of some of these clauses so that the draftsman may decide what he should include and, where appropriate, how the relevant clause should be composed.

(The references are to the model clauses in the second part of this chapter.)

5.1.1 Arbitration

See **Clauses 5A** and **5B**.

Arbitration is not an automatic choice in a commercial contract. Its suitability or not will tend to depend upon the subject matter of the agreement and the relative strength of the parties. Where the contract is international in character careful thought should be given to where the seat of any arbitration should be. The method of choosing an arbitrator is also of importance.

5.1.2 Assignment and non-assignment

See **Clauses 5C–5F**.

In any commercial contract where the identity of the other contracting party is material a non-assignment clause should be included (see also **5.1.9**). This may be absolute or discretionary. Most protection comes from an absolute prohibition – a party could, of course, always waive this if commercially advantageous. Non-assignment clauses are frequently not mutual.

In other cases where a contracting party may envisage that it may wish to assign it can insert a clause specifically permitting assignment to avoid any contention that some form of prohibition was implied or followed from the form and subject matter of the contract.

5.1.3   Confidentiality

See **Clauses 5G** and **5H**.

Wherever there is a medium- or long-term commercial relationship between two parties it is likely that situations will arise, or will be intrinsic to the relationship, where one party will entrust the other with commercially sensitive information. It is important to lay down a marker as the law on implied confidentiality is not as clear as it might be. In corporate situations it is important to ensure that not only the party itself but its employees and directors are expressly bound. Where assignment of the contract is permitted, or where a change in a party's business structure or ownership is permitted, it is advisable to ensure that the clause is wide enough to encompass legal persons or individuals who may not be parties to the contract.

5.1.4   Further action

See **Clause 5I**.

A very useful provision to put in many commercial contracts where either party may be obliged to carry out future acts such as re-assigning rights, completing licences, etc.

5.1.5   Indemnity

See **Clauses 5J** and **5K**.

An indemnity clause is intended to apportion risk so that if B suffers loss as a result of the claims of a third party in specified situations A undertakes to make good that loss. It is not appropriate in all commercial contracts to include an indemnity provision (either unilateral or bilateral). However, in many it is, especially where, for example, the misuse of the *proferens'* product, name, logo, etc. could result in the *proferens* facing loss of reputation, goodwill or legal action.

Where the intention or effect of an indemnity clause is to limit or exclude liability as between the contracting parties, e.g. where A has to indemnify B against loss B has caused to A, rather than addressing the effect of loss caused by a third party, the effect is that of an exclusion clause and it is so treated under the common law and statute.

There is an alternative form of indemnity clause from the usual in which A is required 'to hold B harmless' in certain situations. The effect of this is that A is undertaking not to pursue B for losses A suffers rather than either party indemnifying the other.

5.1.6   Insolvency

See **Clause 5L**.

It is normal and sensible to include in any executory contract a break clause in the event of the insolvency or similar of the other party.

5.1.7   Jurisdiction and proper law

See **Clause 5M**.

It may be helpful briefly to review the position in English law regarding the proper or applicable law of a contract. The applicable law of a contract, in the absence of express provision in the agreement, is now determined by the application of the provisions in Regulation 593/2008/EC (Rome I). For example, it is often the place of business or residence of the party whose performance is characteristic of the contract (Article 4). Similarly, in most cases where a contract is made within the EU the court or courts having jurisdiction will be determined by the application of Regulation 44/2001/EC.

In any contract, therefore, which has an international aspect to it, whether because of the place of business of one or both of the parties or the place or places of performance it is highly desirable to include a jurisdiction and applicable law provision. Jurisdiction need not be exclusive though it is usually wise to make it so. There may also be more than one applicable law where that is appropriate because of the nature of the subject matter or the surrounding circumstances of the agreement.

5.1.8   Non-compete

See **Clauses 5N** and **5O**.

Non-compete clauses frequently arise in connection with employment contracts which are outside the scope of this work. However they also have their place in commercial contracts between business entities.

In **Chapter 7** there is a consideration of non-compete clauses in the case of sale and purchases of businesses. The other principal types of commercial contracts which are specifically covered in this title and in which they have a role are agency, exclusive (and sole) distribution, and franchising. The question always is whether the clause is intending to protect a legitimate business interest rather than stifle fair competition. A necessary safety net when any non-compete clause is deployed is a severability clause.

5.1.9   Re-organisation of the business structure

See **Clause 5P**.

Where the identity of a contracting party is important to the *proferens*, thought needs to be given to whether there should be restrictions on change of that identity even if such change does not amount to a novation or variation. An example of where such a restriction may sometimes be appropriate but is not always so is a distribution contract. Where Y has exclusive or sole rights then the relationship is far more interdependent than when Y is one of many. In the former case the personal identity of the participants in Y company may be a very important consideration, but is much less likely to be so where Y is one of many. Moreover, an exclusive or sole distributor is far more likely to be amenable to such a restriction than one who is not.

5.1.10   Retention of title

See **Clause 5Q**.

Retention of title is inherent in a hire purchase or lease agreement (although should nonetheless be expressly stated) but not in a sale agreement where there is either part or no payment prior to delivery.

A retention of title clause will be effective where the goods sold are not then subsumed in a new product by the purchaser. Provided that the whole title is retained there is no need for registration of a charge under the provisions of the Companies Act 2006, s.860. The creation of a fiduciary relationship may enable goods to be traced to subsequent sub-purchasers – *Aluminium Industrie Vaassen BV v. Romalpa Aluminium Ltd* [1976] 2 All ER 552, [1976] 1 WLR 676, CA.

5.1.11   Set off

See **Clause 5R**.

Set off arises in two guises:

(a) the *proferens* denying the other party the right to set off; and
(b) the *proferens* entitling itself to set off any sum owed to it by the other party against anything it may itself owe.

In practice (a) above is rare in commercial contracts though common in property leases and the like. On the other hand, (b) is a common provision where the *proferens* is providing the service and most payment will flow in its direction but there may be some situations in which it will be obliged to make some payment to the other party.

5.1.12   Severability and substitution

See **Clauses 5S** and **5T**.

A severance clause enables a contract or part of a term to survive when the rest is struck down for illegality or unreasonableness, etc. Options as to what will happen in that eventuality are available to the draftsman (and the parties), such as substitution of an alternative by agreement.

5.1.13   Third party rights

See **Clause 5U**.

Under the provisions of the Contracts (Rights of Third Parties) Act (CRTPA) 1999 a named third party may seek to enforce benefits it is given under the agreement notwithstanding the fact that it is not a party. In summary CRTPA 1999 provides as follows:

1.   One of two conditions must be met (s.1). Either:

(a) there must be an *express* term providing that a third party may enforce the term in question; or
(b) the term purports to confer a benefit upon him.

2. The third party must be expressly identified in the contract:
   (a) by name; and/or
   (b) as member of a class; and/or
   (c) as answering a particular description.

3. There is no right conferred on a third party to enforce a term of the contract otherwise than in accordance with other relevant terms of the contract.

4. The third party may avail himself of any of the enforcement remedies available to a contracting party, e.g. specific performance, etc.

5. A third party may rely upon an exclusion clause in favour of that third party.

6. The original parties cannot usually vary the original contract without the third party's consent. There are, however, some exceptions to this.

7. There is provision for dispensing with the third party's consent to variation, etc. on application to the arbitral tribunal or court.

8. Where a third party brings proceedings all defences (but not counterclaims) that would have been available in an action brought by the promisee are available to the promisor (i.e. the person against whom the third party is seeking to enforce the term). It may, therefore, be desirable either to exclude the operation of CRTPA 1999 or, if it is desired to make its application effective, to ensure that the contract contains all the details necessary.

9. In principle the existence of rights of enforcement by the third party against the promisor do not affect the rights of the other contracting party. This is subject to the avoidance of double recovery (ss.4, 5).

10. CRTPA 1999 does not apply to contracts for the carriage of goods.

11. A third party cannot rely upon CRTPA 1999 to challenge a term restricting or avoiding the liability of the promisor for negligently causing damage or loss (other than injury or death) (s.7(2)).

12. An arbitration clause is binding in a dispute between a third party and the promisor where the third party is seeking to enforce a term of the contract against the promisor.

As a general rule parties tend to exclude the operation of CRTPA 1999 in commercial contracts (although an example of an exception is the franchise agreement where provision is made for third party rights being conferred upon the master franchisor).

5.1.14　Waiver

See **Clauses 5V** and **5W**.

A waiver clause which protects the *proferens* (or either party if desired) is a sensible safety measure giving the beneficiary flexibility in dealing with any breach. Waiver can result in an estoppel and can prove fatal to a party's ability to enforce its rights.

5.1.15　Whole contract

See **Clause 5X**.

A whole contract clause is intended to reduce the scope for a party contending that there are implied terms resulting from pre-contract representations incorporated into the written agreement. It cannot entirely remove the risk of there being found to be a collateral contract but it is usually a prudent inclusion.

CLAUSE 5A   Arbitration

1. Arbitration

1.1. In the event that any dispute arises in connection with or out of this Agreement it shall be referred to an arbitrator ('the Arbitrator') under the Rules of the Chartered Institute of Arbitrators ('the Rules').

1.2. If a dispute is referred to the Arbitrator under the provisions of this Clause 1 the Rules shall be deemed to be incorporated into this Agreement.

or

CLAUSE 5B   Arbitration

1. Arbitration

1.1. Any dispute or difference between the Parties which arises in connection with this Agreement shall be referred for arbitration by a single arbitrator ('the Arbitrator').

1.2. The seat of the arbitration shall be [*specify location*].

1.3. The Arbitrator shall be appointed by the Parties by Agreement within [...] weeks of either Party informing the other of the existence of a dispute or difference between them.

1.4. If the Parties are unable to agree the appointment of an Arbitrator within the time specified in Clause 1.3, or such further time as they shall both agree, then the [President of the Law Society *or other*] will be invited by the Parties jointly to make an appointment.

1.5. The procedure for the arbitration shall be agreed by the Parties, or failing agreement by them within [...] weeks of the appointment of the Arbitrator, or such further period as they shall both agree, by the Arbitrator himself.

1.6. [If either Party fails to comply with any procedural order by the Arbitrator the Arbitrator may make an award in the defaulting Party's absence.]

CLAUSE 5C   Assignment not permitted

1. Assignment not permitted

1.1. No novation, assignment or delegation of the obligations and benefits of this Agreement by X is permitted.

or

CLAUSE 5D   Agreement personal to one party

1. Agreement personal to X

1.1. This Agreement is personal to X. X may not assign his rights or liabilities under this Agreement without the express prior written permission of Y which permission shall be in Y's absolute discretion.

or

CLAUSE 5E Assignment

1. Assignment

1.1. Neither Party may assign, charge, mortgage, sub-contract, delegate or otherwise assign or transfer its rights or obligations under this Agreement save where express provision is made for the same in this Agreement, without the prior written consent of the other Party.

1.2. A Party may assign or transfer its rights under this Agreement if such assignment or transfer takes place in the context of the disposal of all of its business to which the Service is related provided that, in the case of a proposed assignment by Y, the proposed assignee or transferee undertakes to X directly in a form reasonably required by X to be bound by the obligations of the proposed assignor.

or

CLAUSE 5F Assignment permitted

1. Assignment permitted

1.1. The Purchaser may assign its rights and benefits under this Agreement in whole or in part at any time prior to or after Completion.

CLAUSE 5G Confidentiality

1. Confidentiality

1.1. Each Party agrees not to disclose any confidential information provided by the other Party during the Term or at any time thereafter to any third party save where the law requires. Each Party also agrees not to use any such confidential information for any purpose other than the performance of this Agreement and will not use the information for any business or other purpose of its own. For the avoidance of doubt such information includes but is not limited either in type, *genus* or subject to:

    1.1.1. all marketing information and intelligence

    1.1.2. all costings and prices

    1.1.3. all trade secrets, processes and formulae.

1.2. Each Party undertakes to procure that its employees, directors, agents and advisers and any other persons to whom it makes available confidential information shall also keep confidential the information the subject of this Clause 1.

or

CLAUSE 5H Confidentiality

1. Confidentiality

1.1. X agrees not to disclose any confidential information provided by Y during the Term or at any time thereafter to any third party save where the law requires. X also agrees not to use any such confidential business information other than for running of the Business and will not use the information for any business or other purpose of its own. For the avoidance of doubt such information includes but is not limited either in type, *genus* or subject to:

1.1.1. all business information supplied to X by Y regarding the Business

1.1.2. all marketing information and intelligence

1.1.3. all trade secrets, processes and formulae.

1.2. For the proper protection of the confidential information X will ensure that:

1.2.1. any employee or member of his staff, whether temporary or permanent, will at the commencement of their employment and no later be provided with a contract of employment or engagement which will include a like obligation to that of X in respect of confidential information

1.2.2. any [director *or* partner] of X or any associated [company *or* firm] will be required to provide, in a form approved by Y, an undertaking in regard to confidential information in like form to that set out above in relation to X before being given access to confidential information.

CLAUSE 5I   Further action

1. Further action

1.1. The Parties agree that they will expeditiously carry out such further acts as may be necessary for the purpose of this Agreement including the execution and delivery of such instruments, deeds, licences, notifications as may be reasonably required by the other Party or by law.

CLAUSE 5J   Indemnity

1. Indemnity

1.1. X will indemnify Y in respect of any losses, damage or liability Y may incur as a result of X's acts or omissions, whether deliberate, accidental, negligent or reckless, in the course of the performance or purported performance of its obligations or rights under this Agreement whether such acts or omissions amount to a breach of an express or implied obligation under this Agreement or a breach of any other legal requirement or obligation, code of practice, licence, consent, forbearance, approval, permission or rule.

1.2. For the avoidance of doubt losses, damage and liability shall include but not be limited to economic and commercial loss, loss of goodwill, legal and other costs associated with legal proceedings of any kind which Y has to bring or to which it has to respond, fines, penalties, damages and any financial consequence whatever flowing directly or indirectly from the matters set out in this Clause 1.

or

CLAUSE 5K   Indemnity

1. Indemnity

1.1. Each Party shall keep the other indemnified in respect of any loss, damage, penalty, surcharge, fine, confiscation, claim or demand of any kind the other shall suffer as a result of the former's negligence, breach of contract or other wrongful act or omission.

CLAUSE 5L   Insolvency

1. Insolvency

1.1. X may terminate this Agreement forthwith in the event that Y:

    1.1.1. is [declared bankrupt *or* wound up due to insolvency]

    1.1.2. makes or seeks a composition with its creditors

    1.1.3. enters into or seeks an insolvent voluntary arrangement

    1.1.4. becomes the subject of the appointment of a manager, receiver or liquidator

    1.1.5. is the subject of an administration order

    1.1.6. has its assets charged or seized for the satisfaction of a debt.

CLAUSE 5M   Jurisdiction and proper law

1. Jurisdiction and proper law

1.1. This Agreement is governed by the law of England and Wales and is subject to the [exclusive] jurisdiction of the courts of England and Wales.

CLAUSE 5N   Non-compete

1. Non-compete

1.1. Each of the Vendors must not for a period of [2] years after the date of this Agreement for any reason be engaged in, involved or associated with, either by himself or in connection or association with any other person or entity, any business within [the United Kingdom *or* the European Union *or* 10 miles of [*specify*] *or* [*other geographical area*]] which is similar to that of the Company [or any subsidiary or associated company thereof] whether as franchisee, agent, principal, adviser, shareholder or in any other capacity.

1.2. Each of the Vendors must not for a period of [12] months after termination either for himself or on behalf of any other entity, seek, solicit or obtain orders from any entity which was a customer of the Company [or any subsidiary or associated company thereof] at the date of this Agreement [or for a period of [2] years prior thereto].

1.3. Each of the Vendors shall not for a period of [12] months after the date of this Agreement seek to entice away or recruit any employee of either the Company [or its subsidiaries or associated companies] who was so employed at the date of this Agreement.

or

CLAUSE 5O   Non-compete

1. Non-compete

1.1. Both during the currency of the Agreement and for a period of [2] years after termination for whatever reason the Exclusive Agent may not act as Agent or Principal or in any other capacity whatsoever in the sale or supply or negotiations for the sale or supply of [Products *or* [*class of products*]] of like or similar description or of a type within the [Territory *or* Territories] which would be likely to interfere with the Principal's sales and supply of the [Products *or* [*class of products*]] without first obtaining the written consent of the Principal.

CLAUSE 5P   Re-organisation of business structure or ownership

1. Re-organisation of business structure or ownership

1.1. X may terminate this Agreement if there is any material re-organisation of Y's business structure unless:

1.1.1. such re-organisation is not the result of insolvency

1.1.2. the resultant company or organisation is bound by the provisions of this Agreement

1.1.3. the beneficial ownership of the resultant entity is not in the hands of competitors of X anywhere in the world except to the extent that such ownership does not exceed [10%] of the total.

CLAUSE 5Q   Retention of title

1. Retention of title

1.1. The title to any consignment of the Goods will remain with X until X has received:

1.1.1. full payment for them

1.1.2. full payment for any other Goods or products supplied under any other contract between X and Y.

1.2. Until full payment is received as specified in this Clause 1 Y hereby acknowledges that he has possession of them solely as bailee and in a fiduciary capacity for X.

1.3. Y will not pledge, charge or in any way encumber the Goods unless and until title has passed.

1.4. Y will store the Goods separately from any other goods on his premises and ensure that they are marked or readily identifiable as the property of X until title has passed.

1.5. X shall have a right of inspection at any reasonable time of the Goods whilst they remain his property and may re-take possession of them at any time if title has not passed.

CLAUSE 5R   Set off

1. Set off

1.1. Notwithstanding any other express or implied term of this Agreement X reserves the right to set off against any sum payable or owed by it to Y any debt or other liability, whether absolute or contingent, owed by Y to X, or any sum, debt or other liability, absolute or contingent, owed by Y to any third party for which X is liable or may be liable in default of payment or discharge by Y. In the event of such set off Y irrevocably authorises X to pay from such sum or sums held by X for Y such sum as will discharge any such debt or liability to a third party or discharge the debt or sum owed to X.

CLAUSE 5S   Severability

1. Severability

1.1. In the event that any term of this Agreement is found to be invalid or otherwise unenforceable then such term shall be regarded and construed as severable from the Agreement so as not to affect the validity and enforceability of the remainder.

or

CLAUSE 5T   Substitution and severability

1. Substitution and severability

1.1. If the time limits or geographical extent of any of the covenants in Clause [...] is found to be unreasonable then there shall be substituted in respect thereof such limitations as shall be decided by any competent court or tribunal required to determine issues arising from this Agreement and the covenants herein as lawful, reasonable and proportionate.

1.2. If notwithstanding the provisions set out in this Clause 1 any term of this Agreement is found to be invalid or otherwise unenforceable then such term shall be regarded and construed as severable from the Agreement so as not to affect the validity and enforceability of the remainder.

CLAUSE 5U   Third party rights

1. Third party rights

1.1. The Parties to this Agreement agree that it is not hereby intended that any rights should be conferred upon or enforceable by any third party as defined in the Contracts (Rights of Third Parties) Act 1999.

CLAUSE 5V   Waiver

1. Waiver

1.1. No failure or delay on the part of X to exercise the whole or any part of any right or remedy under this Agreement shall be construed or operate as a waiver of that right in whole or in part.

or

CLAUSE 5W   Waiver

1. Waiver

1.1. No failure, neglect or delay in enforcing any of the terms of this Agreement may be construed as a waiver of any of X's rights in respect thereof nor such neglect, failure or delay a variation of the express terms of the Agreement.

1.2. X may at its absolute discretion in whole or in part release, compound or compromise, or grant time or indulgence to any party for any liability under this Agreement without affecting its rights against that or any other party under the same or any other liability.

CLAUSE 5X   Whole agreement

1. Whole agreement

1.1. This Agreement supersedes and replaces any previous agreement between the Parties whether oral or in writing in relation to the Project. The Parties hereby agree that in entering into this Agreement neither has relied upon any warranty or representation made by or on behalf of the other Party save where expressly stated in this Agreement. The Parties hereby agree that this Agreement constitutes the whole agreement between the Parties in respect of the Project. The Parties agree that no variation may be made to it unless such variation is in writing and signed by both Parties.

1.2. Nothing in this Clause 1 shall be construed as limiting or excluding either Party's liability to the other for fraud or deceit in inducing the making of this Agreement.

Specific commercial agreements

6

Agency

6.1   Introduction

This chapter is concerned with agencies which arise from agreements between principals and agents who are not employees of the principal.

There are essentially three main types of such agency:

1. An agency where the agent has the principal's authority to negotiate contracts and, where appropriate, to enter into binding agreements on his behalf.
2. An agency where the agent is effectively a representative of the principal but has no authority to enter into contractual arrangements on his behalf. Such an agent is sometimes called an introducer.
3. A *del credere* agent where the agent guarantees to the principal the performance by the other party to a contract into which the agent has entered on behalf of the principal.

Each type of agency may be exclusive or non-exclusive. It is important to be clear when drafting which type of agency is intended and exactly what its parameters are.

Provided they relate to the sale and purchase of goods, it is likely that all such agencies are now subject to the Commercial Agents (Council Directive) Regulations 1993, SI 1993/3053 (as amended), which are the British version of Council Directive 86/653/EEC (the Commercial Agents Directive). In *PJ Pipe and Valve Co Ltd* v. *Audco India Ltd* [2005] EWHC 1904, QB it was established that even an introducer may be a commercial agent for the purposes of the Regulations. This decision was applied in *Accentuate Ltd* v. *Asigra Inc* [2009] 2 Lloyd's Rep. 59 where a negotiating introducer was found to be capable of being a commercial agent provided that he was not forbidden from soliciting contractual offers, following the decision in *Nigel Fryer Joinery Services Ltd* v. *Ian Firth Hardware Ltd* [2008] 2 Lloyd's Rep. 108.

Although the Regulations contain various provisions which affect the relationship, in part reflecting continental practice, the principal effect is that they provide for two methods of compensation to the agent if the principal terminates the relationship, apart from and in possible addition to any contractual remedy that might be available – see regs. 16 and 17. There can be no derogation from the Regulations.

There can be complications over which national version of the Commercial Agents Directive applies but these are largely avoided when the agency agreement contains a choice of law provision.

There is effectively no way of avoiding payment of one year's commission if the agreement comes within the Regulations and the agent's contract is terminated by the principal without cause. However the following steps (mostly in the alternative) may avoid or limit the effect of the Regulations:

1. Avoid a self-employed agency contract by providing for a fixed-term employment contract.
2. Do not give the agent the authority to negotiate a contract even if non-binding on the principal.
3. Fix the indemnity payable at a maximum of one year's lost commission.
4. Tightly define the agent's responsibilities and include a provision that he cannot vary any responsibility which keeps him outside the Regulations without the principal's written consent.

In practical terms, although the UK Regulations can be more generous than those adopted by other EU countries in relation to compensation, it may be possible to limit the effect of making the UK Regulations applicable by appropriate measures such as those set out in (2)–(4) above.

The precedents provided (**Precedents 6A** and **6B**) both allow the draftsman to include options which are intended to put the agency outside the scope of the Regulations. However, it must be borne in mind that the jurisprudence is developing and therefore it is not possible to guarantee that the Regulations will not apply where the agent is involved in the sale and supply of goods save in very clear cases where he has only a very minimal role and does not actually develop the principal's business.

PRECEDENT 6A   Agreement for exclusive agency

AGREEMENT FOR EXCLUSIVE AGENCY

(Drafted on behalf of the Principal)

THIS AGREEMENT is dated [...] and is made BETWEEN:

1. [*Name of Principal*] [of [*address*] *or* whose registered office is at [*address*]], [*company registration number*] ('the Principal'); and
2. [*Name of Exclusive Agent*] [of [*address*] *or* [whose registered office is at [*address*]], [*company registration number*] ('the Exclusive Agent').

RECITALS

1. The Principal carries on the business of [...] and wishes to appoint the Exclusive Agent to promote the [Products *or* [*class of products, etc.*]] as defined below.
2. The Exclusive Agent wishes to act as agent for the Principal in the promotion of the [Products *or* [*class of products, etc.*]].

DEFINITIONS

In this Agreement and the Schedules, the following words shall have the following meanings:

'Agency'	The right and obligation of the Exclusive Agent to act as exclusive agent of the Principal within the Exclusive [Territory *or* Territories] in respect of the [Products *or* [*class of products*]].
'Agreed Address/es'	Any address agreed by the Parties as an address for service of any notices under this Agreement as set out in Schedule 4 and as may be varied by agreement from time to time.
'Commission'	Sums earned by the Exclusive Agent in consideration of his carrying out his agency duties under this Agreement.
'Completed Sales'	1. Where the Principal has accepted an order and the transaction has been concluded as a result of the Exclusive Agent's action or where the transaction is concluded with a third party whom the Exclusive Agent has previously acquired as a customer for transactions of the same kind. 2. Where the transaction has been entered into with a customer belonging to the [Territory *or* Territories].
'Directive'	Council Directive 86/653/EEC.
'Exclusive [Territory *or* Territories]'	That territory or those territories as specified in Schedule 2 or as may be varied by written agreement between the Parties from time to time.
'Intellectual Property'	All copyrights, trade names, trade marks, designs and devices relating to the [Products *or* [*class of products*]].
'Parties'	The Principal and the Exclusive Agent.
'Previous Agent'	Any agent of the Principal who was [an] agent for the [Territory *or* Territories] prior to the commencement of this Agreement.
['Products' *or* '[*Class of products, etc.*]']	Those products specified in Schedule 1.
'Regulations'	The Commercial Agents (Council Directive) Regulations 1993 SI 1993/3053 as amended.
'Schedule/s'	The Schedules attached to this Agreement.
'Target[s]'	Target[s] as set out in Schedule 3 or as varied by written agreement between the Parties from time to time.

INTERPRETATION

In this Agreement:

1. The singular includes the plural and one gender includes all.
2. References to Schedules and Clauses are to those in this Agreement.
3. Reference to a statutory provision includes any amendment or replacement provision relevant to the Agreement.
4. Reference to a document includes that document as amended, altered or replaced subsequent to the date of this Agreement.

5.   Reference to writing includes facsimile transmission, e-mail and similar media unless the context otherwise expressly provides.

6.   Time expressed in days excludes the first day but includes the last day. If the last day does not fall on a normal business day in [both] England and Wales [and the [Territory or Territories]] then the last day will be deemed to be the first normal business day thereafter in [the [Territory or Territories] and] England and Wales].

7.   The headings in this document do not form part of the Agreement.

OPERATIVE PROVISIONS

1. Appointment of the Exclusive Agent

1.1. By this Agreement the Principal appoints the Exclusive Agent from [date] to be an Exclusive Agent for the sale of the [Products or [class of products]] in the Exclusive [Territory or Territories].

1.2. If the Exclusive Agent fails to meet the Target for each period the Exclusive Agent shall immediately lose his exclusivity in the Exclusive [Territory or Territories].

2. Duration of the Agency

2.1. The Exclusive Agent is appointed for a term of [...] years.

2.2. Either Party may terminate this Agreement. Termination may be effected by either Party giving the other written notice as follows (*Note: These are the minimum periods under reg.15 of the Regulations.*):

   2.2.1. in the first calendar year from the date of this Agreement at least 1 month

   2.2.2. in the second calendar year at least 2 months

   2.2.3. in the third calendar year at least 3 months.

2.3. Notice may be given and end on any day of the month.

3. Obligations of the Principal

3.1. The Principal must at all material times act in good faith towards the Exclusive Agent.

3.2. The Principal must provide the Exclusive Agent at all material times with such information and materials as he reasonably requires for the carrying out of his duties as Exclusive Agent including samples, catalogues and price lists. Any such materials and information shall remain the exclusive property of the Principal to whom they must be returned on termination of the Agency for whatever reason.

3.3. The Principal must provide the Exclusive Agent with the necessary information relating to the Products and necessary for the performance of his duties under this Agreement.

3.4. [Within [...] month[s] after the completion of each quarter starting on the [... day of ...] the Principal will provide the Exclusive Agent in writing which may include by fax or e-mail transmission, with a detailed statement of Commission earned during that quarter.]

or

[The Principal must give to the Exclusive Agent a detailed statement of the Commission due not later than the last day of the month following the quarter in which the Commission has become due. If requested by the Exclusive Agent, the Principal must give to the Exclusive Agent such information as the Exclusive Agent may reasonably require to verify the amount of Commission earned by him.]

3.5. In the event of difficulties with supply of the [Product or [class of products]] the Principal must inform the Exclusive Agent as soon as reasonably possible.

3.6. At all material times the Principal will use his best endeavours to ensure that the Exclusive Agent is kept appraised of current prices, specifications and other information originating from the Principal relevant to the Exclusive Agent's duties as Exclusive Agent.

3.7. On receipt of any order from the Exclusive Agent which the Principal accepts, the Principal will use its best endeavours to ensure that the Products are dispatched to the customer as soon as reasonably practicable.

3.8. The Principal will notify the Exclusive Agent within a reasonable period if it anticipates that the volume of commercial transactions will be significantly lower than that which the Exclusive Agent could normally have expected.

3.9. The Principal will inform the Exclusive Agent within a reasonable period of its acceptance or refusal of, and of any non-execution by it of, a commercial transaction which the Exclusive Agent has procured for it.

4. Obligations of the Exclusive Agent

4.1. It is the obligation of the Exclusive Agent during the term of this Agreement:

4.1.1. to serve the Principal faithfully and diligently

4.1.2. to promote with his best endeavours the [Products *or* [*class of products*]] in the Exclusive [Territory *or* Territories].

4.2. In all transactions the Exclusive Agent must disclose to the customer or potential customer or relevant third party that he is the agent of the Principal.

4.3. [The Exclusive Agent may not bind the Principal to any contractual agreement without the Principal's prior written authority.] [The Exclusive Agent may not negotiate any terms with potential customers, whether contractually binding or otherwise, other than to inform them of prices, availability and other like information about the [Products *or* [*class of products*]].] [The Exclusive Agent may only take orders for the [Products *or* [*class of products*]] at the Principal's list prices and at its standard trading terms]. (*Note: This clause is likely to have the effect of placing the contract outside the Regulations provided other requirements are met – see commentary.*)

or

[The Exclusive Agent may take orders provided that the customer is expressly told prior to the taking of such orders that it is subject to approval by the Principal.] (*Note: This exclusion may disengage the Regulations but the outcome is uncertain – see commentary.*)

4.4. [The Principal has the right to refuse any order obtained by the Exclusive Agent without providing any explanation for such refusal. In the event that any order is refused by the Principal for the avoidance of doubt no commission will be payable in respect thereof.]

4.5. The Exclusive Agent may not act as agent on behalf of the Principal outside the Exclusive [Territory *or* Territories].

4.6. Both during the currency of the Agreement and for a period of [2] years after termination for whatever reason the Exclusive Agent may not act as Agent or Principal or in any other capacity whatsoever in the sale or supply or negotiations for the sale or supply of [Products *or* [*class of products*]] of like or similar description or of a type within the [Territory *or* Territories] which would be likely to interfere with the Principal's sales and supply of the [Products *or* [*class of products*]] without first obtaining the written consent of the Principal.

4.7. On the obtaining of any order the Exclusive Agent will transmit it to the Principal as soon as reasonably practicable.

4.8. The Exclusive Agent does not have authority to make any representations or provide any warranty in respect of the [Products *or* [*class of products*]] without the express written authority of the Principal.

4.9. The Exclusive Agent does not have the authority nor must he hold himself out as having the authority of the Principal to pledge the Principal's credit.

4.10. The Exclusive Agent is not authorised to accept any money on behalf of the Principal nor to enter into any compromise or similar agreement with any of the Principal's customers.

4.11. The Principal is not responsible for any costs incurred by the Exclusive Agent save where he has agreed to be so responsible in advance in writing.

4.12. The Exclusive Agent must provide the Principal with a monthly written report of his activities.

4.13. The Exclusive Agent must achieve the Target[s]. Failure to do so is a fundamental breach of this Agreement. The attainment of the Target[s] will be monitored by the Principal as set out in Schedule 3. The Exclusive Agent must procure orders from customers or purchasers located within the Exclusive [Territory *or* Territories] for delivery of the Products resulting in minimum annual sales equivalent to the Target[s].

4.14. The Exclusive Agent may not vary, increase or decrease his obligations under this Agreement without the express prior written consent of the Principal. In the event that the Exclusive Agent voluntarily assumes increased or different obligations from those set out in this Agreement without such prior written consent such obligations do not constitute terms of the Agreement or obligations under the Agency.

5. Remuneration

5.1. The Exclusive Agent shall be entitled to Commission on Completed Sales made to a customer which is situated within the Exclusive [Territory *or* Territories].

5.2. The Exclusive Agent shall be entitled to receive Commission on sales made to a customer which is situated within the [Territory *or* Territories] as soon as, and to the extent that, one of the following circumstances occurs:

5.2.1. the Principal has executed the transaction or

5.2.2. the Principal should, according to his agreement with the third party, have executed the transaction or

5.2.3. the third party has executed the transaction.

5.3. The Exclusive Agent shall not be entitled to Commission if that Commission is payable to the Previous Agent, unless it is equitable because of the circumstances for the Commission to be shared between the agents.

5.4. Any Commission which the Exclusive Agent receives to which he is not entitled shall be repayable by him on demand.

5.5. The amount of Commission payable shall be [...]% of the nett price of the [Products *or* [*class of products*]].

5.6. The Exclusive Agent shall be entitled to Commission on any Completed Sales made after the termination of this Agreement which directly resulted from orders placed by him with the Principal prior to the termination provided that the Completed Sales are made within a reasonable time and in any event not later than [...] months after the termination.

5.7. The Exclusive Agent will also be entitled to Commission on any Completed Sales made on orders placed after the termination of this Agreement but which emanate from customers within the Exclusive [Territory *or* Territories] and which are largely attributable to the efforts of the Exclusive Agent provided that:

5.7.1. the Completed Sale takes place within [...] months of the termination of the Agreement and

5.7.2. the Completed Sale was wholly or largely attributable to the efforts of the Exclusive Agent.

5.8. The Commission shall become payable not later than the last day of the month following the quarter in which it became due.

5.9. The right to Commission can be extinguished only if and to the extent that:

5.9.1. it is established that the contract between the third party and the Principal will not be executed and

5.9.2. that fact is due to a reason for which the Principal is not to blame.

5.10. Any Commission which the Exclusive Agent has already received shall be refunded if the right to it is extinguished.

6. Indemnity on termination

6.1. In the event that:

6.1.1. the Exclusive Agent is found by a court of competent jurisdiction to be a commercial agent within the meaning of the Regulations and/or Directive and

6.1.2. this Agreement is terminated in such a way as to entitle the Exclusive Agent to an indemnity or compensation within the meaning of the Regulations and/or Directive

then it is agreed by the Parties that the Exclusive Agent will be entitled to an indemnity and not compensation within the meaning of the Regulations and Directive. The amount of the indemnity may not exceed a figure equivalent to an indemnity for one year calculated from the Exclusive Agent's average annual remuneration over the preceding five years and if the contract goes back less than five years the indemnity shall be calculated on the average for the period in question. *(Note: This wording is taken from reg. 17 of the Regulations and Article 17 of the Directive.)*

7. Intellectual Property

7.1. The Intellectual Property belongs [exclusively] to the Principal and the Exclusive Agent has no proprietary right or interest in it whatever.

7.2. The Exclusive Agent may use the Intellectual Property and such literature [and other media] as may be provided by the Principal only as the Principal expressly authorises.

7.3. The Exclusive Agent must not infringe the rights of the Principal in respect of the Intellectual Property and must inform the Principal of any infringement or threatened infringement by any third party of which he is aware, including passing off, as expeditiously as is reasonably possible and if reasonably required by the Principal thereinafter assist the Principal in any remedial action.

8. Confidential information

8.1. The Exclusive Agent agrees not to disclose any confidential information provided by the Principal during the currency of this Agreement or at any time thereafter to any third party save where the law requires.

9. Waiver

9.1. No failure, neglect or delay in enforcing any of the terms of this Agreement may be construed as a waiver of any of the Principal's rights in respect thereof nor such neglect, failure or delay a variation of the express terms of the Agreement.

10. Variation

10.1. Any variation of the terms of this Agreement must be in writing signed by the Principal and the Exclusive Agent.

11. Agreement personal to the Exclusive Agent

11.1. This Agreement is personal to the Exclusive Agent. The Exclusive Agent may not assign his rights or liabilities under this Agreement without the express prior written permission of the Principal which permission shall be in the Principal's absolute discretion.

12. Termination of this Agreement

12.1. The Principal may summarily terminate this Agreement by written notice to the Exclusive Agent in any of the following circumstances:

12.1.1. the Exclusive Agent is made bankrupt

12.1.2. the Exclusive Agent is unable due to health or other personal reasons to carry out his duties under this Agreement for a period of more than [28 days]

12.1.3. the Exclusive Agent commits a breach of any term in this Agreement and where it is capable of remedy fails to do so within [28] days of being notified of the breach in writing by the Principal

12.1.4. the Exclusive Agent dies.

13. Notices

13.1. All notices under this Agreement shall be in writing and shall be delivered personally [or by first class, registered or recorded post] [or by facsimile transmission] in every case to the other Party's Agreed Address. [In the case of first class post notice will be deemed to be received [3] business days after the date of posting.]

14. *Force majeure*

14.1. In the event that either Party is unable to perform, or is delayed in its performance of its obligations under this Agreement due to circumstances beyond its reasonable control then it shall not be deemed to be in breach thereof providing that it gives prompt written notice thereof to the other Party.

15. Previous agreements

15.1. This Agreement supersedes and replaces any previous agreement between the Exclusive Agent and the Principal in relation to the Agency.

16. Law and jurisdiction

16.1. This Agreement is governed by the law of England and Wales and is subject to the [exclusive] jurisdiction of the courts of England and Wales. (*Note: This clause in either form will usually have the effect of engaging the UK Regulations if the agency is otherwise within their ambit – see commentary.*)

17. Schedules

17.1. The Schedules form part of this Agreement including any subsequent amendments made thereto.

Signed, etc.

SCHEDULE 1

The Products

[*Set out details of the Products*]

Signed, etc.

SCHEDULE 2

The Exclusive [Territory *or* Territories]

[*Set out particulars of the Exclusive Territory/Territories*]

Signed, etc.

SCHEDULE 3

The Target[s]

1. The Target will be as follows and will be reviewed on each anniversary of the Agreement or such other time as the Parties may agree:
    [*Sales first quarter, etc.*]
2. At the end of each quarter beginning on the last day of the month in which the Agreement is made or at such other time as the Parties may agree, the Principal will provide the Exclusive Agent with a schedule of sales made against the target for that quarter as 25% of the (annual) Target.
3. If the Exclusive Agent falls short of the Target by more than [...]% over a period of 12 months, such failure will constitute a failure to reach the Target.

Signed, etc.

SCHEDULE 4

Agreed Addresses

[*Set out details of Agreed Addresses*]

Signed, etc.

PRECEDENT 6B   Agreement for non-exclusive agency

AGREEMENT FOR NON-EXCLUSIVE AGENCY

(Drafted on behalf of the Principal)

THIS AGREEMENT is dated [...] and is made BETWEEN:

1. [*Name of Principal*] [of [*address*] *or* whose registered office is at [*address*]], [*company registration number*] ('the Principal'); and
2. [*Name of Agent*] [of [*address*] *or* whose registered office is at [*address*]], [*company registration number*] ('the Agent').

RECITALS

1.   The Principal carries on the business of [*specify*] and wishes to appoint the Agent to promote the [Products *or* [*class of products, etc.*]] as defined below.
2.   The Agent wishes to act as agent for the Principal in the promotion of the [Products *or* [*class of products, etc.*]].

DEFINITIONS

'Agency'	The Right and Obligation of the Agent to act as Agent of the Principal within the [Territory *or* Territories] in respect of the [Products *or* [*class of products*]].
'Agreed Address'	Any address agreed by the Parties as an address for service of any notices under this Agreement as set out in Schedule 4 and as may be varied by agreement from time to time.
'Commission'	Sums earned by the Agent in consideration of his carrying out his agency duties under this Agreement.
'Completed Sales'	Where the Principal has accepted an order and the transaction has been concluded as a result of the Agent's action or where the transaction is concluded with a third party whom the Agent has previously acquired as a customer for transactions of the same kind.
'Directive'	Council Directive 86/653/EEC
'Intellectual Property'	All copyrights, trade names, trade marks, designs and devices relating to the [Products *or* [*class of products*]].
'Parties'	The Principal and the Agent.
'Previous Agent'	Any agent of the Principal who was [an] agent for the [Territory *or* Territories] prior to the commencement of this Agreement.
'[Products *or* [*class of products, etc.*]]'	Those products specified in Schedule 1.
'Regulations'	The Commercial Agents (Council Directive) Regulations SI 1993/3053 as amended.
'Target[s]'	Target[s] as set out in Schedule 3 or as varied by written agreement between the parties from time to time.
'[Territory *or* Territories]'	That territory or those territories as specified in Schedule 2 or as may be varied by written agreement between the parties from time to time.

INTERPRETATION

In this Agreement:

1.   The singular includes the plural and one gender includes all.
2.   References to Schedules and Clauses are to those in this Agreement.
3.   Reference to a statutory provision includes any amendment or replacement provision relevant to the Agreement.
4.   Reference to a document includes that document as amended, altered or replaced subsequent to the date of this Agreement.

5. Reference to writing includes facsimile transmission, e-mail, and similar media unless the context otherwise expressly provides.
6. Time expressed in days excludes the first day but includes the last day. If the last day does not fall on a normal business day in [both] England and Wales [and the [Territory *or* Territories]] then the last day will be deemed to be the first normal business day thereafter in the [Territory *or* Territories and] [England and Wales].
7. The headings in this document do not form part of the Agreement.

OPERATIVE PROVISIONS

1. Appointment of the Agent

1.1. By this Agreement the Principal appoints the Agent from [*date*] to be an Agent for the sale of the [Products *or* [*class of products*]] in the [Territory *or* Territories].

2. Duration of the Agency

2.1. The Agent is appointed for a term of [3] years.

2.2. Either Party may terminate this Agreement. Termination may be effected by either Party giving the other written notice as follows (*Note: These are the minimum periods under reg. 15 of the Regulations.*):

2.2.1. in the first calendar year from the date of this Agreement at least 1 month

2.2.2. in the second calendar year at least 2 months

2.2.3. in the third calendar year at least 3 months.

2.3. Notice may be given and end on any day of the month.

3. Obligations of the Principal

3.1. The Principal must at all material times act in good faith towards the Agent.

3.2. The Principal must provide the Agent at all material times with such information and materials as he reasonably requires for the carrying out of his duties as Agent including samples, catalogues and price lists. Any such materials and information shall remain the exclusive property of the Principal to whom they must be returned on termination of the Agency for whatever reason.

3.3. The Principal must provide the Agent with the necessary information relating to the Products and necessary for the performance of his duties under this Agreement.

3.4. [Within [*1 month*] after the completion of each quarter starting on the [... day of ...] the Principal will provide the Agent in writing, which may include by fax or e-mail transmission, a detailed statement of Commission earned during that quarter.]

or

[The Principal must give to the Agent a detailed statement of the Commission due not later than the last day of the month following the quarter in which the Commission has become due. If requested by the Agent, the Principal must give to the Agent such information as the Agent may reasonably require to verify the amount of Commission earned by him.]

3.5. In the event of difficulties with supply of the [Products *or* [*class of products*]] the Principal must inform the Agent as soon as reasonably possible.

3.6. At all material times the Principal will use his best endeavours to ensure that the Agent is kept appraised of current prices, specifications and other information originating from the Principal relevant to the Agent's duties as agent.

3.7. On receipt of any order from the Agent which the Principal accepts it will use its best endeavours to ensure that the Products are dispatched to the customer as soon as reasonably practicable.

3.8. The Principal will notify the Agent within a reasonable period if it anticipates that the volume of commercial transactions will be significantly lower than that which the Agent could normally have expected.

3.9. The Principal will inform the Agent within a reasonable period of its acceptance or refusal of, and of any non-execution by it of, a commercial transaction which the Agent has procured for it.

4. Obligations of the Agent

4.1. It is the obligation of the Agent during the term of this Agreement to:

4.1.1. serve the Principal faithfully and diligently

4.1.2. promote with his best endeavours the [Products *or* [*class of products*]] through the [Territory *or* Territories]

4.2. In all transactions the Agent must disclose to the customer or potential customer or relevant third party that he is the agent of the Principal.

4.3. [The Agent may not bind the Principal to any contractual agreement without the Principal's prior written authority.] [The Agent may not negotiate any terms with potential customers, whether contractually binding or otherwise, other than to inform them of prices, availability and other like information about the [Products *or* [*class of products*]].] [The Agent may only take orders for the [Products *or* [*class of products*]] at the Principal's list prices and at its standard trading terms.] (*Note: This clause is very likely to have the effect of placing the contract outside the Regulations provided other requirements are met – see commentary.*)

or

[The Agent may take orders provided that the customer is expressly told prior to the taking of such order that it is subject to approval by the Principal.] (*Note: This exclusion may disengage the Regulations but the outcome is uncertain – see commentary.*)

4.4. [The Principal has the right to refuse any order obtained by the Agent without providing any explanation for such refusal. In the event that any order is refused by the Principal for the avoidance of doubt no Commission will be payable in respect thereof.]

4.5. The Agent may not act as Agent on behalf of the Principal outside the [Territory *or* Territories].

4.6. Both during the currency of the Agreement and for a period of [2] years after termination for whatever reason the Agent may not act as Agent or Principal or in any other capacity whatsoever in the sale or supply or negotiations for the sale or supply of [Products *or* [*class of products*]] of like or similar description or of a type which would be likely to interfere with the Principal's sales and supply of the [Products *or* [*class of products*]] within the [Territory *or* Territories] without first obtaining the written consent of the Principal.

4.7. On the obtaining of any order the Agent will transmit it to the Principal as soon as reasonably practicable.

4.8. The Agent does not have authority to make any representations or provide any warranty in respect of the [Products *or* [*class of products*]] without the express written authority of the Principal.

4.9. The Agent does not have the authority nor must he hold himself out as having the authority of the Principal to pledge the Principal's credit.

4.10. The Agent is not authorised to accept any money on behalf of the Principal nor to enter into any compromise or similar agreement with any of the Principal's customers.

4.11. The Principal is not responsible for any costs incurred by the Agent save where he has agreed to be so responsible in advance in writing.

4.12. The Agent must provide the Principal with a monthly written report of his activities.

4.13. The Agent must achieve the Target[s]. Failure to do so is a fundamental breach of this Agreement. The attainment of the Target[s] will be monitored by the Principal as set out in Schedule 3. The Agent must procure orders from customers or purchasers located within the [Territory *or* Territories] for delivery of the Products resulting in minimum annual sales equivalent to the Target[s].

4.14. The Agent may not vary, increase or decrease his obligations under this Agreement without the express prior written consent of the Principal. In the event that the Agent voluntarily assumes increased or different obligations from those set out in this Agreement without such prior written consent such obligations do not constitute terms of the Agreement or obligations under the Agency.

5. Remuneration

5.1. The Agent shall be entitled to Commission on sales concluded during the period covered by this Agreement where:

5.1.1. the transaction has been concluded as a result of his action or

5.1.2. the transaction is concluded with a third party whom he has previously acquired as a customer for transactions of the same kind and

5.1.3. the Principal has executed the transaction or

5.1.4. the Principal should, according to his agreement with the third party, have executed the transaction or

5.1.5. the third party has executed the transaction.

5.2. The amount of Commission payable shall be [*10*]% of the nett price of the [Products *or* [*class of products*]].

5.3. The Agent shall not be entitled to Commission if that Commission is payable to the Previous Agent, unless it is equitable because of the circumstances for the Commission to be shared between the Agents.

5.4. Any Commission which the Agent receives to which he is not entitled shall be repayable by him on demand.

5.5. The Agent shall be entitled to Commission on any Completed Sales made after the termination of his Agreement which directly resulted from orders placed by him with the Principal prior to the termination provided that the Completed Sales are made within a reasonable time and in any event not later than [*3 months*] after the termination.

5.6. The Agent will also be entitled to Commission on any Completed Sales made on orders placed after the termination of this Agreement but which emanate from customers within the [Territory *or* Territories] and which are largely attributable to the efforts of the Agent provided that the Completed Sale takes place within [*3 months*] of the termination of the Agreement.

5.7. The Commission shall become payable not later than the last day of the month following the quarter in which it became due.

5.8. The right to Commission can be extinguished only if and to the extent that:

5.8.1. it is established that the contract between the third party and the Principal will not be executed and

5.8.2. that fact is due to a reason for which the Principal is not to blame.

5.9. Any Commission which the Exclusive Agent has already received shall be refunded if the right to it is extinguished.

6. Indemnity on termination

6.1. In the event that:

6.1.1. the Agent is found by a court of competent jurisdiction to be a commercial agent within the meaning of the Regulations and/or Directive and

6.1.2. this Agreement is terminated in such a way as to entitle the Agent to an indemnity or compensation within the meaning of the Regulations and/or Directive

then it is agreed by the Parties that the Agent will be entitled to an indemnity and not compensation within the meaning of the Regulations and Directive. The amount of the indemnity may not exceed a figure equivalent to an indemnity for one year calculated from the commercial agent's average annual remuneration over the preceding five years and if the contract goes back less than five years the indemnity shall be calculated on the average for the period in question. (Note: The wording is taken from reg.17 of the Regulations and Article 17 of the Directive.)

7. Intellectual Property

7.1. The Intellectual Property belongs [exclusively] to the Principal and the Agent has no proprietary right or interest in it whatever.

7.2. The Agent may use the Intellectual Property and such literature [and other media] as may be provided by the Principal only as the Principal expressly authorises.

7.3. The Agent must not infringe the rights of the Principal in respect of the Intellectual Property and must inform the Principal of any infringement or threatened infringement by any third party of which he is aware, including passing off, as expeditiously as is reasonably possible and if reasonably required by the Principal thereinafter assist the Principal in any remedial action.

8. Confidential information

8.1. The Agent agrees not to disclose any confidential information provided by the Principal during the currency of this Agreement or at any time thereafter to any third party save where the law requires.

9. Waiver

9.1. No failure, neglect or delay in enforcing any of the terms of this Agreement may be construed as a waiver of any of the Principal's rights in respect thereof nor such neglect, failure or delay a variation of the express terms of the Agreement.

10. Variation

10.1. Any variation of the terms of this Agreement must be in writing signed by the Principal and the Agent.

11. Agreement personal to the Agent

11.1. This Agreement is personal to the Agent. The Agent may not assign his rights or liabilities under this Agreement without the express prior written permission of the Principal which permission shall be in the Principal's absolute discretion.

12. Termination of this Agreement

12.1. The Principal may summarily terminate this Agreement by written notice to the Agent in any of the following circumstances:

12.1.1. the Agent is made bankrupt

12.1.2. the Agent is unable due to health or other personal reasons to carry out his duties under this Agreement for a period of more than [*28 days*]

12.1.3. the Agent commits a breach of any term in this Agreement and where it is capable of remedy fails to do so within [28] days of being notified of the breach in writing by the Principal

12.1.4. the Agent dies.

13. Notices

13.1. All notices under this Agreement shall be in writing and shall be delivered personally [or by first class, registered or recorded post] [or by facsimile transmission] in every case to the other Party's Agreed Address. [In the case of first class post notice will be deemed to be received [3] business days after the date of posting.]

14. *Force majeure*

14.1. In the event that either Party is unable to perform, or is delayed in its performance of its obligations under this Agreement due to circumstances beyond its reasonable control then it shall not be deemed to be in breach thereof providing that it gives prompt written notice thereof to the other Party.

15. Previous agreements

14.1. This Agreement supersedes and replaces any previous agreement between the Agent and the Principal in relation to the Agency.

16. Law and jurisdiction

16.1. This Agreement is governed by the law of England and Wales and is subject to the [exclusive] jurisdiction of the courts of England and Wales. (*Note: This clause in either form will usually have the effect of engaging the UK Regulations if the agency is otherwise within their ambit – see commentary.*)

17. Schedules

17.1. The Schedules form part of this Agreement including any subsequent amendments made thereto.

Signed, etc.

SCHEDULE 1

The Products

[*Set out details of the Products*]

Signed, etc.

SCHEDULE 2

The Territory/Territories

[*Set out particulars of the Territory/Territories*]

Signed, etc.

SCHEDULE 3

The Targets

1. The Target will be as follows and will be reviewed on each anniversary of the Agreement or such other time as the Parties may agree:
    [*Sales first quarter, etc.*]
2. At the end of each quarter beginning on the last day of the month in which the Agreement is made or at such other time as the Parties may agree, the Principal will provide the Agent with a schedule of sales made against the target for that quarter as 25% of the (annual) Target.
3. If the Agent falls short of the Target by more than [*10*]% over a period of 12 months, such failure will constitute a failure to reach the Target.

SCHEDULE 4

Agreed Addresses

[*Set out details of Agreed Addresses*]

Signed, etc.

7

Buying and selling businesses

7.1   Introduction

The buying and selling of businesses essentially takes one of two forms. It either amounts to a transfer of share ownership (in the case of a company) or the purchase of a business's assets. This chapter is intended to provide a practical guide and precedents for simple acquisitions and sales in either form. For more complex acquisitions a specialist publication should be consulted.

The choice of which form to use may be largely determined by fiscal considerations which are beyond the scope of this publication. In the simplest terms, however, the principal considerations in the majority of cases will be the following.

7.2   Sale of shares

See **Precedent 7A**.

The simple transfer of shares enables a business to be transferred intact without the need to realise any of its assets and as a going concern. This may minimise potential problems over continued employment of employees, capital gains tax associated with particular assets, transfer of licences and consents, VAT, tax allowances, etc.

The principal disadvantage to the vendor is that it is usually necessary for it to provide extensive warranties and guarantees as well as a likely withholding of part of the purchase price as security for those warranties.

7.3   Sale of assets of a business

See **Precedent 7B**.

The sale of assets is unlikely to involve the need for any withholding of purchase consideration or the provision of warranties. However, transfer of undertaking complications may arise in the case of employees who will be continuing to work in the business under its new owners. There may also be complex tax issues to be addressed.

Certain businesses, for example banking, are governed by specific regulations and there are also controls on transfers which involve companies with significant market share. Neither of these issues is addressed in this chapter as both lie outside the scope of the title, as do company formations.

7.4   Pre-contract due diligence

It should go without saying that any purchase, save between connected parties, should be preceded by appropriate financial and legal investigation. The Financial Services and Markets Act 2000, s.397 makes it an offence to undertake misleading practices or make misleading statements in relation to the buying and selling of shares. The Act has less application in the case of a sale of assets rather than shares.

7.5   Restraint of trade

The principal modern authority is *Nordenfelt* v. *Maxim Nordenfelt Guns and Ammunition Co* [1894] AC 535 at 565. In essence, the courts recognise the difference between restraint of trade clauses in employment contracts and those in contracts for the sale and purchase of a business. A much greater degree of leniency is shown in the latter type of transaction.

It is for the benefiting party to establish that any restriction on competition is to protect a legitimate business interest. Broadly, a geographical restriction will only be justified to the extent that the business traded in that area. Duration may reflect consideration paid. It is worth noting that the restriction in the case of *Nordenfelt* was to last 25 years and was upheld.

Restrictions on solicitation and non-dealing are treated more leniently than in the case of employment-related contracts and may not be limited in geographical application. This is especially so where the customer contact is part of the consideration provided by the vendor. In general, a non-dealing clause will be expected to be of shorter duration than a non-solicitation clause.

Poaching of staff may be restricted but it does not follow that any restriction longer than that which would be acceptable in an employment contract will necessarily be upheld.

Confidential information may be given a more liberal meaning in the case of a sale and purchase agreement than in an employment context.

7.6   The position of vendors who remain employed by the business

It should be noted that where a vendor remains employed, possibly in an earn-out, by the business he has sold, restrictions may be imposed in his employment contract. If they are then they are subject to the employment law regime for the purpose of deciding whether they are justifiable, not the more lenient regime to which reference has been made.

7.7 Taxation

As stated above, detailed consideration of this topic is beyond the scope of this chapter. However, it should be noted that where part or the whole of the purchase price is paid for in share issues to the vendor, Her Majesty's Revenue and Customs (HMRC) may regard the transaction as amounting to a distribution under the Corporation Tax Act 2010, s.1000 and therefore liable to income tax as opposed to the generally more favourable capital gains tax.

7.8 Public limited companies

The City Code on Takeovers and Mergers applies to all acquisitions of public companies, whether listed or unlisted.

PRECEDENT 7A Sale and purchase agreement for whole of company's shares

SALE AND PURCHASE AGREEMENT FOR WHOLE OF COMPANY'S SHARES

THIS AGREEMENT is made on [date].

BETWEEN:

1. The persons whose names and addresses are set out in Schedule 1 ('the Vendors').
2. [Name of company] [registration number] whose registered office is at [address] ('the Purchaser').

RECITALS

1. [Name of company] is a company registered in England and Wales under number [registration number] ('the Company') and has an authorised share capital of £[...] divided into [number] [ordinary] shares of £[...] each, of which [number] [ordinary] shares of £[...] each have been issued and are fully paid.
2. The Vendors are the beneficial owners of the whole of the issued and allotted share capital in the Company and each of the Vendors is the sole beneficial owner and registered holder of the number of the Sale Shares as set out in Schedule 2.
3. The Vendors have agreed to sell, and the Purchaser has agreed to buy, all the issued shares in the Company on the following terms.

DEFINITIONS

In this Agreement the following definitions apply:

'Agreed Address'	The address of each Party as set out in Schedule 1.
'Completion'	The completion of the sale and purchase of the shares in the Company.
'Completion Accounts Date'	The date set out in Schedule 3.
'Consideration Shares'	[number] [ordinary] shares in the Purchaser each having a denomination of £[...].

'Disclosure Letter'	The disclosure letter of the date of this Agreement from the Vendors' solicitors to the Purchaser's solicitors together with the documents annexed thereto, a copy of which is annexed hereto in Schedule 6.
'Last Accounting Date'	The date set out in Schedule 3.
'Party' and 'Parties'	Each of the Purchaser and the Vendors.
['The Properties']	[Those properties set out in Schedule 4].
'Purchaser's Solicitors'	Messrs [...].
'Retention'	The sum of £[...].
'Retention Account'	An account at [...] Bank plc to be in the joint names of each of the Purchaser's Solicitors and the Vendors' Solicitors.
'Retention Payment Date'	[...] day of [...] 20[...].
'Sale Shares'	All of the [ordinary] shares in the Company as issued and allotted at the time of this Agreement as set out in Schedule 2.
['The Subsidiaries']	[The companies set out in Schedule 5].
'Vendors' Solicitors'	Messrs [...].
'Warranties'	The warranties set out in Schedule 6.

INTERPRETATION

In this Agreement:

1. The singular includes the plural and one gender includes all.
2. References to Schedules and Clauses are to those in this Agreement.
3. Reference to a statutory provision includes any amendment or replacement provision relevant to the Agreement.
4. Reference to a document includes that document as amended, altered or replaced subsequent to the date of this Agreement.
5. Reference to writing includes facsimile transmission, e-mail, and similar media unless the context otherwise expressly provides.
6. Time expressed in days excludes the first day but includes the last day. If the last day does not fall on a normal business day in both England and Wales then the last day will be deemed to be the first normal business day.
7. The headings in this document do not form part of the Agreement.

OPERATIVE PROVISIONS

1. Sale and purchase

1.1. The Vendors shall each sell to the Purchaser the number of the Sale Shares allotted to and held by them as set out in Schedule 2 with [full *or* limited] title guarantee free from any encumbrance whatever.

1.2. The sale and purchase of all Sale Shares must be completed simultaneously in accordance with this Agreement otherwise the Purchaser shall not be bound to complete the purchase of any.

2. Consideration

2.1. The consideration for the Sale Shares shall be:

2.1.1. the sum of £[...] which is to be paid to the Vendors' Solicitors at Completion [by way of banker's draft] less £[...] being the Retention.

2.1.2. the issue and allotment to the Vendors of the Consideration Shares in the amounts set out in Schedule 2.

3. Retention

3.1. The Purchaser shall provide the Vendors' Solicitors with the Retention at Completion [by way of banker's draft] which shall be paid by the Vendors' Solicitors into the Retention Account forthwith. For the avoidance of doubt the Retention is not and is not intended by the Parties to be a limitation on the amount the Purchaser may claim from the Vendors for breach of the Warranties or for any other cause or reason connected with or arising out of this Agreement.

4. Completion

4.1. Completion shall take place at the offices of the Purchaser's Solicitors [immediately following the making of this Agreement].

4.2. The Vendors shall deliver to the Purchaser (where necessary as agent of the Company) the following at the time of Completion:

4.2.1. share transfers of all of the Sale Shares executed by the respective holders and made in favour of the Purchaser or such other person or persons as the Purchaser may direct together with the relevant share certificates or such other or additional documents as are needed to give good title to the Purchaser and to enable the Purchaser to procure registration of the Sale Shares as it may direct

4.2.2. [certificates for the shares in the Subsidiaries held by the Company and transfers in favour of the Purchaser (or as the Purchaser may direct) in respect of any shares in the Subsidiaries not held by the Company]

4.2.3. confirmation by the Vendors executed as a deed by each of them in the form set out in Schedule 7 that they have no claims against the Company [or any of the Subsidiaries]

4.2.4. a deed of resignation in the form set out in Schedule 7 from:

4.2.4.1. each director [excluding those remaining with the agreement of the Purchaser]

4.2.4.2. the Company Secretary

4.2.4.3. [the directors and company secretaries of the Subsidiaries]

4.2.5. a letter of resignation from the Company's auditors [and those of the Subsidiaries] in the form set out in Schedule 7

4.2.6. the Company's [and each Subsidiary's] certificate of incorporation, certificate of incorporation on change of name (if applicable), Common Seal, statutory registers, minute books, share certificate books and all other books (all duly written up to date)

4.2.7. certified copies of resolutions of the board of the Company [and of the Subsidiaries] as set out in Schedule 7

4.2.8. [title deeds and all ancillary documents in respective of the Properties]

4.2.9. the power of attorney under which any document required to be delivered under this Clause 4.2 has been executed.

4.3. Upon completion of the obligations set out in Clause 4.2 the Purchaser shall:

4.3.1. pay to the Vendors' Solicitors [by bankers' draft] the sum of £[...] in sterling

4.3.2. pay to the Vendors' Solicitors the sum of £[...] in sterling to be placed by them into the Retention Account

4.3.3. allot and issue to the Vendors the Consideration Shares in the amounts set out in Schedule 2 credited as fully paid

4.3.4. deliver share certificates to the Vendors' Solicitors in respect of the Consideration Shares.

4.4. In the event that the requirements set out in Clause 4.2 are not met in full the Purchaser shall be entitled to:

4.4.1. continue to Completion in which case the Vendors will be obliged to use their best endeavours to comply with the outstanding requirements of Clause 4.2 or

4.4.2. substitute a new date for Completion

4.4.3. rescind this Agreement.

Nothing in this Clause 4.4 shall prejudice the right of the Purchaser to exercise any other right or remedy it may have.

4.5. For the avoidance of doubt delivery by and to the Vendors' or the Purchaser's Solicitors shall be deemed to be delivery by and to the respective Party.

5. Warranties

5.1. The Vendors jointly and severally warrant, undertake and represent to the Purchaser that:

5.1.1. the statements made in Schedule 6 are and will be at Completion true, correct and a fair presentation of the facts referable thereto subject only to those matters fully and accurately set out in the Disclosure Letter

5.1.2. [the statements in Schedule 6 are true, correct and a fair presentation of the facts referable thereto insofar as they are applicable to each of the Subsidiaries if additionally and separately each of the Subsidiaries' names were substituted for that of the Company therein]

5.1.3. the contents of the Disclosure Letter are true, correct and a fair presentation of the facts referable thereto

5.1.4. in no case referred to in this Clause 5 has there been any omission of any material information.

6. Vendors' liability

6.1. The Vendors shall be jointly and severally liable for any breach of any obligation under this Agreement.

7. Indemnities

7.1. The Vendors will indemnify the Purchaser for any loss or cost of whatever kind which it may suffer as a result of the Vendors being in breach of the Warranties and/or of any of the Warranties being untrue, misleading or in any way incomplete or incorrect for whatever reason.

8. The Consideration Shares

8.1. The Consideration Shares and the ordinary shares of £[...] issued at the date of this Agreement shall rank *pari passu* in all respects [save that they shall not rank for the [interim] dividend for the accounting year [20../..]].

8.2. The Purchaser [confirms that application has been made to the appropriate listing authority for the Consideration Shares to be admitted when allotted to trade on [the London

Stock Exchange *or* the Alternative Investment Market] [and] warrants that it has authority pursuant to the provisions of Sections 349–351 of the Companies Act 2006 to allot such Consideration Shares].

9. Payment of Retention

9.1. The Purchaser shall procure that the Retention shall be paid to the Vendors' Solicitors in whole or in part from the Retention Account on the Retention Payment Day upon the happening of the following:

9.1.1. written confirmation from the Purchaser's Solicitors to the Vendors' Solicitors that no claim has been made upon the Warranties in respect of which there is any sum outstanding to the Purchaser in which case the whole Retention shall be paid to the Vendors' Solicitors

9.1.2. written confirmation from the Purchaser's Solicitors that a claim has been made upon the Warranties in respect of which until resolved there is a sum outstanding in which case the said confirmation shall specify the sum that has been claimed or, if less, outstanding. In such case that part of the Retention if any which exceeds the sum claimed or outstanding (whichever of which is the lesser) shall be paid to the Vendors' Solicitors

9.1.3. interest earned on the Retention shall be paid to the recipient or recipients rateably according to the proportion receivable by them.

9.2. If any sum has been retained under this Clause 9 beyond the Retention Payment Date due to the existence of a claim:

9.2.1. in the event that a sum remains due and owing to the Purchaser after resolution or settlement of any claim by the Purchaser arising from the Warranties the Vendors shall procure that such sum be paid to the Purchaser's Solicitors from the Retention Account

9.2.2. in the event that the sum retained is more than that which is payable to the Purchaser under the claim as resolved or settled the Purchaser shall procure that the balance is paid to the Vendors' Solicitors from the Retention Account within 7 days of settlement or resolution together with interest earned thereon.

9.3. Such confirmation as is set out in this Clause 9 must be provided in writing to the Vendors' Solicitors not less than [7] days prior to the Retention Payment Date. In the event that no confirmation is provided by the due date then the Purchaser must procure that the Retention is paid to the Vendors' Solicitors on the Retention Payment Date in full together with interest earned thereon.

10. Waivers

10.1. All or any rights of pre-emption to which any of the Vendors is entitled is irrevocably waived by this Agreement in the Sale Shares.

10.2. No failure or delay on the part of the Purchaser to exercise the whole or any part of any right or remedy under this Agreement against any other Party shall be construed or operate as a waiver of that or any other right in whole or in part against that or any other Party.

10.3. The Purchaser may at its absolute discretion in whole or in part release, compound or compromise, or grant time or indulgence to any party for, any liability under this Agreement without affecting its rights against that or any other party under the same or any other liability.

11. Assignment

11.1. The Purchaser may assign its rights and benefits under this Agreement in whole or in part at any time prior to or after Completion.

12. Whole agreement

12.1. This Agreement supersedes and replaces any previous agreement between the Parties whether oral or in writing in relation to the sale and purchase of the Company. The Parties hereby agree that in entering into this Agreement they have not relied upon any warranty or representation made by or on behalf of the other Party save where expressly stated in this Agreement and its Schedules. The Parties hereby agree that this Agreement constitutes the whole agreement between the Parties in respect of the sale and purchase of the Company.

12.2. Nothing in this Clause shall be construed as limiting or excluding either Party's liability to the other for fraud or deceit in inducing the making of this Agreement.

12.3. The Vendors warrant that they have been advised by the Purchaser to seek independent legal and financial advice before entering into this Agreement and that their decision to make this Agreement is based solely upon their own judgment and assessment of the commerciality of the sale of the Company.

13. Costs of this transaction

13.1. Each of the Parties shall bear its own costs of this Agreement and transaction save that if the Purchaser is entitled to and does lawfully rescind the Agreement the Purchaser shall be entitled to have its reasonable legal and other costs of the transaction and the Agreement paid by the Vendors who, for the avoidance of doubt, shall be jointly and severally liable in respect thereof.

14. Confidentiality

14.1. The contents of this Agreement and the matters involved in this transaction are confidential to the Parties and their advisers and may not be communicated to any third party at any time before or after Completion except as required by law [and/or by the rules and regulations of the London Stock Exchange or the Financial Services Authority].

15. Non-compete

15.1. As a separate and additional covenant each of the Vendors covenants that:

15.1.1. he will not for a period of [...] years after the date of this Agreement for any reason be engaged in, involved or associated with, either by himself or in connection or association with any other person or entity, any business within [the United Kingdom *or* the European Union *or* 10 miles of [*specify*] *or* [*other geographical area*]] which is similar to that of the Company [and/or the Subsidiaries] whether as franchisee, agent, principal, adviser or in any other capacity.

15.1.2. he will not for a period of [...] years after termination either for himself or on behalf of any other entity, seek, solicit or obtain orders from any entity which was a customer of the Company [and/or the Subsidiaries] at the date of this Agreement [or for a period of [...] years prior thereto].

15.1.3. he will not for a period of [...] months after the date of this Agreement seek to entice away or recruit any employee of either the Company [and/or the Subsidiaries] who was so employed at the date of this Agreement.

16. Substitution and severability

16.1. If the time limits or geographical extent of any of the covenants in Clause 15 is found to be unreasonable then there shall be substituted in respect thereof such limitations as shall be decided by any competent court or tribunal required to determine issues arising from this Agreement and the covenants herein as lawful, reasonable and proportionate.

16.2. If notwithstanding the provisions set out in Clause 16.1 any term of this Agreement is found to be invalid or otherwise unenforceable then such term shall be regarded and construed as severable from the Agreement so as not to affect the validity and enforceability of the remainder.

17. Notices

17.1. All notices under this Agreement shall be in writing and shall be delivered personally [or by first class, registered or recorded post] [or by facsimile transmission] in every case to the other Party's Agreed Address. [In the case of first class post notice will be deemed to be received [3] business days after the date of posting.]

18. Variation of this Agreement

18.1. Any variation of the terms of this Agreement must be in writing signed by all of the Parties.

19. Further action

19.1. The Parties agree that they will expeditiously carry out such further acts as may be necessary for the purpose of this Agreement including the execution and delivery of such instruments, deeds, licences, notifications as may be reasonably required by the other Party or by law.

20. Law and jurisdiction

20.1. This Agreement is governed by the law of England and Wales and is subject to the [exclusive] jurisdiction of the courts of England and Wales.

21. Schedules

21.1. The Schedules form part of this Agreement including any subsequent amendments made thereto.

Signed, etc.

SCHEDULE 1

Agreed Addresses

[*Set out the Addresses of the Parties*]

Signed, etc.

SCHEDULE 2

Details of Vendors, Sale Shares and Consideration Shares

[*Set out details of the Vendors, the Sale Shares and the Consideration Shares*]

Signed, etc.

SCHEDULE 3

Last Accounting Date and Completion Accounts Date

[*Set out the Last Accounting Date and Completion Accounts Date*]

Signed, etc.

[SCHEDULE 4

The Properties

Part I

[*List of Freehold Properties*]

Part II

[*List of Leasehold Properties*]

Signed, etc.

[SCHEDULE 5

Subsidiary Companies

[*List of Subsidiary Companies*]

Signed, etc.

SCHEDULE 6

Part 1

Disclosure Letter

Date: [...]

From: [*Vendors' Solicitors*]

To: [*Purchaser's Solicitors*]

Dear Sirs

[*Name of company*] ('the Company')

This letter is the Disclosure Letter referred to in the Agreement of [today's date *or* [*date*] ('the Agreement') to be made between our clients [*names of Vendors*] ('the Vendors') and your client [*name of purchaser*] ('the Purchaser') for the sale and purchase of [*name of the company*] ('the Company'). Where this letter uses terms defined in the Agreement they have the same meaning as therein defined.

The Warranties are given expressly subject to the contents of this letter. Even where a specific disclosure is made by reference to a particular paragraph of the Warranties such disclosure is deemed to be made in respect of all of the Warranties.

This letter is written on the express instructions of the Vendors and has been approved by each of them. It is written on the strict understanding that the Purchaser accepts that this firm has no liability whatever to the Purchaser for its contents or omissions.

We are instructed to make the following disclosures on behalf of the Vendors:

1) Deemed disclosures
    The following matters shall be deemed to be disclosed to the Purchaser:

    (a) the contents of the records of the Company [and the Subsidiaries] obtainable from Companies House on [*date*];

(b) all matters disclosed in response to all inquiries from and on behalf of your clients and which are included in the Disclosure Bundle, a copy of which is appended hereto as Annexe 1;

(c) all matters which are apparent from [the management and] audited accounts of the Company [and the Subsidiaries] as requested and disclosed for the years [...] including the directors' reports and accompanying notes;

(d) any matters relating to the Company [and the Subsidiaries] which would be available from the search of any publicly available register or record [including but not limited to:

　　(i)　HM Land Registry
　　(ii)　HM Land Charges Registry
　　(iii)　Registers held by Local Authorities];

(e) all matters contained within the Disclosure Bundle provided to the Purchaser. The Purchaser is deemed to have knowledge of all matters whether express or implied contained within them;

(f) all matters contained within the statutory books of the Company [and the Subsidiaries] which have been made available to the Purchaser and its advisers for inspection.

2) Specific disclosures
[Here set out details of specific disclosures being made, if possible by reference to the appropriate paragraph or paragraphs of the Warranties].

Please sign and return the enclosed copy of this letter thereby acknowledging receipt thereof together with Annexe 1. Receipt by us of your signed copy of this letter will constitute acceptance by you and your clients of its terms.

Yours faithfully

[signature on behalf of Vendors' Solicitors]

[[on duplicate] We acknowledge receipt of the above letter (including its Schedules) and of the copies of the documents contained in Annexe 1, and we accept its terms].

ANNEXE 1

[Contents of the Disclosure Bundle]

Part 2

Warranties

1) In these Warranties reference to the Company is also a reference to and includes each of the Subsidiaries unless the context does not so permit.

2) Recitals (1) and (2) above are true and accurate and will be so at Completion.

3) There is no indebtedness between each of the Vendors and the Company nor will any arise.

4) The Vendors between them are the owners of all of the Sale Shares and are able to transfer them unencumbered at Completion.

5) The Company has no legal or other obligation either actual or contingent at the date of this Agreement or at Completion to allot to any person any share or loan capital.

6) The Company will have no actual or contingent liabilities at the date of Completion other than those set out below:
[Set out details of all mortgages, charges, contractual obligations, outstanding tax liabilities, etc. by reference to or inclusion of appropriate documents].

7) The list of Subsidiaries as set out in Schedule 5 is full and accurate.

8) The accounts of the Company for the [*last 5 accounting years*] and at the Last Accounting Date are a true and accurate record and fair representation of the financial standing of the Company including but not limited to its assets, liabilities, profits or losses and comply with the relevant statutory and accounting standards requirements.

9) The nett assets of the Company at the time of Completion are not materially different from those reflected in the accounts at the Last Accounting Date.

10) The financial position of the Company including but not limited to its profits, losses, assets and liabilities have not materially changed since the Last Accounting Date save insofar as they have followed the usual course of business so that the accounts at the Last Accounting Date are a fair, true and accurate representation of the Company's position at Completion.

11) No dividend or other distribution has been declared or paid, and no capital distribution made or agreed to be made in respect of, any share capital of the Company since the Last Accounting Date.

12) The Company has continued to trade since the Last Accounting Date in materially the same way as before the Last Accounting Date.

13) All book and other debts included in the accounts at the Last Accounting Date are collectable in the ordinary course of business and in any event should be received within [3] months of Completion.

14) All debts to the Company included in the accounts at the Last Accounting Date are the sole property of the Company.

15) All assets of the Company included in the accounts at the Last Accounting Date are the unencumbered property of the Company to which the Company has sole marketable and good title.

16) The Company is the sole beneficial owner of the Properties to which it has good and provable title.

17) There are no lawsuits, enforcement actions, arbitrations, mediations, prosecutions or other proceedings or actions pending or already begun against the Company or its directors of which the Vendors have or should have knowledge. The Vendors do not know of any act or omission which may or is likely to give rise any such proceeding or action as mentioned herein.

18) The Company has accounted to HM Revenue and Customs for all taxes which were required to be deducted from other persons and payable to them.

19) All VAT records together with supporting documentation are complete.

20) The Company and its directors have submitted all necessary tax returns, information and payments timeously and there is no outstanding penalty, surcharge, dispute, inquiry or issue with the tax authorities of which the Company and its directors have knowledge or which is likely to arise as a result of any act or omission on the directors' or the Company's part.

21) All information of material relevance to the Purchaser's purchase of the Sale Shares has been disclosed to the Purchaser in writing.

22) All information supplied to the Purchaser and the Purchaser's Solicitors whether in the Disclosure Letter or otherwise is accurate, true, complete and a fair representation of the underlying facts.

23) There is no fact or circumstance which would affect the Purchaser's decision to purchase the Sale Shares.

24) All steps have been taken and obligations discharged which are necessary to ensure the continuation in business of the Company and the preservation of its assets.

25) The Company does not have any obligations or commitments to future capital or other expenditure which it has not disclosed to the Purchaser's Solicitors.

26) There are no obligations, whether legally binding or otherwise, on the part of the Company to make payments either now or at some future date to former employees of the Company as a result of termination of their employment or retirement which are not included in the Pension scheme which is fully funded.

27) There is no existing obligation, either legal or otherwise, to increase the remuneration of any employee or officer of the Company either now or in the future.

28) The Company has not entered into any guarantees, indemnities or similar obligations.

29) There is no reason to believe that the fact of this Agreement and the transaction therein contemplated will lead to the Company losing any of its present customers or suppliers.

Signed, etc.

SCHEDULE 7

Resignation of directors/secretary

To: The Directors of [*company*] [Ltd *or* plc] ('the Company')

[*date*]

Dear Sirs

I resign my office as [director *or* secretary] of the Company with effect from [...].

I acknowledge that I have no claim against the Company [or the Subsidiaries as defined in the sale and purchase Agreement dated ... in respect of the Company] for compensation for loss of office, in respect of any loan or pension or any other matter other than my outstanding fees of £[...]. which it has been agreed will be discharged on [... 20..].

EXECUTED AS A DEED, etc.

[*signature of director or secretary*]

[*signatures of witnesses*]

Resignation of auditors

To: The Directors of [*company*] ('the Company')

[*date*]

Dear Sirs

We hereby resign as auditors of the Company with effect from [...].

We confirm that, save for the sum of £[...] due to us in respect of outstanding audit fees, we do not have any claim against the Company whatsoever.

We certify that we are not aware of any circumstances connected with our resignation which we are required to bring to the notice of members or creditors of the Company by virtue of the provisions of Section 519 of the Companies Act 2006.

We enclose a signed duplicate of this letter for the registrar of companies.

Yours faithfully

[*signatures of resigning auditors*]

Deed of confirmation by Vendor

To: The Directors of [*company*] ('the Company')

[*date*]

Dear Sirs

I hereby confirm that I have no claim whatever against the Company [or any of the Subsidiaries as defined in the sale and purchase Agreement of ...].

EXECUTED AS A DEED, etc.

[*signature of Vendor*]

[*signatures of witnesses*]

Signed, etc.

PRECEDENT 7B   Sale and purchase of small/medium business and premises

SALE AND PURCHASE OF SMALL/MEDIUM BUSINESS AND PREMISES

THIS AGREEMENT FOR SALE AND PURCHASE is made the [... of ...] BETWEEN:

1. [*Name of seller*] of [*address*] ('the Seller'); and
2. [*Name of buyer*] of [*address*] ('the Purchaser').

RECITALS

1. The Seller is the owner of the business known as [*Smiths*] which trades under the name ['*Smiths*'] and [*retails fancy goods from its premises*].
2. The Purchaser intends under the terms of this Agreement to purchase the business including its assets and goodwill as a going concern.

DEFINITIONS

In this Agreement the following definitions apply:

'Business'	The business known as [*Smiths*] and trading under the Trading Name.
'Completion Date'	The date on which the sale and purchase of the business is to be completed.
'Fixtures and Fittings'	The fixtures and fittings belonging to the Seller at the Premises [and as set out in Schedule 1 hereto].
'Goodwill'	The goodwill associated exclusively with the Business as carried on by the Seller including but not limited to the right to use the Trading Name and to hold itself out as carrying on the Business.
'Landlord'	The lessor of the Premises as defined in the copy lease at Schedule 2.
'Lease'	The lease of the Premises in Schedule 2.
'Premises'	The premises the subject of the Lease.

'Purchase Price'	The sum of £[...] apportioned as set out in Clause 2.
'Purchaser's Solicitors'	Messrs [...].
'Seller's Solicitors'	Messrs [...].
'Standard Conditions'	The Standard Commercial Property Conditions edition [...].
'Stock'	The stock of the Business as set out in Schedule 3 as at the date of exchange of this Agreement.
'Trading Name'	'[*Smith's Fancy Goods*]'.
'Warranties'	The warranties provided by the Seller as set out in Schedule 4.

INTERPRETATION

In this Agreement:

1. The singular includes the plural and one gender includes all.
2. References to Schedules and Clauses are to those in this Agreement.
3. Reference to a statutory provision includes any amendment or replacement provision relevant to the Agreement.
4. Reference to a document includes that document as amended, altered or replaced subsequent to the date of this Agreement.
5. Reference to writing includes facsimile transmission, e-mail, and similar media unless the context otherwise expressly provides.
6. Time expressed in days excludes the first day but includes the last day. If the last day does not fall on a normal business day in both England and Wales then the last day will be deemed to be the first normal business day.
7. The headings in this document do not form part of the Agreement.

OPERATIVE PROVISIONS

1. Sale and purchase

1.1. The Seller shall sell and the Purchaser agrees to buy at the Purchase Price subject to the terms and conditions of this Agreement and with the benefit of the Warranties, upon which the Purchaser is deemed to have relied, the Business consisting of:

1.1.1. the Fixtures and Fittings

1.1.2. the Goodwill

1.1.3. the Lease

1.1.4. the Stock.

1.2. This Agreement will incorporate the Standard Conditions insofar as the Standard Conditions are consistent with this Agreement save that:

1.2.1. the contract rate shall be [...]% above the minimum lending rate of [...] Bank plc

1.2.2. [any other variations required].

2. Apportionment of the Purchase Price

2.1. The Purchase Price shall be apportioned as follows:

2.1.1. the Fixtures and Fittings £[...]

2.1.2. the Goodwill £[...]

2.1.3. the Lease   £[...]

2.1.4. the Stock   £[...].

3. Completion

3.1. Completion of the sale and purchase shall take place at the premises of the Purchaser's Solicitors on the Completion Date which will be [...] am on [... day of ... 20..].

3.2. At the Completion Date the Seller shall effect completion of the terms of this Agreement (including compliance with the Standard Conditions) including:

3.2.1. an assignment of the remainder of the term of the Lease

3.2.2. delivering to the Purchaser the Fixtures and Fittings and the Stock

3.2.3. [an assignment of the Goodwill to the Purchaser].

4. Deposit

4.1. The Purchaser shall pay to the Seller's Solicitors the sum of £[...] [by banker's draft] as deposit on the signing and exchange of this Agreement [to be held by them as stakeholder].

5. Licence to assign the Lease

5.1. In accordance with the Standard Conditions this Agreement is subject to the obtaining by the Seller of a licence to assign the remainder of the term of the Lease to the Purchaser.

6. Transfer of assets and obligations

6.1. Stock levels

6.1.1. The Seller undertakes to ensure that stock is maintained after exchange and at completion at levels commensurate with those set out in Schedule 3 and in any event to the value of at least £[...].

6.1.2. The Seller shall be responsible for all outgoings, expenses and overheads in connection with the Business up to but not including the Completion Date.

7. [Book debts of the Business prior to completion

7.1. The book debts of the Business prior to Completion (if any) shall remain the property of the Seller and the Purchaser [shall direct the relevant debtors to the Seller *or* shall receive them as agent of the Seller].

8. Books of account

8.1. The existing books of account prior to the Completion Date shall be retained by the Seller who will provide the Purchaser with such copies as it requires at the Purchaser's reasonable expense. The Seller shall retain the books for at least 6 years.

9. Business sold as going concern

9.1. The Seller and Purchaser each undertakes to use its reasonable endeavours to provide such information as is required by HM Revenue and Customs to establish that the Business was sold under this Agreement as a going concern. If any VAT is determined to be payable for any thing sold and purchased or supplied under this Agreement then the Purchaser shall bear the cost thereof [together with any penalty, costs, interest or expenses] upon receipt from the Seller of an appropriate VAT invoice in connection therewith.

10. Non-compete

10.1. The Seller covenants:

10.1.1. for a period of [2] years after the date of this Agreement that he will not be for any reason engaged in, involved or associated with, either by himself or in connection or association with any other person or entity, any business [within 10 miles of [*specify*] *or* [*other geographical area*]] which is similar to that of the Business whether as franchisee, agent, principal, adviser or in any other capacity

10.1.2. for a period of [12] months after completion that he will not either for himself or on behalf of any other entity, seek, solicit or obtain orders from any entity which was a customer of the Business at the date of this Agreement [or for a period of [2] years prior thereto]

10.1.3. for a period of [12] months after the date of this Agreement that he will not seek to entice away or recruit any employee of the Business who was so employed at the date of this Agreement.

11. Substitution and severability

11.1. If the time limits or geographical extent of any of the covenants in Clause 10 is found to be unreasonable then there shall be substituted in respect thereof such limitations as shall be decided by any competent court or tribunal required to determine issues arising from this Agreement and the covenants herein as lawful, reasonable and proportionate.

11.2. If notwithstanding the provisions set out in Clause 11.1 any term of this Agreement is found to be invalid or otherwise unenforceable then such term shall be regarded and construed as severable from the Agreement so as not to affect the validity and enforceability of the remainder.

12. Further action

12.1. The Seller and the Purchaser agree that they will expeditiously carry out such further acts as may be necessary for the purpose of this Agreement including the execution and delivery of such instruments, deeds, licences, notifications as may be reasonably required by the other party or by law.

13. [Law and jurisdiction

13.1. This Agreement is governed by the law of England and Wales and is subject to the [exclusive] jurisdiction of the courts of England and Wales].

14. Whole agreement

14.1. This Agreement supersedes and replaces any previous agreement between the Seller and the Purchaser in relation to the sale and purchase of the Business whether oral or in writing. Each of the Seller and the Purchaser hereby agrees that in entering into this Agreement it has not relied upon any warranty or representation made by or on behalf of the other party save where expressly stated in this Agreement. The Seller and the Purchaser hereby agree that this constitutes the whole agreement between them in respect of the sale and purchase of the Business.

15. Schedules

15.1. The Schedules form part of this Agreement including any subsequent amendments made thereto.

Signed, etc.

SCHEDULE 1

Fixtures and Fittings

[*Insert schedule of Fixtures and Fittings*]

Signed, etc.

SCHEDULE 2

Copy Lease

[*Insert copy of the Lease of the premises*]

Signed, etc.

SCHEDULE 3

Stock

[*Insert details of Stock*]

Signed, etc.

SCHEDULE 4

The Warranties

1. The Seller warrants to the Purchaser:

1.1. the Fixtures and Fittings, Lease and Stock are the unencumbered property solely of the Seller and will be transferred to the Purchaser free from any charge, lien, bill of sale, hire purchase agreement or other encumbrance upon completion

1.2. the accounts of the Business for the [*last 5 accounting years*] and at the end of the last accounting period are a true and accurate record and fair representation of the financial position of the Business including but not limited to its assets and profits or losses and comply with the relevant [statutory and] accounting standards requirements

1.3. there has been no material change in the financial position of the Business since the end of the last of the periods to which those accounts relate

1.4. the Seller will carry on the business from the date hereof until completion in a way which is not materially different from the way in which it was carried on during the period to which the last set of accounts relates so as to preserve and maintain the Goodwill and reputation of the Business

1.5. there are no lawsuits, enforcement actions, arbitrations, mediations, prosecutions or other proceedings or actions pending or already begun concerning the Business [of which the Seller has or should have knowledge]. The Seller does not know of any act or omission which may or is likely to give rise any such proceeding or action as mentioned herein

1.6. the Seller is not in breach of the terms of the Lease

1.7. the replies to any inquiries, requests or requisitions received by the Seller and his advisers are true, fair and accurate.

2. **Continuing obligations**

2.1. Notwithstanding the Completion of the Sale and Purchase under this Agreement the terms and conditions thereof shall remain in full force until all obligations contained herein are fully satisfied.

Signed, etc.

8

Contractor services

8.1 Introduction

This chapter provides a useful general purpose contract for services by a contractor (**Precedent 8A**). It can be used for any service contract which does not require a specialised form, from professional services to office cleaning.

The precedent contains numerous possible variations. For instance, there is a provision for Retail Prices Index (RPI) linked fee uplifts where the contract may be of considerable duration. A confidentiality clause is included but this may not be appropriate for some contexts.

The agreement may be used either for a long-term contract, e.g. maintenance or servicing, or for a one-off project or job.

For some contracts many of the commercial clauses could be omitted.

PRECEDENT 8A   Contractor services contract

CONTRACTOR SERVICES CONTRACT

THIS AGREEMENT dated [*date*] is made by and between:

1. [*Name*] a company incorporated in England and Wales under company number [*number*] and whose registered office is at [*address*] ('the Contractor'); and
2. [*Name*] a company incorporated in England and Wales under company number [*number*] and whose registered office is at [*address*] ('the Customer').

RECITALS

1. The Contractor supplies [a range of [*short description of service*] *or* services connected with [*identify the type of business*]].
2. The Contractor is willing to provide the Services (as defined below) and the Customer is willing to appoint the Contractor to provide the Services in accordance with the provisions of this Agreement.

DEFINITIONS

In this Agreement and the Schedules, the following words shall have the following meaning:

'Commencement Date'	The date on which a Service is commenced as set out in Schedule 1.
'Delivery Date'	The delivery date for a Service or phase of a Service as set out in Schedule 2, if applicable.
'Fee'	The amounts set out in Schedule 2 as may be varied from time to time.
'Party' and 'Parties'	The Contractor and the Customer, and 'Party' shall mean either one of them.
'Review Date'	Any date from which the Contractor is entitled to increase the Fees for a Service as set out in Schedule 1 to this Agreement.
'Review Period'	A period beginning on any Review Date and ending on the day before the next Review Date, and qualified uses of the term are to be construed accordingly.
['RPI'	The Retail Price Index maintained and published by the Office for National Statistics.]
'Schedules'	The Schedules attached to this Agreement and as varied or added to from time to time by written agreement.
'Service' and 'Services'	The service or services set out in Schedule 2 which the Customer has agreed from time to time to receive from the Contractor and as may be varied or added to by the Parties by written agreement from time to time.
['Site[s]'	The Customer's premises where the Contractor will be performing the Services].

INTERPRETATION

In this Agreement:

1. The singular includes the plural and one gender includes all.
2. References to Schedules and Clauses are to those in this Agreement.
3. Reference to a statutory provision includes any amendment or replacement provision relevant to the Agreement.
4. Reference to a document includes that document as amended, altered or replaced subsequent to the date of this Agreement.
5. Reference to writing includes facsimile transmission, e-mail, and similar media unless the context otherwise expressly provides.
6. Time expressed in days excludes the first day but includes the last day. If the last day does not fall on a normal business day in both England and Wales then the last day will be deemed to be the first normal business day.
7. The headings in this document do not form part of the Agreement.

OPERATIVE PROVISIONS

1. Duration of this Agreement

1.1. This Agreement shall continue from the date of its signing [until the ... of ... 20.. *or* for a period of [...] years *or* until terminated by either Party under the provisions of clause 14 *or* until completion of the project specified in Schedule 2].

2. Services

2.1. The Contractor will provide the Services as set out in Schedule 2 as may be varied from time to time.

2.2. The Contractor shall provide the Services from the Commencement Date.

3. Consideration

3.1. In consideration for the Contractor providing the Services the Customer shall pay the Fee as set out in Schedule 2.

4. Provision of the Service

4.1. Where applicable the Contractor shall use its best endeavours to provide the Services within the time limits set out in Schedule 2. If it is unable to do so for any reason it will notify the Customer as soon as practically possible and inform the Customer of:

4.1.1. the reason for its being unable to provide the Service

4.1.2. when the Service will be resumed.

4.2. Failure to provide a Service will not arise if the reason for the failure is a breach of this Agreement by the Customer or a *force majeure* event.

5. Services to be provided

5.1. The Services which the Contractor will provide are set out in Schedule 2. The Customer and the Contractor shall agree the provision of an individual Service including service levels, specification, Delivery Date (if applicable), details of delivery, the period of provision (if applicable) and the Fee payable and their agreement shall be signified by the signing of a copy of Schedule 2 as varied from time to time.

5.2. Schedule 2 may be varied or added to as agreed by the Parties from time to time, in writing. Any variation or addition to Schedule 2 shall be clearly indicated (including the additional or different Fee to be paid by the Customer) and a like procedure followed to that set out in sub-paragraph 5.1.

6. Obligations of the Customer

6.1. During the currency of this Agreement the Customer will ensure that the Customer's staff and agents cooperate and assist the Contractor.

6.2. Where required the Customer shall provide, where applicable:

6.2.1. [access to a safe and reliable power supply on the Site[s]]

6.2.2. [access to the Customer's computer network together with all necessary passwords, codes, keys and the like necessary for the carrying out of the Services by the Contractor [whether on site or remotely]]

6.2.3. [temporary use during the provisions of a Service of such computer and other equipment as the Contractor shall reasonably require]

6.2.4. [access to all parts of the Site[s]where the Services are to be rendered]

6.2.5. [reasonable canteen and refreshment facilities [at its own expense] for the use of the Contractor's employees whilst providing a Service on the Site[s]]

6.2.6. [adequate and secure parking on site during all time spent working at the Site[s]]

6.2.7. access to the Customer's premises at all times reasonably necessary [including where appropriate outside normal office hours] for the purpose of carrying out the Services on site

6.2.8. such information as the Contractor reasonably requires for the performance of the Services

6.2.9. [all such other physical or other requirements the Contractor may have on or off site].

6.3. In the event that the Customer receives any notice, decision, notification or is the object of any enforcement action by a governmental or regulatory agency or body which is likely to affect the delivery of the Services by the Contractor, it will immediately inform the Contractor in writing indicating what action it is proposing to take in respect thereof.

7. Payment of Fee

7.1. A Fee shall be paid upon invoicing by the Contractor for each Service. [If the Customer wishes to raise a purchase order to the Contractor prior to its being invoiced then it must do so and supply the order to the Contractor at least [1 month] before the Fee for the relevant Service is payable. For the avoidance of doubt the Fee will be due and payable on the relevant payment date whether any purchase order has been provided as set out herein and absent the timeous provision of a purchase order the Customer will be invoiced prior to the beginning of the provision of a Service and required to pay as set out in Schedule 2].

7.2. If the Customer does not make a payment by the date stated in an invoice or as otherwise provided for in this Agreement then the Contractor shall be entitled to:

7.2.1. charge interest on the outstanding amount at the rate of [...]% a year above the base lending rate of [...] Bank plc

7.2.2. require the Customer to pay, in advance, for any Service (both including and in addition to the Service in respect of which it is in default) which has not yet been performed and

7.2.3. not perform any further Service.

8. Determination of revised Fees

8.1. The Fee for any Review Period is to be determined by the Contractor and notified in writing to the Customer not less than [1 month] prior to the relevant Review Date. [A Fee for any Review Period may not increase by a greater percentage than any percentage increase in the RPI between the beginning and end of the previous Review Period (or in the case of the first Review Period between the Commencement Date for a Service and its first Review Date)].

8.2. [The Parties may agree a different figure from that set out in Clause 8.1, but in default of such agreement prior to the Review Date, the Fee payable shall be that set out in Clause 8.1].

8.3. Where the relevant Schedule provides for charging for the Service on an hourly or other time basis then the references in this Clause 8 to the Fee shall be construed as a reference to the hourly or other time rate.

9. [Confidentiality

9.1. Each Party agrees not to disclose any confidential information provided by the other Party during the currency of this Agreement or at any time thereafter to any third party save where the law requires. Each Party also agrees not to use any such confidential information for any other purpose other than in connection with the provision of the Service and will not use the information for any business or other purpose of its own.

9.2. Each Party undertakes to procure that its employees, directors, agents and advisers and any other persons to whom it makes available confidential information shall also keep confidential the information the subject of this Clause 9.

9.3. The obligations in this Clause 9 shall continue after the termination of this Agreement].

10. [Use of sub-contractor

10.1. The Contractor may employ the services of a sub-contractor in order to deliver Services to the Customer. The Contractor shall in such case be responsible for ensuring that the Service provided by the sub-contractor is to the same or a comparable standard to that delivered or intended to be delivered by the Contractor].

11. Liability of the Contractor

11.1. The liability of the Contractor [(and of any sub-contractor)] under or in connection with this Agreement for the provision of the Services whether arising in contract, tort, negligence, breach of statutory duty or otherwise howsoever shall not exceed [a refund of that part of the Fee for that Service which has been paid by the Customer to the Contractor under this Agreement. The relevant Fee for the purpose of this Clause 11 will be that which relates to the particular Service in respect of which a successful claim is brought by the Customer *or* the amount of professional negligence insurance cover carried by the Contractor which shall not be less than £[...]].

11.2. [The Contractor shall not be liable to the Customer for any indirect, consequential or economic loss including but not limited to damage, costs or expenses of any description, loss of profit, business, goodwill, turnover or any other loss arising from its performance or non-performance of its obligations in connection with this Agreement whether arising from breach of contract, tort, breach of duty, negligence or any other cause of action].

11.3 Nothing in this Clause 11 shall limit or remove the Contractor's liability for causing personal injury or death.

12. Indemnity

12.1. The Customer will indemnify the Contractor in respect of any losses, damage or liability the Contractor may incur as a result of the Customer's acts or omissions, whether deliberate, accidental, negligent or reckless, in the course of the provision by the Contractor of the Service to the Customer under this Agreement whether such acts or omissions amount to a breach of an express or implied obligation under this Agreement or a breach of any other legal requirement or obligation, code of practice, licence, consent, forbearance, approval, permission or rule.

12.2. For the avoidance of doubt losses, damage and liability shall include but not be limited to economic and commercial loss, loss of goodwill, legal and other costs associated with legal proceedings of any kind which the Contractor has to bring or to which it has to respond, fines, penalties, damages and any financial consequence whatever flowing directly or indirectly from the matters set out in this Clause 12.

13. Whole agreement and previous agreements

13.1. This Agreement supersedes and replaces any previous agreement between the Parties whether oral or in writing in relation to the provision of the Service. The Parties hereby agree that in entering into this Agreement they have not relied upon any warranty or representation made by or on behalf of the other Party save where expressly stated in this Agreement. The Parties hereby agree that this Agreement including the Schedules constitutes the whole agreement between the Parties in relation to the provision of the Services.

13.2. Nothing in this Clause 13 shall be construed as limiting or excluding either Party's liability to the other for fraud or deceit in inducing the making of this Agreement.

14. Termination

14.1. The Service[s] will start on the Commencement Date and will continue until:

14.1.1. terminated by either Party giving at least [3 *months*] written notice

14.1.2. where applicable the completion of a specific project or task.

14.2. In the event that all Services under Schedule 2 have been terminated for whatever reason this Agreement shall itself lapse within [28 *days*] of the end of the provision of the last remaining Service.

14.3. Without prejudice to the other remedies or rights a Party may have, the Contractor may terminate the provision of any Service at any time, on written notice to the Customer, subject to completing any work or project for which full payment has already been made, if the Customer:

14.3.1. is [declared bankrupt *or* wound up due to insolvency]

14.3.2. makes or seeks a composition with its creditors

14.3.3. enters into or seeks an insolvent voluntary arrangement

14.3.4. becomes the subject of the appointment of a manager, receiver or liquidator

14.3.5. is the subject of an administration order

14.3.6. has its assets charged or seized for the satisfaction of a debt

14.3.7. divulges confidential business information obtained from the Contractor

14.3.8. fails to comply with the terms of any software or data licence in connection with the Service

14.3.9. has any sum due under this Agreement which remains unpaid for more than [28 *days*]

14.3.10. does not furnish any document or other information which the Customer is obliged to provide within [28 *days*] of its due date

14.3.11. is in breach of its obligations under this Agreement and in the case of a breach capable of remedy fails to remedy the same within [21 *days*] after receipt of the notice giving full particulars of the breach and requiring it to be remedied.

15. Consequences of termination of the Services and/or this Agreement

15.1. Upon termination of the Services the Customer must pay for the Services provided prior to the date of termination as well as any further expenditure incurred by the Contractor after the date of termination arising from commitments reasonably entered into by the Contractor prior to the date of termination but payable by the Contractor afterwards.

15.2. [Upon termination of the last of the Services provided to the Customer and consequently the termination of this Agreement, the Customer shall return or destroy (as reasonably required by the Contractor) all documents, materials or other information, whether in hard copy or electronic form, in its possession or control which constitute or include any confidential information of the Contractor].

16. *Force majeure*

16.1. The Contractor shall not have any liability to the Customer for any delay, omission, failure or inadequate performance of this Agreement which is the result of circumstances beyond the reasonable control of the Contractor. Where the Contractor is so affected in its performance of this Agreement it will notify the Customer as soon as is reasonably possible in writing.

17. Amendments

17.1. This Agreement may only be amended or varied in writing signed by the Parties or their duly authorised representatives.

18. [Assignment

18.1. Neither Party may assign, charge, mortgage, sub-contract, delegate or otherwise assign or transfer its rights or obligations under this Agreement save where express provision is made for the same in this Agreement, without the prior written consent of the other Party.

18.2. A Party may assign or transfer its rights under this Agreement if such assignment or transfer takes place in the context of the disposal of all of its business to which the Service is related provided that the proposed assignee or transferee undertakes to the Contractor directly in a form reasonably required by the Contractor to be bound by the obligations of the proposed assignor].

19. Waiver

19.1. No failure, neglect or delay in enforcing any of the terms of this Agreement by one Party may be construed as a waiver of any of that Party's rights in respect thereof nor such neglect, failure or delay a variation of the express terms of the Agreement.

20. [No agency, partnership, etc.

20.1. Neither Party is for any purpose the agent or partner of the other as a result of anything arising from this Agreement and each Party hereby undertakes not to represent to any third party that it has any authority to act on that other Party's behalf].

21. Further action

21.1. The Parties agree that they will expeditiously carry out such further acts as may be necessary for the purpose of this Agreement including the execution and delivery of such instruments, deeds, licences, notifications as may be reasonably required by the other Party or by law.

22. Severance

22.1. In the event that any term of this Agreement is found to be invalid or otherwise unenforceable then such term shall be regarded and construed as severable from the Agreement so as not to affect the validity and enforceability of the remainder.

23. Notices

23.1. All notices under this Agreement shall be in writing and shall be delivered personally, [or by first class, registered or recorded post] [or by facsimile transmission] in every case to the other Party's address. [In the case of first class post notice will be deemed to be received [3] business days after the date of posting.]

24. [Non-solicitation

24.1. Neither of the Parties shall during the currency of this Agreement and for a period of [...] months after its termination seek to entice away or recruit any employee of the other Party [or its associated companies] who is or was so employed during the duration of this Agreement].

25. Law and jurisdiction

25.1. This Agreement is governed by the law of England and Wales and is subject to the [exclusive] jurisdiction of the courts of England and Wales.

26. Third party rights

26.1. The Parties to this Agreement agree that it is not hereby intended that any rights should be conferred upon or enforceable by any third party as defined in the Contracts (Rights of Third Parties) Act 1999.

27. Schedules

27.1. The Schedules form part of this Agreement including any subsequent amendments made thereto.

Signed, etc.

SCHEDULE 1

Commencement Date [and Review Date]

[*Set out Commencement Date and, where applicable, the Review Date*]

Signed, etc.

SCHEDULE 2

Services to be provided, Delivery Dates and Fees

[*Set out details of services to be provided*]

Signed, etc.

9

Distribution agreements

9.1 Introduction

A distribution agreement has similarities to and differences from both franchise agreements and agency agreements. It is important not to confuse the three as very different legal consequences can flow.

An agency agreement will involve the principal in direct contractual relationships with the end user or customer. It will also potentially be subject to the regulations regarding commercial agents (see **Chapter 6**).

A franchise agreement will not usually involve direct contractual relationships between franchisor and franchisee but the goodwill of the franchisee is usually that of the franchisor (see **Chapter 1**). Both relationships tend to involve significant post-contractual term ramifications.

A distribution agreement will not usually involve any direct contractual relationship between the originating supplier or manufacturer and the end customer except by way of manufacturer warranties and guarantees. There may, of course, also be product liability.

It is important to distinguish between exclusive, non-exclusive and sole distribution agreements. In a sole agreement the manufacturer retains the right to supply directly himself in the relevant territory.

9.2 Exclusive and sole agreements

Exclusivity provisions may engage Community legislation, i.e. Regulation 2790/99/EC which permits such an arrangement only if:

(a) it comes within the block exemption for vertical restraints;
(b) has been granted exemption under the provisions of Article 81(3) of the Rome Treaty; or
(c) it is *de minimis*.

In both exclusive and sole agreements the contract needs to be more tightly drawn than a non-exclusive agreement because both parties have more at stake and the relationship is much closer to that of a franchise.

An example of both types is included in this chapter (**Precedents 9A** and **9B**). Only a slight variation is required to convert the exclusive agreement (**Precedent 9A**) into a sole agreement and the variation is indicated.

PRECEDENT 9A   Exclusive/sole distribution agreement

[EXCLUSIVE *or* SOLE] DISTRIBUTION AGREEMENT

THIS [EXCLUSIVE *or* SOLE] DISTRIBUTION AGREEMENT is dated [...] and is made

BETWEEN:

1. [*Name of Manufacturer*] [of [*address*] *or* whose registered office is at [*address*]], [*company registration number*] ('the Manufacturer'); and
2. [*Name of Distributor*] [of [*address*] *or* whose registered office is at [*address*]], [*company registration number*] ('the Distributor').

RECITALS

1. The Manufacturer manufactures the Goods.
2. By this Agreement the Manufacturer wishes to appoint the Distributor as [exclusive *or* sole] distributor of the Goods within the [Territory *or* Territories] as defined below.

DEFINITIONS

The following words have the meanings set out below in this Agreement:

'Commencement Date'	The date upon which the supply of the Goods will begin under this Agreement.
'Confirmation of Receipt'	Written confirmation of receipt of a Purchase Order.
'Goods'	Goods manufactured by the Manufacturer, as listed and described in Schedule 1.
'Intellectual Property'	All copyrights, trade names, trademarks, designs and devices relating to the Goods.
'Manufacturer's Usual Terms and Conditions'	The Manufacturer's usual terms and conditions as set out in Schedule 2 or as subsequently notified to the Purchaser from time to time during the Term.
'Marks'	The marks, trademarks and get-up associated with the Goods.
'Minimum Value'	Minimum value of Goods to be purchased under this Agreement in each year of the Term as set out in Schedule 3 to this Agreement as may be amended from time to time by agreement.
'Party' and 'Parties'	The Manufacturer and Distributor.
'Party's Agreed Address/es'	Addresses for service as set out in Schedule 5 and as varied from time to time.
'Price List'	The Manufacturer's price list for the Goods in Schedule 4 as varied from time to time.
'Purchase Order'	Orders in writing provided to the Manufacturer by the Distributor under the terms of this Agreement.

'Schedule' and 'Schedules'	The Schedules to this Agreement.
'Target[s]'	Target or targets as set out in Schedule 3 or as varied by written agreement between the parties from time to time.
'Term'	The duration of this Agreement as defined in Schedule 3.
'[Territory *or* Territories]'	As set out in Schedule 6 to this Agreement.

INTERPRETATION

In this Agreement:

1. The singular includes the plural and one gender includes all.
2. References to Schedules and Clauses are to those in this Agreement.
3. Reference to a statutory provision includes any amendment or replacement provision relevant to the Agreement.
4. Reference to a document includes that document as amended, altered or replaced subsequent to the date of this Agreement.
5. Reference to writing includes facsimile transmission, e-mail, and similar media unless the context otherwise expressly provides.
6. Time expressed in days excludes the first day but includes the last day. If the last day does not fall on a normal business day in [both] England and Wales [and the [Territory *or* Territories]] then the last day will be deemed to be the first normal business day thereafter in [the [Territory *or* Territories] and] England and Wales.
7. The headings in this document do not form part of the Agreement.

OPERATIVE PROVISIONS

1. Appointment of Distributor

1.1. The Commencement Date of this Agreement shall be [...].

1.2. The Manufacturer hereby grants to the Distributor the [exclusive *or* sole] right to distribute from the Commencement Date the Goods for the Term subject to the terms and conditions of this Agreement only within the [Territory *or* Territories] and no where else worldwide.

1.3. The Manufacturer shall not:

1.3.1. appoint any other Distributor within the [Territory *or* Territories]

1.3.2. [sell the Goods itself directly within the [Territory *or* Territories]].

1.4. The Distributor shall not sell or distribute the Goods through any sub-distributor or sales agent without the prior written permission of the Manufacturer.

2. Supply of Goods

2.1. The Distributor may place and the Manufacturer will accept Purchase Orders for Goods from the Commencement Date.

2.2. Each Purchase Order must be in writing and must state:

2.2.1. the delivery date [which unless agreed otherwise in writing will not be less than [...] days]

2.2.2. the quantity of the Goods required. [The Manufacturer will not be bound to accept a Purchase Order for [more *or* less] than [*number*] items of Goods for delivery within [...] weeks].

2.3. Upon receipt of a Purchase Order the Manufacturer shall send to the Distributor within [...] days a Confirmation of Receipt of the Purchase Order which shall specify the price.

2.4. [The Distributor will purchase Goods to at least the Minimum Value during each calendar year during the Term beginning with the Commencement Date].

2.5. In order to assist the Manufacturer in providing the best service to the Distributor the Distributor will use its best endeavours not less than [...] weeks before the commencement of each new year of the Term to provide an estimate of the likely volume of the Goods it anticipates purchasing during that year. If that estimate should change thereafter the Distributor will notify the Manufacturer at the first practical opportunity.

2.6. The Manufacturer will use its best endeavours to maintain sufficient stocks to meet the anticipated sales to the Distributor based upon the Distributor's estimates.

2.7. The Manufacturer reserves the right to change the specification of the Goods or to cease to supply some or all of them. If it does so it will notify the Distributor in writing as soon as reasonably practical.

3. Individual contracts of sale

3.1. Each Confirmation of Receipt of a Purchase Order shall constitute the acceptance of a separate contract to sell the Goods to the Distributor under the terms of this Agreement and subject to the Manufacturer's Usual Terms and Conditions provided that the Confirmation of Receipt does not expressly state that the Purchase Order is not accepted. In the event that the Purchase Order is not accepted the Manufacturer will specify in the Confirmation of Receipt the reason or reasons for its non-acceptance. For the avoidance of doubt the Manufacturer may subsequently rely, in resisting any claim for breach of contract or other legal action by the Distributor, upon any further or other ground for being entitled to reject the Purchase Order even if such was not specified in the Confirmation of Receipt.

3.2. In the event that there is any inconsistency between the terms of this Agreement and the Manufacturer's Usual Terms and Conditions the terms of this Agreement shall prevail.

3.3. The Manufacturer undertakes to give the Distributor at least [...] weeks written notice of any material change in the Manufacturer's Usual Terms and Conditions.

3.4. For the avoidance of doubt default by the Manufacturer in relation to any one Purchase Order shall not entitle the Distributor to treat this Agreement as terminated.

4. Retention of title

4.1. The title to any consignment of the Goods will remain with the Manufacturer until the Manufacturer has received:

4.1.1. full payment for them

4.1.2. full payment for any other Goods or products supplied under any other contract between the Manufacturer and the Distributor.

4.2. Until full payment is received as specified in this Clause 4 the Distributor hereby acknowledges that he has possession of them solely as bailee and in a fiduciary capacity for the Manufacturer.

4.3. The Distributor will not pledge, charge or in any way encumber or allow or cause to be encumbered the Goods unless and until title has passed.

4.4. The Distributor will store the Goods separately from any other goods on his premises and ensure that they are marked or readily identifiable as the property of the Manufacturer until title has passed.

4.5. The Manufacturer shall have a right of inspection of the Goods at any reasonable time whilst they remain his property and may re-take possession of them at any time if title has not passed.

5. Payment for the Goods

5.1. The Distributor shall pay the list price as set out in the Price List for the Goods less [...]%. The Manufacturer will give the Distributor at least [...] months written notice of any change to the prices of the Goods. Payment shall consist of a part payment of [...]% with the Purchase Order and thereafter payment of the balance within [...] days of delivery, [all in Sterling].

5.2. The list price of the Goods does not include delivery to the Distributor or any place of delivery nominated by him. If the Distributor wishes the Manufacturer to effect or arrange delivery then the costs shall be as set out in Schedule 4 as varied from time to time or as otherwise agreed by the parties. Payment of the delivery costs shall be on the same basis and terms as payment of the list price.

5.3. If the Distributor wishes to insure the Goods during the process of delivery then it shall either arrange its own or pay the premium set out in Schedule 4. For the purpose of this Agreement risk in the Goods, though not title unless the purchase price has already been paid in full, shall be that of the Distributor from the time Goods are received by the carrier.

5.4. If the full part payment is not received by the Manufacturer within [...] days of receipt of the Purchase Order the Manufacturer may:

5.4.1. cancel or suspend any further delivery to the Distributor under any Purchase Order

5.4.2. sell or otherwise dispose of any Goods that have been ordered by the Distributor and apply the proceeds of sale to the overdue payment

5.4.3. charge the Distributor interest on the amount outstanding at the rate of [...]% a year above the base rate of [*name of bank*] from time to time, from the date the payment was due until receipt of the full price regardless of whether the Manufacturer has obtained judgment prior thereto.

5.5. The provisions of this Clause 5 are strictly without prejudice and in addition to the Manufacturer's rights and remedies as set out in Clause 4.

6. The Marks

6.1. During the Term the Manufacturer will permit the Distributor to use the Marks as set out below. For the avoidance of doubt the Manufacturer gives no warranty as to the validity of the Marks.

6.2. The Marks are to be used by the Distributor solely for purposes authorised by the Manufacturer and connected with distribution of the Goods, for which sole purpose the Distributor is hereby granted licence.

6.3. The Marks are not to be altered, abbreviated, modified or used in connection with any other marks, brands, or the like without the express prior written approval of the Manufacturer, which permission is at the Manufacturer's absolute discretion. The Manufacturer may however at any time modify the Marks and/or substitute new Marks for those existing at the time of this Agreement and the new or modified Marks will be deemed to be the Marks as defined in this Agreement. For the avoidance of doubt the Distributor will not be eligible for any compensation in such circumstances as those set out herein in this Clause 6.3.

6.4. No other marks are to be used by the Distributor in connection with the distribution of the Goods.

6.5. No copies or imitations of the Marks are to be used by the Distributor for any purpose during the Term or thereafter. At no time is the Distributor to register or attempt to register any Mark in connection with the Goods.

6.6. The Distributor is not to commit any act or omission which is likely adversely to affect the Manufacturer's goodwill in the Marks and/or the Goods and/or to damage the Manufacturer's reputation.

6.7. The Distributor is to report to the Manufacturer any infringement of the Marks by any third party and to assist it in taking such steps as may be necessary.

6.8. In all uses of the Marks the Distributor must include a clear and appropriate indication of whether the Mark is registered or unregistered.

6.9. If any recording of a Mark at a Trade Marks Registry is required the Distributor will provide all reasonable assistance to the Manufacturer during the Term.

6.10. The Distributor may not use the name of the Manufacturer or any of the Marks as part of its own name. It may however trade as an authorised distributor of the Goods during the Term.

6.11. The Marks will remain at all times both during the Term and thereafter the property of the Manufacturer and/or its successors or assignees.

7. Training

7.1. [The Distributor will ensure that [it attends *or* its employees/staff attend] the initial training provided by the Manufacturer prior to the commencement of distribution of the Goods under this Agreement. The course will be provided at the reasonable expense of the Distributor] *or* [The Manufacturer will provide initial and refresher training for the employees of the Distributor at regular intervals in order to acquaint them with the Goods and developments connected therewith. Such training will be provided at the Distributor's premises at the Manufacturer's expense save that the Distributor will pay all associated costs such as reasonable hotel expenses and travelling costs] *or* [The Distributor will have a continuing obligation [to attend *or* to ensure that its employees/staff attend] such further training as the Manufacturer reasonably requires].

7.2. [If during the Term the Manufacturer reasonably considers that [an employee *or* a member of staff] has not completed the Training to its satisfaction then it may require that the [employee *or* member of staff] is not employed to work in the distribution of the Goods under this Agreement].

8. Conduct of the Distributor

8.1. The Distributor must at all times during the Term:

8.1.1. carry out the distribution of the Goods to the highest business and ethical standards

8.1.2. without prejudice to the generality of the foregoing the Distributor must ensure there is compliance with all relevant law and regulation including, whether national or supra-national, but not limited to, employment law and regulation, money laundering law and regulation, health and safety requirements and all other statutory and common law requirements relating to the operation of its business

8.1.3. [inform the Manufacturer forthwith of proposed changes in its business arrangements and obtain its prior written approval before implementation including but not limited to changes in ownership of more than [...]% of the nominal share capital or equity of the Distributor or any business, company or firm with which it is associated in the distribution of the Goods]

8.1.4. inform the Manufacturer of changes in the [directors *or* partners] of the Distributor.

9. Accounts and records

9.1. The Distributor must maintain throughout the Term proper accounts, books and records in relation to the distribution of the Goods.

9.2. Copies of the accounts, books and records must be available to the Manufacturer upon reasonable notice.

9.3. In the event that the Manufacturer requires any supporting documentation in relation to details of gross turnover of the Goods the Distributor agrees to provide the same within [...] days of being notified in writing of such request.

9.4. The obligation to provide supporting documentation in this Clause 9 will remain if this Agreement has terminated but the supporting documentation has not been provided prior to the termination thereof. In such circumstances the time limits for compliance will be [...] days and [...] days respectively from the date of the end of the current financial year of the Term or [...] days and [...] days respectively from the date of termination of this Agreement, whichever is the sooner.

10. Targets

10.1. It shall be an express obligation of this Agreement that the Distributor achieves the Target[s] from year to year. Failure to so is a breach of this Agreement.

11. Marketing, advertising and promotion of the Goods

11.1. The Distributor is responsible at all times during the Term for the promotion of the Goods within the [Territory *or* Territories]. [This must be conducted [as agreed *or* in consultation] from time to time with the Manufacturer]. The marketing and advertising associated with the promotion of the Goods is to be financed by the Distributor who must undertake to spend at least £[...] per annum in relation thereto.

11.2. In all marketing and advertising the Distributor must make clear that he does not act as the agent in any way of the Manufacturer.

11.3. The Distributor may sell the Goods at a price to be determined by him.

11.4. The Distributor shall supply the Manufacturer on a quarterly basis with:

11.4.1. an up to date price list in relation to the Goods

11.4.2. full details of how many units of the Goods have been sold in the [Territory *or* Territories]

11.4.3. copies of all promotional materials used or intended to be used in relation to the Goods which will be subject to the Manufacturer's prior approval.

11.5. Throughout the Term the Distributor shall:

11.5.1. maintain a properly trained and efficient sales force in respect of the Goods

11.5.2. comply with all legal requirements in the [Territory *or* Territories] in respect of storage, promotion and sales of the Goods

11.5.3. permit representatives of the Manufacturer to inspect premises, transport and promotional literature associated with the promotion and sale of the Goods

11.5.4. provide a full after sales service to the purchasers of the Goods.

11.6. The Distributor warrants that it will not make any warranties or representations to any third parties regarding the Goods save those which have been expressly approved by the Manufacturer in writing or which are included and approved in any literature about the Goods provided by the Manufacturer from time to time.

12. Financial capability

12.1. The Distributor must ensure that it has at all material times the financial means, including but not limited to working capital, to discharge its obligations under this Agreement and to maintain the integrity and reputation of the Goods.

13. No competing Goods

13.1. During the Term the Distributor shall not obtain from any other supplier, nor distribute or sell either directly or indirectly, save with the prior written consent of the Manufacturer, any goods which are similar, identical or compete with the Goods. The Manufacturer may at any time at its sole discretion withdraw such consent on the giving of not less than [...] months written notice.

13.2. The Distributor may not have any direct or indirect financial or other interest in any business which may be reasonably considered to be a competitor of the Manufacturer anywhere in the world other than the direct or indirect holding of shares in a public listed company where that shareholding amounts to less than [...]% of the total nominal share capital of the public listed company.

14. No agency

14.1. The Distributor is not for any purpose the agent of the Manufacturer. The Distributor must ensure that in all promotional literature, advertising and any other communications with customers and any other third parties it is made clear that it is acting and trading on its own behalf as Principal and not as agent of the Manufacturer.

15. Confidential information

15.1. The Distributor agrees not to disclose any confidential information provided at any time by the Manufacturer either during the Term or at any time thereafter to any third party save where the law requires. The Distributor also agrees not to use any such confidential information for any other purpose other than for the purposes of this Agreement and will not use the information for any business or other purpose of its own. For the avoidance of doubt such information includes but is not limited either in type, *genus* or subject to:

15.1.1. all business information supplied to the Distributor by the Manufacturer regarding the Goods

15.1.2. all marketing information and intelligence

15.1.3. all trade secrets, processes and formulae.

15.2. For the proper protection of the confidential information the Distributor will ensure that:

15.2.1. any employee or member of his staff, whether temporary or permanent, will at the commencement of their employment and no later be provided with a contract of employment or engagement which will include a like obligation to that of the Distributor in respect of confidential information

15.2.2. any [director *or* partner] of the Distributor or any associated [company *or* firm] will be required to provide, in a form approved by the Manufacturer, an undertaking in regard to confidential information in like form to that set out above in relation to the Distributor before being given access to confidential information.

16. Goodwill

16.1. All goodwill in the Marks and the Goods belongs to the Manufacturer, whether generated by the Distributor or otherwise and the Distributor agrees to make no claim in respect thereof.

17. [Customers

17.1. The Distributor will maintain an up to date record of all its customers for the Goods in the [Territory *or* Territories] full details of which it will provide on demand to the Manufacturer].

18. Right of inspection

18.1. The Distributor and/or its appointed agent will be entitled to inspect the operation of the Distributor's business in connection with the distribution of the Goods during any normal business hours in the [Territory *or* Territories] without further notice.

19. Market information

19.1. The Distributor must at all times keep the Manufacturer aware of developments in market conditions within the [Territory *or* Territories] including but not limited to:

19.1.1. actions by competitors or potential competitors of the Goods

19.1.2. plans and proposals for business development by the Distributor.

20. Compliance with laws of the [Territory *or* Territories]

20.1. The Distributor will ensure that it complies at all material times with the laws of the [Territory *or* Territories] relevant to the distribution of the Goods including, but not limited to, those relating to:

20.1.1. data protection and freedom of information

20.1.2. import licences and duties (which the Distributor will be responsible for obtaining and discharging at its own expense)

20.1.3. certificates of origin or other requisite documents

20.1.4. taxes, tariffs and other duties

20.1.5. health and safety

20.1.6. equal opportunities

20.1.7. employment

20.1.8. insurance

20.1.9. occupiers' liability

20.1.10. business registration [and company returns]

20.1.11. the prevention of money laundering

20.1.12. storage, promotion and sale of the Goods.

21. Warranty as to conformity with description

21.1. The Manufacturer warrants that the Goods supplied under this Agreement will correspond, at the time of delivery, with the description it has given to the Distributor. All other warranties, terms or conditions relating to quality, fitness for purpose or condition, whether implied by common law or statute, or express are excluded save where to do so would be by law impermissible.

22. Liability for breach

22.1. Whilst the Manufacturer will endeavour at all times to comply with its legal and contractual obligations to the Distributor it does not accept liability for any loss suffered by the Distributor as a result of any misrepresentation, misdescription, breach of contract, breach of duty or other act or omission (unless fraudulent) however made or caused which constitutes more than a refund of any sum paid or the waiver of any sum contractually payable by the Distributor for the Goods.

22.2. The Manufacturer does not accept liability for any consequential economic or other losses suffered by the Distributor whether resulting from misrepresentation, misdescription, breach of contract, breach of duty or other act or omission (unless fraudulent) however caused.

22.3. Nothing in these Conditions shall limit the right of either Party to seek to recover damages for personal injury or death occasioned by breach of contract or breach of duty by the other Party, its employees or agents.

23. Indemnity

23.1. The Distributor will indemnify the Manufacturer in respect of any losses, damage or liability the Manufacturer may incur as a result of the Distributor's acts or omissions, whether deliberate, accidental, negligent or reckless, in the course of the performance or purported performance of its obligations or rights under this Agreement whether such acts or omissions amount to a breach of an express or implied obligation under this Agreement or a breach of any other legal requirement or obligation, code of practice, licence, consent, forbearance, approval, permission or rule.

23.2. For the avoidance of doubt losses, damage and liability shall include but not be limited to economic and commercial loss, loss of goodwill, legal and other costs associated with legal proceedings of any kind which the Manufacturer has to bring or to which it has to respond, fines, penalties, damages and any financial consequence whatever flowing directly or indirectly from the matters set out in this Clause 23.

24. Organisation of the distribution of the Goods within the [Territory *or* Territories]

24.1. The Distributor must ensure that it sets up and maintains such structures as will enable it to monitor and organise the distribution of the Goods within the [Territory *or* Territories].

25. Novation

25.1. No novation, assignment or delegation of the obligations and benefits of this Agreement by the Distributor is permitted.

25.2. The Manufacturer may novate, assign or delegate the benefits and obligations of this Agreement on giving 21 days written notice to the Distributor.

26. Termination of this Agreement

26.1. This Agreement may expire by effluxion of time or in accordance with the following provisions:

26.1.1. in the event that the Distributor fails to remedy any remediable breach of which it has been notified in writing by the Manufacturer within [...] days the Manufacturer may at its absolute discretion terminate forthwith this Agreement

26.1.2. in the event that the Distributor commits any irremediable material breach or persistently commits any remediable breach of this Agreement the Manufacturer may terminate this Agreement forthwith.

26.2. The Manufacturer may terminate this Agreement forthwith in the event that the Distributor:

26.2.1. is [declared bankrupt *or* wound up due to insolvency]

26.2.2. makes or seeks a composition with its creditors

26.2.3. enters into or seeks an insolvent voluntary arrangement

26.2.4. becomes the subject of the appointment of a manager, receiver or liquidator

26.2.5. is the subject of an administration order

26.2.6. has its assets charged or seized for the satisfaction of a debt

26.2.7. seeks to challenge the Manufacturer's Intellectual Property rights in relation to the Intellectual Property connected with the Goods

26.2.8. behaves in a way which is likely to bring the Goods or the Manufacturer into disrepute including but not limited to conviction for an indictable criminal offence

26.2.9. divulges confidential business information in connection with the Goods to an unauthorised third party

26.2.10. fails to commence, carry on or terminate as appropriate its distribution business in relation to the Goods

26.2.11. fails to pay any sum due under this Agreement for more than [28 *days*] after its due date

26.2.12. neglects to furnish any document or other information which the Distributor is obliged to provide within [28 *days*] of its due date.

27. Re-organisation of business structure or ownership

27.1. The Manufacturer may terminate this Agreement if there is any material re-organisation of the Distributor's business structure unless:

27.1.1. such re-organisation is not the result of insolvency

27.1.2. the resultant company or organisation is bound by the provisions of this Agreement

27.1.3. the beneficial ownership of the resultant entity is not in the hands of competitors of the Manufacturer anywhere in the world except to the extent that such ownership does not exceed [...]% of the total.

28. Legislative change

28.1. In the event that there is a change in legislation which materially affects the legitimate interests of the Manufacturer in respect of this Agreement the Manufacturer will be entitled to terminate this Agreement upon giving reasonable notice to the Distributor which must be not less than [...] days and in no instance more than [...] days.

29. Post termination rights and obligations

29.1. Termination of this Agreement for any reason shall not affect the rights of either Party in respect of the period after termination nor either Party's rights which may have arisen as a result of any breach pre-dating the termination.

29.2. In order to ensure the proper protection of the Goods, including their Marks and Goodwill upon termination of the Term the Distributor must:

29.2.1. cease the promotion, advertising or sale of the Goods

29.2.2. remove all signage, Marks, names, advertisements and other material indicating that the Distributor remains an authorised distributor of the Goods

29.2.3. return all samples of the Goods

29.2.4. return all copies of literature and material supplied for or associated with the distribution of the Goods other than that which is not branded or specific to the Manufacturer

29.2.5. return all copies of software, business information documentation and other materials containing business information connected with the implementation and operation of this Agreement

29.2.6. remove or erase from all computers and other electronic equipment all copies and versions of any software specific to the operation of this Agreement

29.2.7. not use any confidential business information received by it during the course of the operation of this Agreement and must not disclose such information to any third party whether within or without the [Territory *or* Territories]

29.2.8. provide all reasonable assistance to the Manufacturer to achieve an orderly transfer of the distribution of the Goods to any person nominated by the Manufacturer.

29.3. The Distributor hereby grants the Manufacturer an irrevocable power of attorney to effect such of these acts as is necessary for any purpose contained in this Clause 29.

29.4. The Manufacturer shall be entitled to purchase back from the Distributor after termination of this Agreement any Goods remaining in the possession of the Distributor and not already paid for by a customer or the subject of a Purchase Order in relation to a customer of the Distributor. The price shall be either the invoice price or the book value according to the Distributor's records, whichever is the lower. The Goods shall be delivered back to the Manufacturer at the Manufacturer's expense and risk.

29.5. The Distributor shall have no claim against the Manufacturer for compensation for loss of distribution rights, loss of goodwill or any similar loss; and subject as otherwise provided in this Agreement and to any rights or obligations that have accrued before termination, neither Party shall have any further obligation to the other under this Agreement.

30. Restrictions on the Distributor

30.1. The Distributor must not during the Term and for a period of [...] months after termination of this Agreement for any reason be engaged in, involved or associated with, either by itself or in connection or association with any other entity, any business which manufactures, sells or distributes goods the same as, similar to or which compete with the Goods within the [Territory *or* Territories]. [Such limitation extends to the [directors] [and] [principal shareholders] of the Distributor].

30.2. [The Distributor shall not for a period of [...] months after termination seek to entice away or recruit any employee of the Manufacturer who was so employed at the time of termination].

30.3. [In order to ensure the effectiveness of the provisions in this Clause 30 the Distributor will obtain from its [directors] [and] [principal shareholders] a deed of agreement in a form approved by the Manufacturer whereby each [director] [and] [principal shareholder] agrees to be bound by the provisions of this Clause 30].

30.4. The copyright and Intellectual Property in all Marks and materials connected with the Goods shall remain the copyright and Intellectual Property of the Manufacturer.

31. Severability

31.1. In the event that any of the restrictions in this Agreement are found by a court of competent jurisdiction to be unenforceable because they are unreasonable but which would be enforceable were specific words, phrases or clauses removed then the restrictions shall apply as if such words, phrases or clauses were removed.

31.2. In the event that any term of this Agreement is found to be invalid or otherwise unenforceable then such term shall be regarded and construed as severable from the Agreement so as not to affect the validity and enforceability of the remainder.

32. Whole agreement

32.1. This Agreement supersedes and replaces any previous agreement between the Parties whether oral or in writing in relation to the distribution of the Goods. The Distributor hereby agrees that in entering into this Agreement it has not relied upon any warranty or representation made by or on behalf of the Manufacturer save where expressly stated in this Agreement. The Parties hereby agree that this Agreement constitutes the whole agreement between the Parties in respect of the distribution of the Goods.

32.2. Nothing in this Clause 32 shall be construed as limiting or excluding either Party's liability to the other for fraud or deceit in inducing the making of this Agreement.

32.3. Without prejudice to the generality of the foregoing the following is agreed between the Parties:

32.3.1. all financial information provided by the Manufacturer to the Distributor is provided in good faith and is intended to be indicative only. The Distributor hereby acknowledges that it accepts that the provision of such information is at the request of the Distributor on the basis that it does not constitute a representation, warranty, or guarantee by the Manufacturer and that the Distributor has not placed reliance upon it for the purpose of entering into this Agreement or for any other purpose

32.3.2. the Distributor accepts that the Manufacturer does not and cannot predict how the distribution of the Goods will perform in the [Territory *or* Territories] either under the Distributor or at all

32.3.3. the Distributor warrants that it has been advised by the Manufacturer to seek independent legal and financial advice before entering into this Agreement and that its decision to make this Agreement is based solely upon its own judgement and assessment of the Goods commerciality in the [Territory *or* Territories].

33. Variation

33.1. Any variation of the terms of this Agreement must be in writing signed by the Parties.

34. Further action

34.1. The Parties agree that they will expeditiously carry out such further acts as may be necessary for the purpose of this Agreement including the execution and delivery of such instruments, deeds, licences, notifications as may be reasonably required by the other Party or by law.

35. Set off

35.1. Notwithstanding any other express or implied term of this Agreement the Manufacturer reserves the right to set off against any sum payable or owed by it to the Distributor any debt or other liability, whether absolute or contingent, owed by the Distributor to the Manufacturer, or any sum, debt or other liability, absolute or contingent, owed by the Distributor to any third party for which the Manufacturer is liable or may be liable in default of payment or discharge by the Distributor. In the event of such set off the Distributor irrevocably authorises the Manufacturer to pay from such sum or sums held by the Manufacturer for the Distributor such sum as will discharge any such debt or liability to a third party or discharge the debt or sum owed to the Manufacturer.

36. Force majeure

36.1. Neither Party shall have any liability to the other for any delay, omission, failure or inadequate performance of this Agreement which is the result of circumstances beyond its reasonable control. Where a Party is so affected in its performance of this Agreement it will notify the other Party in writing as soon as is reasonably practical.

36.2. If performance of this Agreement is materially prevented by *force majeure* for a period of more than [...] months then either Party may serve upon the other a written notice effecting termination in not less than [...] weeks thereafter. [In the event that *force majeure* ceases to prevent performance of the Agreement within the notice period then the notice shall be null and void and the obligations of the Parties will continue under this Agreement].

37. Waiver

37.1. No failure, neglect or delay in enforcing any of the terms of this Agreement may be construed as a waiver of any of the Manufacturer's rights in respect thereof nor such neglect, failure or delay a variation of the express terms of the Agreement.

38. Third party rights

38.1. The Parties to this Agreement agree that it is not hereby intended that any rights should be conferred upon or enforceable by any third party as defined in the Contracts (Rights of Third Parties) Act 1999.

39. Notices

39.1. All notices under this Agreement shall be in writing and shall be delivered personally [or by first class, registered or recorded post] [or by facsimile transmission] in every case to the other Party's Agreed Address. [In the case of first class post notice will be deemed to be received [3] business days after the date of posting].

40. Law and jurisdiction

40.1. This Agreement is governed by the law of England and Wales and is subject to the [exclusive] jurisdiction of the courts of England and Wales.

41. Schedules

41.1. The Schedules form part of this Agreement including any subsequent amendments made thereto.

Signed, etc.

SCHEDULE 1

The Goods

[Insert list and description of the Goods]

Signed, etc.

SCHEDULE 2

The Manufacturer's Usual Terms and Conditions

[Attach a copy]

Signed, etc.

SCHEDULE 3

Targets, Term and Minimum Order

[Insert details]

Signed, etc.

SCHEDULE 4

Price list, delivery and insurance costs

[*Insert details*]

Signed, etc.

SCHEDULE 5

Parties' Agreed Addresses

[*Insert Agreed Addresses*]

Signed, etc.

SCHEDULE 6

The [Territory *or* Territories]

[*Insert list and/or description of the Territory/Territories*]

Signed, etc.

PRECEDENT 9B   Non-exclusive distribution agreement

NON-EXCLUSIVE DISTRIBUTION AGREEMENT

THIS DISTRIBUTION AGREEMENT is dated [...] and is made

BETWEEN:

1. [*Name of Manufacturer*] [of [*address*] *or* whose registered office is at [*address*]], [*company registration number*] ('the Manufacturer'); and
2. [*Name of Distributor*] [of [*address*] *or* whose registered office is at [*address*]], [*company registration number*] ('the Distributor').

RECITALS

1. The Manufacturer manufactures the Goods.
2. By this Agreement the Manufacturer wishes to appoint the Distributor as a distributor of the Goods within the [Territory *or* Territories] as defined below.

DEFINITIONS

The following words have the meanings set out below in this Agreement:

'Commencement Date'	The date upon which the supply of the Goods will begin under this Agreement.
'Confirmation of Receipt'	Written confirmation of receipt of a Purchase Order.
'Goods'	Goods manufactured by the Manufacturer, as listed and described in Schedule 1.

'Intellectual Property' and 'Intellectual Property Rights'	All copyrights, trade names, trademarks, designs and devices relating to the Goods.
'Manufacturer's Usual Terms and Conditions'	The Manufacturer's usual terms and conditions as set out in Schedule 2 or as subsequently notified to the Purchaser from time to time during the Term.
'Marks'	The marks, trademarks and get-up associated with the Goods.
'Party' and 'Parties'	The Manufacturer and the Distributor.
'Party's Agreed Address/es'	Addresses for service as set out in Schedule 5 and as varied from time to time.
'Price List'	The Manufacturer's price list for the Goods in Schedule 4 as varied from time to time.
'Purchase Order'	Orders in writing provided to the Manufacturer by the Distributor under the terms of this Agreement.
'Schedule' and 'Schedules'	The Schedules to this Agreement.
'Term'	The duration of this Agreement as defined in Schedule 3.
'[Territory or Territories]'	As set out in Schedule 6 to this Agreement.

INTERPRETATION

In this Agreement:

1. The singular includes the plural and one gender includes all.
2. References to Schedules and Clauses are to those in this Agreement.
3. Reference to a statutory provision includes any amendment or replacement provision relevant to the Agreement.
4. Reference to a document includes that document as amended, altered or replaced subsequent to the date of this Agreement.
5. Reference to writing includes facsimile transmission, e-mail, and similar media unless the context otherwise expressly provides.
6. Time expressed in days excludes the first day but includes the last day. If the last day does not fall on a normal business day in [both] England and Wales [and the [Territory or Territories]] then the last day will be deemed to be the first normal business day thereafter in [the [Territory or Territories] and] England and Wales.
7. The headings in this document do not form part of the Agreement.

OPERATIVE PROVISIONS

1. Appointment of Distributor

1.1. The Commencement Date of this Agreement shall be [...].

1.2. The Manufacturer hereby grants to the Distributor the right to distribute from the Commencement Date the Goods for the Term subject to the terms and conditions of this Agreement only within the [Territory or Territories] and no where else worldwide.

1.3. The Distributor shall not sell or distribute the Goods through any sub-distributor or sales agent without the prior written permission of the Manufacturer.

2. Supply of Goods

2.1. The Distributor may place and the Manufacturer will accept Purchase Orders for Goods from the Commencement Date.

2.2. Each Purchase Order must be in writing and must state:

2.2.1. the delivery date [which unless agreed otherwise in writing will not be less than [...] days]

2.2.2. the quantity of the Goods required. [The Manufacturer will not be bound to accept a Purchase Order for [more *or* less] than [*number*] items of Goods for delivery within [...] weeks].

2.3. Upon receipt of a Purchase Order the Manufacturer shall send to the Distributor within [...] days a Confirmation of Receipt of the Purchase Order which shall specify the price.

2.4. [In order to assist the Manufacturer in providing the best service to the Distributor the Distributor will use its best endeavours not less than [...] weeks before the commencement of each new year of the Term to provide an estimate of the likely volume of the Goods it anticipates purchasing during that year. If that estimate should change thereafter the Distributor will notify the Manufacturer at the first practical opportunity.

2.5. The Manufacturer will use its best endeavours to maintain sufficient stocks to meet the anticipated sales to the Distributor based upon the Distributor's estimates].

2.6. The Manufacturer reserves the right to change the specification of the Goods or to cease to supply some or all of them. If it does so it will notify the Distributor in writing as soon as reasonably practical.

3. Individual contracts of sale

3.1. Each Confirmation of Receipt of a Purchase Order shall constitute the acceptance of a separate contract to sell the Goods to the Distributor under the terms of this Agreement and subject to the Manufacturer's Usual Terms and Conditions provided that the Confirmation of Receipt does not expressly state that the Purchase Order is not accepted. In the event that the Purchase Order is not accepted the Manufacturer will specify in the Confirmation of Receipt the reason or reasons for its non-acceptance. For the avoidance of doubt the Manufacturer may subsequently rely, in resisting any claim for breach of contract or other legal action by the Distributor, upon any further or other ground for being entitled to reject the Purchase Order even if such was not specified in the Confirmation of Receipt.

3.2. In the event that there is any inconsistency between the terms of this Agreement and the Manufacturer's Usual Terms and Conditions the terms of this Agreement shall prevail.

3.3. The Manufacturer undertakes to give the Distributor at least [...] weeks written notice of any material change in the Manufacturer's Usual Terms and Conditions.

3.4. For the avoidance of doubt default by the Manufacturer in relation to any one Purchase Order shall not entitle the Distributor to treat this Agreement as terminated.

4. Retention of title

4.1. The title to any consignment of the Goods will remain with the Manufacturer until the Manufacturer has received:

4.1.1. full payment for them

4.1.2. full payment for any other Goods or products supplied under any other contract between the Manufacturer and the Distributor.

4.2. Until full payment is received as specified in this Clause 4 the Distributor hereby acknowledges that he has possession of them solely as bailee and in a fiduciary capacity for the Manufacturer.

4.3. The Distributor will not pledge, charge or in any way encumber or allow or cause to be encumbered the Goods unless and until title has passed.

4.4. The Distributor will store the Goods separately from any other goods on his premises and ensure that they are marked or readily identifiable as the property of the Manufacturer until title has passed.

4.5. The Manufacturer shall have a right of inspection at any reasonable time of the Goods whilst they remain his property and may re-take possession of them at the Distributor's expense at any time if title has not passed.

5. Payment for the Goods

5.1. The Distributor shall pay the list price as set out in the Price List for the Goods less [...]%. The Manufacturer will give the Distributor at least [...] months written notice of any change to the prices of the Goods. Payment shall consist of a part payment of [...]% with the Purchase Order and thereafter payment of the balance within [...] days of delivery, [all in Sterling].

5.2. The list price of the Goods does not include delivery to the Distributor or any place of delivery nominated by him. If the Distributor wishes the Manufacturer to effect or arrange delivery then the costs shall be as set out in Schedule 4 as varied from time to time or as otherwise agreed by the parties. Payment of the delivery costs shall be on the same basis and terms as payment of the list price.

5.3. If the Distributor wishes to insure the Goods during the process of delivery then it shall either arrange its own or pay the premium set out in Schedule 4. For the purpose of this Agreement risk in the Goods, though not title unless the purchase price has already been paid in full, shall be that of the Distributor from the time Goods are received by the carrier.

5.4. If the full part payment is not received by the Manufacturer within [...] days of receipt of the Purchase Order the Manufacturer may:

5.4.1. cancel or suspend any further delivery to the Distributor under any Purchase Order

5.4.2. sell or otherwise dispose of any Goods that have been ordered by the Distributor and apply the proceeds of sale to the overdue payment

5.4.3. charge the Distributor interest on the amount outstanding at the rate of [...]% a year above the base rate of [name of bank] from time to time, from the date the payment was due until receipt of the full price regardless of whether the Manufacturer has obtained judgment prior thereto.

5.5. The provisions of this Clause 5 are strictly without prejudice and in addition to the Manufacturer's rights and remedies as set out in Clause 4.

6. The Marks

6.1. During the Term the Manufacturer will permit the Distributor to use the Marks as set out below. For the avoidance of doubt the Manufacturer gives no warranty as to the validity of the Marks.

6.2. The Marks are to be used by the Distributor solely for purposes authorised by the Manufacturer and connected with distribution of the Goods, for which sole purpose the Distributor is hereby granted licence.

6.3. The Marks are not to be altered, abbreviated, modified or used in connection with any other marks, brands, or the like without the express prior written approval of the Manufacturer, which permission is at the Manufacturer's absolute discretion. The Manufacturer may however at any time modify the Marks and/or substitute new Marks for those existing at the time of this Agreement and the new or modified Marks will be deemed to be the Marks as defined in this Agreement. For the avoidance of doubt the Distributor will not be eligible for any compensation in such circumstances as those set out herein in this Clause 6.3.

6.4. No other marks are to be used by the Distributor in connection with the distribution of the Goods.

6.5. No copies or imitations of the Marks are to be used by the Distributor for any purpose during the Term or thereafter. At no time is the Distributor to register or attempt to register any Mark in connection with the Goods.

6.6. The Distributor is not to commit any act or omission which is likely adversely to affect the Manufacturer's goodwill in the Marks and/or the Goods and/or to damage the Manufacturer's reputation.

6.7. The Distributor is to report to the Manufacturer any infringement of the Marks by any third party and to assist it in taking such steps as may be necessary.

6.8. In all uses of the Marks the Distributor must include a clear and appropriate indication of whether the Mark is registered or unregistered.

6.9. If any recording of a Mark at a Trade Marks Registry is required the Distributor will provide all reasonable assistance to the Manufacturer during the currency of this Agreement.

6.10. The Distributor may not use the name of the Manufacturer or any of the Marks as part of its own name. It may however trade as an authorised distributor of the Goods during the Term.

6.11. The Marks will remain at all times both during the Term and thereafter the property of the Manufacturer and/or its successors or assignees.

7. Training

7.1. [The Distributor will ensure that [it attends *or* its employees/staff attend] the initial training provided by the Manufacturer prior to the commencement of the distribution of the Goods under this Agreement. The course will be provided at the reasonable expense of the Distributor] *or* [The Manufacturer will provide initial and refresher training for the employees of the Distributor at regular intervals in order to acquaint them with the Goods and developments connected therewith. Such training will be provided at the Distributor's premises at the Manufacturer's expense save that the Distributor will pay all associated costs such as reasonable hotel expenses and travelling costs] *or* [The Distributor will have a continuing obligation [to attend *or* to ensure that its employees/staff attend] such further training as the Manufacturer reasonably requires].

7.2. [If during the Term the Manufacturer reasonably considers that [an employee *or* a member of staff] has not completed the Training to its satisfaction then it may require that the [employee *or* member of staff] is not employed to work in the distribution of the Goods under this Agreement].

8. Conduct of the Distributor

8.1. The Distributor must at all times during the Term:

8.1.1. carry out the distribution of the Goods to the highest business and ethical standards

8.1.2. without prejudice to the generality of the foregoing the Distributor must ensure there is compliance with all relevant law and regulation including, whether national or supra-national, but not limited to, employment law and regulation, money laundering law and regulation, health and safety requirements and all other statutory and common law requirements relating to the operation of its business

8.1.3. [inform the Manufacturer forthwith of proposed changes in its business arrangements and obtain its prior written approval before implementation including but not limited to changes in ownership of more than […]% of the nominal share capital or equity of the Distributor or any business, company or firm with which it is associated in the distribution of the Goods]

8.1.4. inform the Manufacturer of changes in the [directors *or* partners] of the Distributor.

9. Accounts and records

9.1. The Distributor must maintain throughout the Term proper accounts, books and records in relation to the distribution of the Goods.

9.2. Copies of the accounts, books and records must be available to the Manufacturer upon reasonable notice.

9.3. In the event that the Manufacturer requires any supporting documentation in relation to details of gross turnover of the Goods the Distributor agrees to provide the same within [...] days of being notified in writing of such request.

9.4. The obligation to provide supporting documentation in this Clause 9 will remain if this Agreement has terminated but the supporting documentation has not been provided prior to the termination thereof. In such circumstances the time limits for compliance will be [...] days and [...] days respectively from the date of the end of the current financial year of the Term or [...] days and [...] days respectively from the date of termination of this Agreement, whichever is the sooner.

10. Marketing, advertising and promotion of the Goods

10.1. The Distributor is responsible at all times during the Term for the promotion of the Goods within the [Territory *or* Territories]. [This must be conducted [as agreed *or* in consultation] from time to time with the Manufacturer]. The marketing and advertising associated with the promotion of the Goods is to be financed by the Distributor.

10.2. In all marketing and advertising the Distributor must make clear that he does not act as the agent in any way of the Manufacturer.

10.3. The Distributor may sell the Goods at a price to be determined by him.

10.4. The Distributor shall supply the Manufacturer on a quarterly basis with:

10.4.1. an up to date price list in relation to the Goods

10.4.2. full details of how many units of the Goods have been sold in the [Territory *or* Territories]

10.4.3. copies of all promotional materials used or intended to be used in relation to the Goods which will be subject to the Manufacturer's prior approval.

10.5. Throughout the Term the Distributor shall:

10.5.1. maintain a properly trained and efficient sales force in respect of the Goods

10.5.2. comply with all legal requirements in the [Territory *or* Territories] in respect of storage, promotion and sales of the Goods

10.5.3. permit representatives of the Manufacturer to inspect premises, transport and promotional literature associated with the promotion and sale of the Goods

10.5.4. provide a full after sales service to the purchasers of the Goods.

10.6. The Distributor warrants that it will not make any warranties or representations to any third parties regarding the Goods save those which have been expressly approved by the Manufacturer in writing or which are included and approved in any literature about the Goods provided by the Manufacturer from time to time.

11. Financial capability

11.1. The Distributor must ensure that it has at all material times the financial means, including but not limited to working capital, to discharge its obligations under this Agreement and to maintain the integrity and reputation of the Goods.

12. No agency

12.1. The Distributor is not for any purpose the agent of the Manufacturer. The Distributor must ensure that in all promotional literature, advertising and any other communications with customers and any other third parties it is made clear that it is acting and trading on its own behalf as principal and not as agent of the Manufacturer.

13. Confidential information

13.1. The Distributor agrees not to disclose any confidential information provided at any time by the Manufacturer either during the Term or at any time thereafter to any third party save where the law requires. The Distributor also agrees not to use any such confidential information for any other purpose other than for the purposes of this Agreement and will not use the information for any business or other purpose of its own. For the avoidance of doubt such information includes but is not limited either in type, *genus* or subject to:

13.1.1. all business information supplied to the Distributor by the Manufacturer regarding the Goods

13.1.2. all marketing information and intelligence

13.1.3. all trade secrets, processes and formulae.

13.2. For the proper protection of the confidential information the Distributor will ensure that:

13.2.1. any employee or member of his staff, whether temporary or permanent, will at the commencement of their employment and no later be provided with a contract of employment or engagement which will include a like obligation to that of the Distributor in respect of confidential information

13.2.2. any [director *or* partner] of the Distributor or any associated [company *or* firm] will be required to provide, in a form approved by the Manufacturer, an undertaking in regard to confidential information in like form to that set out above in relation to the Distributor before being given access to confidential information.

14. Goodwill

14.1. All goodwill in the Marks and the Goods belongs to the Manufacturer, whether generated by the Distributor or otherwise and the Distributor agrees to make no claim in respect thereof.

15. Right of inspection

15.1. The Distributor and/or its appointed agent will be entitled to inspect the operation of the Distributor's business in connection with the distribution of the Goods during any normal business hours in the [Territory *or* Territories] without further notice.

16. Market information

16.1. The Distributor must at all times keep the Manufacturer aware of developments in market conditions within the [Territory *or* Territories] including but not limited to:

16.1.1. actions by competitors or potential competitors of the Goods

16.1.2. plans and proposals for business development by the Distributor.

17. Compliance with laws of the [Territory *or* Territories]

17.1. The Distributor will ensure that it complies at all material times with the laws of the [Territory *or* Territories] relevant to the distribution of the Goods including, but not limited to, those relating to:

17.1.1. data protection and freedom of information

17.1.2. import licences and duties (which the Distributor will be responsible for obtaining and discharging at its own expense)

17.1.3. certificates of origin or other requisite documents

17.1.4. taxes, tariffs and other duties

17.1.5. health and safety

17.1.6. equal opportunities

17.1.7. employment

17.1.8. insurance

17.1.9. occupiers' liability

17.1.10. business registration [and company returns]

17.1.11. the prevention of money laundering

17.1.12. storage, promotion and sale of the Goods.

18. Warranty as to conformity with description

18.1. The Manufacturer warrants that the Goods supplied under this Agreement will correspond, at the time of delivery, with the description it has given to the Distributor. All other warranties, terms or conditions relating to quality, fitness for purpose or condition, whether implied by common law or statute, or express are excluded save where to do so would be by law impermissible.

19. Liability for breach

19.1. Whilst the Manufacturer will endeavour at all times to comply with its legal and contractual obligations to the Distributor it does not accept liability for any loss suffered by the Distributor as a result of any misrepresentation, misdescription, breach of contract, breach of duty or other act or omission (unless fraudulent) however made or caused which constitutes more than a refund of any sum paid or the waiver of any sum contractually payable by the Distributor for the Goods.

19.2. The Manufacturer does not accept liability for any consequential economic or other losses suffered by the Distributor whether resulting from misrepresentation, misdescription, breach of contract, breach of duty or other act or omission (unless fraudulent) however caused.

19.3. Nothing in these Conditions shall limit the right of either Party to seek to recover damages for personal injury or death occasioned by breach of contract or breach of duty by the other Party, its employees or agents.

20. Indemnity

20.1. The Distributor will indemnify the Manufacturer in respect of any losses, damage or liability the Manufacturer may incur as a result of the Distributor's acts or omissions, whether deliberate, accidental, negligent or reckless, in the course of the performance or purported performance of its obligations or rights under this Agreement whether such acts or omissions amount to a breach of an express or implied obligation under this Agreement or a breach of any other legal requirement or obligation, code of practice, licence, consent, forbearance, approval, permission or rule.

20.2. For the avoidance of doubt losses, damage and liability shall include but not be limited to economic and commercial loss, loss of goodwill, legal and other costs associated with legal proceedings of any kind which the Manufacturer has to bring or to which it has to respond, fines, penalties, damages and any financial consequence whatever flowing directly or indirectly from the matters set out in this Clause 19.

21. Organisation of the distribution of the Goods within the [Territory *or* Territories]

21.1. The Distributor must ensure that it sets up and maintains such structures as will enable it to monitor and organise the distribution of the Goods within the [Territory *or* Territories].

22. Novation

22.1. No novation, assignment or delegation of the obligations and benefits of this Agreement by the Distributor is permitted.

22.2. The Manufacturer may novate, assign or delegate the benefits and obligations of this Agreement on giving 21 days written notice to the Distributor.

23. Termination of this Agreement

23.1. This Agreement may expire by effluxion of time or in accordance with the following provisions:

23.1.1. in the event that the Distributor fails to remedy any remediable breach of which it has been notified in writing by the Manufacturer within [...] days the Manufacturer may at its absolute discretion terminate forthwith this Agreement

23.1.2. in the event that the Distributor commits any irremediable material breach or persistently commits any remediable breach of this Agreement the Manufacturer may terminate this Agreement forthwith.

23.2. The Manufacturer may terminate this Agreement forthwith in the event that the Distributor:

23.2.1. is [declared bankrupt *or* wound up due to insolvency]

23.2.2. makes or seeks a composition with its creditors

23.2.3. enters into or seeks an insolvent voluntary arrangement

23.2.4. becomes the subject of the appointment of a manager, receiver or liquidator

23.2.5. is the subject of an administration order

23.2.6. has its assets charged or seized for the satisfaction of a debt

23.2.7. seeks to challenge the Manufacturer's Intellectual Property Rights in relation to the Intellectual Property connected with the Goods

23.2.8. behaves in a way which is likely to bring the Goods or the Manufacturer into disrepute including but not limited to conviction for an indictable criminal offence

23.2.9. divulges confidential business information in connection with the Goods to an unauthorised third party

23.2.10. fails to commence, carry on or terminate as appropriate its distribution business in relation to the Goods

23.2.11. fails to pay any sum due under this Agreement for more than [*28 days*] after its due date

23.2.12. neglects to furnish any document or other information which the Distributor is obliged to provide within [*28 days*] of its due date.

24. [Re-organisation of business structure or ownership

24.1. The Manufacturer may terminate this Agreement if there is any material re-organisation of the Distributor's business structure unless:

24.1.1. such re-organisation is not the result of insolvency

24.1.2. the resultant company or organisation is bound by the provisions of this Agreement

24.1.3. the beneficial ownership of the resultant entity is not in the hands of competitors of the Manufacturer anywhere in the world except to the extent that such ownership does not exceed [...]% of the total].

25. Legislative change

25.1. In the event that there is a change in legislation which materially affects the legitimate interests of the Manufacturer in respect of this Agreement the Manufacturer will be entitled to terminate this Agreement upon giving reasonable notice to the Distributor which must be not less than [...] days and in no instance more than [...] days.

26. Post termination rights and obligations

26.1. Termination of this Agreement for any reason shall not affect the rights of either Party in respect of the period after termination nor either Party's rights which may have arisen as a result of any breach pre-dating the termination.

26.2. In order to ensure the proper protection of the Goods, including their Marks and Goodwill upon termination of the Term the Distributor must:

26.2.1. cease the promotion, advertising or sale of the Goods

26.2.2. remove all signage, Marks, names, advertisements and other material indicating that the Distributor remains an authorised distributor of the Goods

26.2.3. return all samples of the Goods

26.2.4. return all copies of literature and material supplied for or associated with the distribution of the Goods other than that which is not branded or specific to the Manufacturer

26.2.5. return all copies of software, business information documentation and other materials containing business information connected with the implementation and operation of this Agreement

26.2.6. remove or erase from all computers and other electronic equipment all copies and versions of any software specific to the operation of this Agreement

26.2.7. not use any confidential business information received by it during the course of the operation of this Agreement and must not disclose such information to any third party whether within or without the [Territory *or* Territories]

26.2.8. provide all reasonable assistance to the Manufacturer to achieve an orderly transfer of the distribution of the Goods to any person nominated by the Manufacturer.

26.3. The Distributor hereby grants the Manufacturer an irrevocable power of attorney to effect such of these acts as is necessary for any purpose contained in this Clause 25.

26.4. The Manufacturer shall be entitled to purchase back from the Distributor after termination of this Agreement any Goods remaining in the possession of the Distributor and not already paid for by a customer or the subject of a Purchase Order from a customer of the Distributor. The price shall be either the invoice price or the book value according to the Distributor's records, whichever is the lower. The Goods shall be delivered back to the Manufacturer at the Manufacturer's expense and risk.

26.5. The Distributor shall have no claim against the Manufacturer for compensation for loss of distribution rights, loss of goodwill or any similar loss.

26.6. Subject as otherwise provided in this Agreement and to any rights or obligations that have accrued before termination, neither Party shall have any further obligation to the other under this Agreement.

27. Severability

27.1. In the event that any of the restrictions in this Agreement are found by a court of competent jurisdiction to be unenforceable because they are unreasonable but which would be enforceable were specific words, phrases or clauses removed then the restrictions shall apply as if such words, phrases or clauses were removed.

27.2. In the event that any term of this Agreement is found to be invalid or otherwise unenforceable then such term shall be regarded and construed as severable from the Agreement so as not to affect the validity and enforceability of the remainder.

28. Whole agreement

28.1. This Agreement supersedes and replaces any previous agreement between the Parties whether oral or in writing in relation to the distribution of the Goods. The Distributor hereby agrees that in entering into this Agreement it has not relied upon any warranty or representation made by or on behalf of the Manufacturer save where expressly stated in this Agreement. The Parties hereby agree that this Agreement constitutes the whole agreement between the Parties in respect of the distribution of the Goods.

28.2. Nothing in this Clause 27 shall be construed as limiting or excluding either Party's liability to the other for fraud or deceit in inducing the making of this Agreement.

28.3. Without prejudice to the generality of the foregoing the following is agreed between the Parties:

28.3.1. all financial information provided by the Manufacturer to the Distributor is provided in good faith and is intended to be indicative only. The Distributor hereby acknowledges that it accepts that the provision of such information is at the request of the Distributor on the basis that it does not constitute a representation, warranty, or guarantee by the Manufacturer and that the Distributor has not placed reliance upon it for the purpose of entering into this Agreement or for any other purpose

28.3.2. the Distributor accepts that the Manufacturer does not and cannot predict how the distribution of the Goods will perform in the [Territory *or* Territories] either under the Distributor or at all

28.3.3. the Distributor warrants that it has been advised by the Manufacturer to seek independent legal and financial advice before entering into this Agreement and that its decision to make this Agreement is based solely upon its own judgement and assessment of the Goods' commerciality in the [Territory *or* Territories].

29. Variation

29.1. Any variation of the terms of this Agreement must be in writing signed by the Parties.

30. Further action

30.1. The Parties agree that they will expeditiously carry out such further acts as may be necessary for the purpose of this Agreement including the execution and delivery of such instruments, deeds, licences, notifications as may be reasonably required by the other Party or by law.

31. Set off

31.1. Notwithstanding any other express or implied term of this Agreement the Manufacturer reserves the right to set off against any sum payable or owed by it to the Distributor any debt or other liability, whether absolute or contingent, owed by the Distributor to the Manufacturer, or any sum, debt or other liability, absolute or contingent, owed by the Distributor to any third party for which the Manufacturer is liable or may be liable in default of payment or discharge by the Distributor. In the event of such set off the Distributor irrevocably authorises the Manufacturer to pay from such sum or sums held by the Manufacturer for the Distributor such sum as will discharge any such debt or liability to a third party or discharge the debt or sum owed to the Manufacturer.

32. *Force majeure*

32.1. Neither Party shall have any liability to the other for any delay, omission, failure or inadequate performance of this Agreement which is the result of circumstances beyond its reasonable control. Where a Party is so affected in its performance of this Agreement it will notify the other Party in writing as soon as is reasonably practical.

32.2. If performance of this Agreement is materially prevented by *force majeure* for a period of more than [...] months then either Party may serve upon the other a written notice effecting termination in not less than [...] weeks thereafter. [In the event that *force majeure* ceases to prevent performance of the Agreement within the notice period then the notice shall be null and void and the obligations of the Parties will continue under this Agreement].

33. Waiver

33.1. No failure, neglect or delay in enforcing any of the terms of this Agreement may be construed as a waiver of any of the Manufacturer's rights in respect thereof nor such neglect, failure or delay a variation of the express terms of the Agreement.

34. Third party rights

34.1. The Parties to this Agreement agree that it is not hereby intended that any rights should be conferred upon or enforceable by any third party as defined in the Contracts (Rights of Third Parties) Act 1999.

35. Notices

35.1. All notices under this Agreement shall be in writing and shall be delivered personally [or by first class, registered or recorded post] [or by facsimile transmission] in every case to the other Party's Agreed Address. [In the case of first class post notice will be deemed to be received [3] business days after the date of posting].

36. Law and jurisdiction

36.1. This Agreement is governed by the law of England and Wales and is subject to the [exclusive] jurisdiction of the courts of England and Wales.

37. Schedules

37.1. The Schedules form part of this Agreement including any subsequent amendments made thereto.

Signed, etc.

SCHEDULE 1

The Goods

[Insert list and description of the Goods]

Signed, etc.

SCHEDULE 2

The Manufacturer's Usual Terms and Conditions

[Attach a copy]

Signed, etc.

SCHEDULE 3

Term

[*Insert details*]

Signed, etc.

SCHEDULE 4

Price list, delivery and insurance costs

[*Insert details*]

Signed, etc.

SCHEDULE 5

Parties' Agreed Addresses

[*Insert Agreed Addresses*]

Signed, etc.

SCHEDULE 6

The [Territory *or* Territories]

[*Insert list and/or description of the Territory/Territories*]

Signed, etc.

10

E-commerce

10.1   Introduction

A great deal of the use of the Internet and World Wide Web for commerce is for retail business. In many instances, therefore, the purchaser or user will be a consumer as the law defines. However, consumer contracts are outside the scope of this work.

The terms and conditions in the precedent (**Precedent 10A**) are therefore only for use in a business to business context as they do not necessarily comply with the requirements of consumer protection legislation.

PRECEDENT 10A   Terms and conditions for World Wide Web business to business service

TERMS AND CONDITIONS FOR WORLD WIDE WEB BUSINESS TO BUSINESS SERVICE

1. Definitions

1.1. In these terms and conditions the following shall have the meaning set out in this Clause unless the context otherwise requires:

'We', 'us', 'our'	Refers to [...] Ltd, its agents and employees.
'You', 'your'	Subscriber to the site.
'this Site'	This website.

2. Subscription to this Site

2.1. By taking out a subscription to this Site you are accepting the terms and conditions of a legally binding agreement.

2.2. You are also agreeing to permit us to store and use information about you which you have provided in accordance with our privacy policy.

3. Scope of our service

3.1. Our service is provided only for United Kingdom based businesses and by taking out a subscription you warrant that:

3.1.1. you have authority to do so on behalf of your business

3.1.2. the service will only be used for your internal business purposes and not offered or exploited by you for any other purpose, whether commercial or otherwise.

4. Our obligations

4.1. We shall use our best endeavours to provide the following:

4.1.1. uninterrupted access to this Site and the services it provides

4.1.2. accurate updating of material and information as often as reasonably possible

4.1.3. protection of your privacy as stated in our privacy policy including the protection of personal and financial data and debit/credit card information.

5. No warranty

5.1. Although as stated above we shall use our best endeavours we do not warrant that:

5.1.1. access to this Site and the services it provides will be uninterrupted

5.1.2. material and information will be accurate.

6. Services

6.1. In respect of services we provide we do not warrant that they will be performed with due care and skill.

7. Goods

7.1. In respect of goods we provide we warrant that they will correspond, at the time of delivery, with the description given on this Site. All other warranties, terms or conditions relating to quality, fitness for purpose or condition, whether implied by common law or statute, or express are excluded save where to do so would be by law impermissible.

8. Limitations and exclusions

8.1. Whilst we will endeavour at all times to comply with our legal and contractual obligations we do not accept liability for any loss suffered by you as a result of any delay, mistake, errors, omissions, unavailability, failed access, misrepresentation, misdescription, breach of contract, breach of duty or other act or omission (unless fraudulent) however made or caused which constitutes more than [a refund of any sum paid for any goods or services the subject of a claim *or* your annual subscription to this Site] [or the waiver of any sum contractually payable to us under these terms and conditions in respect of the services or goods the subject of the claim].

8.2. We do not accept liability for any consequential economic or other losses suffered by you whether resulting from misrepresentation, misdescription, breach of contract, breach of duty or other act or omission (unless fraudulent) however caused.

8.3. Nothing in these conditions shall limit the right of any party to seek to recover damages for personal injury or death occasioned by breach of contract or breach of duty by us, our employees or agents.

8.4. Each of the above exclusions or limitations shall be construed as a separate, and severable, provision of these terms and conditions.

9. Payments

9.1. Continued use of this Site is dependent upon prompt payment of all sums due to us. In the event that payments are not made in full and on time we may exclude you from use of those parts of this Site which are not available to non-subscribers.

10. Termination of subscription

10.1. You may terminate your subscription to this Site on [...] days notice to us.

10.2. We may terminate your use of this Site if:

10.2.1. you fail to pay sums due to us promptly

10.2.2. you are in material breach of any of these terms and conditions.

10.3. Any rights that have accrued to either party at the date of termination will remain enforceable after termination.

11. Variations to these terms and conditions

11.1. We may at any time:

11.1.1. vary the services and goods we provide

11.1.2. vary these terms and conditions. We shall notify users of changes on this Site. Your continued use of this Site thereafter will constitute acceptance of them.

12. VAT

12.1. Our goods and services are advised at prices nett of VAT. Any import duties or costs are borne by us.

13. Intellectual property rights

13.1. All intellectual property rights in the design and contents of this Site including but not limited to trademarks, product names, logos, designs and get-up belong to us. You may only take copies of any part of this Site for the purpose of using this Site.

14. *Force majeure*

14.1. We shall not have any liability for any delay, omission, failure or inadequate performance by us in relation to this Site or the supply of goods or services through it which is the result of circumstances beyond our reasonable control. Where we are so affected in our performance of our obligations under these terms and conditions we will notify you as soon as is reasonably possible.

14.2. *Force majeure* includes but is not limited to civil commotion, war and terrorist action, state action, industrial action whether lawful or otherwise, non-availability of raw materials, components and labour at commercially viable prices, unavoidable accident, fire, flood, earthquake, subsidence, epidemic and other natural or physical disasters.

15. Law and jurisdiction

15.1. These terms and conditions shall be governed by the laws of England and Wales and are subject to the [exclusive] jurisdiction of the courts of England and Wales.

16. Invalid clauses

16.1. In the event that any of these terms and conditions is found to be invalid or otherwise unenforceable then such term shall be regarded and construed as severable from the remaining terms and conditions so as not to affect the validity and enforceability of the remainder.

11

Franchising

11.1　Introduction

This chapter is concerned with agreements which entitle a third party (the franchisee) to represent and provide to customers and potential customers goods and services under the style and brand of another party (the franchisor) in return for the payment to that other party of a fixed fee, a percentage of sales take or other monetary consideration.

An agreement may include, and usually does, provision for the supply of a product by the franchisor to the franchisee. The fundamental characteristic of the arrangement is that the franchisee does not acquire any equity or other interest in the franchisor's business but is licensed to act as franchisee for a fixed or indefinite period.

The franchisee will usually own his own business, including premises, fixtures and fittings but not the goodwill generated by the franchisor's business.

The franchisee is not an agent of the franchisor.

A franchise can arise in various ways. Where there is an existing franchisor:

- An existing business may add to its portfolio a franchise from a new franchisor.
- An existing business may replace one franchisor with another.
- A new business may be formed to operate a franchise.

Conversely, an existing business may turn itself into a franchisor whilst either retaining some direct sales itself or becoming a wholly franchised business. This can be a quick way of developing a brand or concept without the need for very large capital injection or high gearing.

In this chapter there is an exclusive franchise agreement (**Precedent 11A**), a non-exclusive master franchise agreement (**Precedent 11B**), and a straightforward non-exclusive direct franchise agreement (which may readily be adapted to an exclusive one) (**Precedent 11C**).

11.2　Comparison with agency or distribution agreements

Apart from the legal distinction there is also a functional distinction between a franchise and an agency or distribution agreement. The latter usually relate solely to a product or products. A franchise is really only suited to a business system or format. For example, a manufacturer of ready-made pizzas might engage self-employed agents to acquire wholesale customers or set up a distribution agreement with a distributor. However, if he had devised a whole business concept which involved the provision of eating places which cooked and sold his pizzas then a franchising arrangement where each eating place was branded with his product may be suitable for franchising. The method of cooking, the menu, the distinctive décor, may all form part of the intellectual property of the franchisor.

11.3   Exclusivity

Exclusivity provisions may engage Community legislation which permits such arrangements only if:

(a) they come within the block exemption for vertical restraints – Regulation 2790/99/EC;

(b) they have been granted exemption under the provisions of Article 81(3) of the Rome Treaty; or

(c) they are *de minimis*.

11.4   Termination

A classic problem with franchise agreements is the termination provisions. Normally these will operate by effluxion of time or on the happening of some event such as a failure by the franchisee to meet his agreed targets.

11.5   Sub-franchising

It is a common commercial practice for the head franchisor to grant sub-franchisor franchises. For example, an American company as head franchisor may grant an English company a sub-franchise so that it may itself grant franchises to individual franchisees. Provision then needs to be made for the head franchisor to step into the sub-franchisor's shoes in certain circumstances.

PRECEDENT 11A   Exclusive master franchise agreement

EXCLUSIVE MASTER FRANCHISE AGREEMENT

THIS EXCLUSIVE MASTER FRANCHISE AGREEMENT is dated [...] and is made BETWEEN:

1. [*Name of Master Franchisor*] [of [*address*] *or* whose registered office is at [*address*]], [*company registration number*] ('the Master Franchisor'); and

2. [*Name of Master Franchisee*] [of [*address*] *or* whose registered office is at [*address*]], [*company registration number*] ('the Master Franchisee').

RECITALS

1. The Master Franchisor has developed the Franchise as defined herein [and has acquired a reputation for [*describe*]] and is the owner of the intellectual property including goodwill associated with the Franchise.
2. By this Agreement the Master Franchisor wishes to appoint the Master Franchisee to [manage and] expand the franchise network for the Franchise on an exclusive basis within the [Territory *or* Territories] as defined below.
3. The Master Franchisee [is an experienced Franchise developer and] wishes to [expand *or* maintain] the network for the Franchise in the [Territory *or* Territories].

DEFINITIONS

In this Agreement the following definitions apply:

'Franchise'	A business model and system as described in Schedule 2 to this Agreement.
'Franchise Agreement'	The agreement a copy of which is set out in Schedule 3 as amended from time to time.
'Franchisee'	Any entity holding a Franchise within the [Territory *or* Territories].
'Initial Franchise Fee'	A sum set out in Schedule 8 to be paid by the Master Franchisee at the commencement of the Master Franchise.
'Initial Training'	The initial training set out in Schedule 7.
'Intellectual Property' and 'Intellectual Property Rights'	All copyrights, trade names, trademarks, designs and devices relating to the Goods.
'Know-how'	The knowledge and expertise of the Master Franchisor in creating [and running] the Franchise as set out in the Manual and any other literature or other media provided by the Master Franchisor in connection with the Franchise or Master Franchise.
'Manual'	An instruction manual which fully describes the operation of the Franchise, a copy of which is in Schedule 6.
'Marks'	The marks, trademarks and get-up associated with the Franchise.
'Master Franchise'	The master franchise granted by the Master Franchisor to the Master Franchisee under this Agreement.
'Materials'	Those materials, literature, computer software and other equipment of whatever nature needed for the operation of the Franchise and supplied by the Master Franchisor.
'Monthly Service Fee'	A monthly charge as set out in Schedule 8 as varied from time to time.
'Party' and 'Parties'	The Master Franchisor and the Master Franchisee.
'Parties' Agreed Addresses'	Addresses for service as set out in Schedule 9 and as varied from time to time.
'Premises'	The premises at [*Master Franchisee's address*].
'Target[s]'	Target or targets as set out in Schedule 4 or as varied by written agreement between the parties from time to time.
'Term'	The duration of this Agreement as defined in Schedule 5.

'[Territory *or* Territories]'   The territory or territories as set out in Schedule 1 to this Agreement.

'Training'   The training set out in Schedule 7.

INTERPRETATION

In this Agreement:

1.   The singular includes the plural and one gender includes all.
2.   References to Schedules and Clauses are to those in this Agreement.
3.   Reference to a statutory provision includes any amendment or replacement provision relevant to the Agreement.
4.   Reference to a document includes that document as amended, altered or replaced subsequent to the date of this Agreement.
5.   Reference to writing includes facsimile transmission, e-mail, and similar media unless the context otherwise expressly provides.
6.   Time expressed in days excludes the first day but includes the last day. If the last day does not fall on a normal business day in [both] England and Wales [and the [Territory *or* Territories]] then the last day will be deemed to be the first normal business day thereafter in [the [Territory *or* Territories] and] England and Wales.
7.   The headings in this document do not form part of the Agreement.

OPERATIVE PROVISIONS

1. The Master Franchise

1.1. The Master Franchisor hereby grants to the Master Franchisee an exclusive Master Franchise for the Term subject to the terms and conditions of this Agreement to be carried on from the Premises, within the [Territory *or* Territories].

2. The Master Franchisor's Obligations

2.1. At the commencement of the Term of the Master Franchise the Master Franchisor will provide the Master Franchisee with the following:

2.1.1. the Manual

2.1.2. the Training

2.1.3. the Materials.

2.2. During the Term the Master Franchisor will:

2.2.1. keep current and where necessary update the contents of the Manual

2.2.2. provide such further training as may be necessary for the exercise of the Master Franchise by the Master Franchisee. Such training shall be at the reasonable cost of the Master Franchisee

2.2.3. provide such further materials as are necessary for the operation of the Master Franchise at the reasonable cost of the Master Franchisee

2.2.4. provide market information, technical assistance and relevant additional Know-how as may be reasonably necessary

2.2.5. permit the Master Franchisee to use the Marks as set out below. For the avoidance of doubt the Master Franchisor gives no warranty as to the validity of the Marks.

3. The Master Franchisee's Obligations

3.1. The Marks

3.1.1. The Marks are to be used by the Master Franchisee solely for purposes authorised by the Master Franchisor and connected with the Franchise and Master Franchise, for which sole purpose the Master Franchisee is hereby granted licence.

3.1.2. The Marks are to be used in ways stipulated from time to time by the Master Franchisor in connection with the Master Franchise and Franchise.

3.1.3. The Marks are not to be altered, abbreviated, modified or used in connection with any other marks, brands, or the like without the express prior written approval of the Master Franchisor, which permission is at the Master Franchisor's absolute discretion. The Master Franchisor may however at any time modify the Marks and/or substitute new Marks for those existing at the time of this Agreement and the new or modified Marks will be deemed to be the Marks as defined in this Agreement. For the avoidance of doubt the Master Franchisee will not be eligible for any compensation in such circumstances as those set out herein in this Clause 3.1.3.

3.1.4. No other Marks are to be used by the Master Franchisee in connection with the Master Franchise or Franchise.

3.1.5. No copies or imitations of the Marks are to be used by the Master Franchisee for any purpose during the currency of this Agreement or thereafter. At no time is the Master Franchisee to register or attempt to register any Mark in connection with the Franchise or Master Franchise.

3.1.6. The Master Franchisee is not to commit any act or omission which is likely adversely to affect the Master Franchisor's goodwill in the Marks and/or Franchise and/or to damage the Master Franchisor's reputation.

3.1.7. The Master Franchisee is to report to the Master Franchisor any infringement of the Marks by any third party and to assist it in taking such steps as may be necessary.

3.1.8. In all uses of the Marks the Master Franchisee must include a clear and appropriate indication of whether the Mark is registered or unregistered.

3.1.9. If any recording of a Mark at a Trade Marks Registry is required the Master Franchisee will provide all reasonable assistance to the Master Franchisor during the currency of this Agreement.

3.1.10. The Master Franchisee may not use the name of the Franchise or any of the Marks as part of its own name. It may however trade under the Franchise name and Marks during the Term.

3.1.11. The Marks will remain at all times both during the Term and thereafter the property of the Master Franchisor and/or its successors or assignees.

3.2. Know-how

3.2.1. The Master Franchisee may not use the Know-how for any purpose other than the operation of the Master Franchise or Franchise nor permit third parties other than Franchisees to do so. During the Term the Master Franchisor must take all reasonable steps to prevent knowledge of the Know-how coming into the hands of third parties other than Franchisees.

3.3. Training

3.3.1. The Master Franchisee will ensure that it [and its employees/staff] attend[s] the Initial Training provided by the Master Franchisor prior to the commencement of the operation of the Master Franchise. The course will be provided at the reasonable expense of the Master Franchisee. If the Master Franchisee [or its employees/staff] fail[s] to complete the course to the reasonable satisfaction of the Master Franchisor then the Master Franchisee's Initial Franchise Fee will be refunded subject to deduction to cover the costs of the Initial Training.

3.3.2. The Master Franchisee will have a continuing obligation to attend [and to ensure that its employees/staff attend] such further Training as the Master Franchisor requires as set out in Schedule 7.

3.3.3. If during the Term the Master Franchisor reasonably considers that [an employee *or* a member of staff] has not completed the Training to its satisfaction then it may require that the [employee *or* member of staff] is not employed to work in the operation of the Master Franchise.

3.4. Conduct of the Master Franchise

3.4.1. The Master Franchisee must at all times comply with any reasonable directions given by the Master Franchisor as to the conduct and management of the Master Franchise and the Franchisees including but not limited to:

3.4.1.1. the implementation of changes or updates to the operation of the Franchise

3.4.1.2. the addition and development of new Franchisees within the [Territory *or* Territories].

3.4.2. The Master Franchisee must at all times operate the Master Franchise to the highest business and ethical standards in full compliance with the Manual.

3.4.3. Without prejudice to the generality of the foregoing the Master Franchisee must ensure there is compliance with all relevant law and regulation including, whether national or supra-national, but not limited to, employment law and regulation, money laundering law and regulation, health and safety requirements and all other statutory and common law requirements relating to the operation of the Master Franchise.

3.4.4. The Master Franchisee must keep insured the premises and business of the Master Franchisee including but not limited to all appropriate third party liabilities as specified in the Manual. The Master Franchisee will provide copies of all insurance documents, including certificates and polices to the Master Franchisor upon demand.

3.4.5. The Master Franchisee must inform the Master Franchisor forthwith of proposed changes in its business arrangements and obtain its prior written approval before implementation including but not limited to:

3.4.5.1. changes in ownership of more than [5%] of the nominal share capital or equity of the Master Franchisee or any business, company or firm with which it is associated in the performance of the Master Franchise

3.4.5.2. material changes (in the case of a limited company) to the memorandum and/or articles of association

3.4.5.3. any share agreements between [shareholders *or* partners] in the Master Franchisee or its associated or connected companies or firms

3.4.5.4. changes in the [directors *or* partners] of the Master Franchisee.

3.5. Premises

3.5.1. The Master Franchise must at all times be carried out from the Premises or such other premises as have been approved in writing by the Master Franchisor prior to the use thereof.

3.6. Accounts and records

3.6.1. The Master Franchisee must maintain throughout the Term proper accounts, books and records in relation to the Master Franchise.

3.6.2. Copies of the accounts, books and records must be available to the Master Franchisor upon reasonable notice and audited details of gross annual turnover and annual profit and loss must be provided to the Master Franchisor within [72 *days*] of the conclusion of each financial year of the Master Franchise.

3.6.3. In the event that the Master Franchisor requires any supporting documentation in relation to the audited details of gross annual turnover and annual profit and loss the Master Franchisee agrees to provide the same within [14 *days*] of being notified in writing of such request.

3.6.4. The obligation to provide audited details of gross annual turnover and annual profit and loss and supporting documentation in this Clause 3.6 will remain if the Master Franchise has terminated but the audited details of gross annual turnover and annual profit and loss and/or supporting documentation have not been provided prior to the termination thereof. In such circumstances the time limits for compliance will be [72 *days*] and [14 *days*] respectively from the date of the end of the current financial year of the Master Franchise or [72 *days*] and [14 *days*] respectively from the date of termination of the Master Franchise, whichever is the sooner.

3.7. Targets

3.7.1. It shall be an express obligation of this Agreement that the Master Franchisee achieves the Target from year to year. Failure to do so is a breach of this Agreement.

3.8. Marketing, advertising and promotion of the Franchise

3.8.1. The Master Franchisee is responsible at all times during the Term for the promotion of the Franchise within the [Territory *or* Territories]. This must be conducted as agreed from time to time with the Master Franchisor and in accordance where applicable with the provisions in the Manual. The marketing and advertising associated with the promotion of the Franchise is to be financed by a fund administered by the Master Franchisee and which is to be funded by the Master Franchisee and the Franchisees.

3.8.2. The Master Franchisee warrants that it will not make any warranties or representations to the Franchisees or any third parties regarding the Master Franchisee and the Franchise save those which have been expressly approved by the Master Franchisor in writing or which are included and approved in the Manual as modified from time to time.

3.9. Financial capability

3.9.1. The Master Franchisee must ensure that it has at all material times the financial means, including but not limited to working capital, to discharge its obligations under this Agreement and to maintain the integrity and reputation of the Franchise.

3.10. Sole business

3.10.1. During the Term the Master Franchisee will not carry on any other business, either directly or indirectly, save with the prior written consent of the Master Franchisor. The Master Franchisor may at any time at its sole discretion withdraw such consent on the giving of not less than [3 *months*] written notice.

3.10.2. The Master Franchisee may not have any direct or indirect financial or other interest in any business which may be reasonably considered to be a competitor of the Franchise anywhere in the world other than the direct or indirect holding of shares in a public listed company where that shareholding amounts to less than [1%] of the total nominal share capital of the public listed company.

4. Audit of Master Franchisee's books by Master Franchisor

4.1. During the Term and for a period of [12 *months*] after its termination the Master Franchisor shall be entitled by itself or through auditors appointed by it to require, having given reasonable written notice, the production of the Master Franchisee's books of accounts for the purpose of auditing them at the premises of the Master Franchisee. Audits will take place during ordinary office hours.

4.2. In the event that any audit referred to in this Clause 4 should disclose an underpayment of more than [3%] of the sums properly payable to the Master Franchisor under this Agreement during any financial year or part thereof of the Master Franchise the Master Franchisee will be required to pay the Master Franchisor the reasonable cost of the audit in addition to the sums properly due under this Agreement. Any such shortfall as mentioned in this Clause 4.2 shall be paid within [7 *days*] of the figure being notified in writing to the Master Franchisee.

5. No agency

5.1. The Master Franchisee is not for any purpose the agent of the Master Franchisor. The Master Franchisee must ensure that a notice is displayed at the Premises in a prominent position stating that the business there carried on is carried on by an independent [company *or* firm] called [*name*] which is the holder of a licence from the Master Franchisor to conduct business under its name but that the Master Franchisee is not in any way an agent of the Master Franchisor for any purpose whatever. A similar notice must be included in all correspondence and literature used in the operation of the Master Franchise.

6. Territory and other variations

6.1. The Master Franchisor reserves the right to require the Master Franchisee under this Agreement to operate differently from other Master Franchisees if the Master Franchisor considers that market and other conditions so require.

7. Confidential information

7.1. The Master Franchisee agrees not to disclose any confidential information provided by the Master Franchisor during the Term or at any time thereafter to any third party save where the law requires. The Master Franchisee also agrees not to use any such confidential information for any other purpose other than for the promotion and running of the Master Franchise and will not use the information for any business or other purpose of its own. For the avoidance of doubt such information includes but is not limited either in type, *genus* or subject to:

7.1.1. all business information supplied to the Master Franchisee by the Master Franchisor regarding the Franchise

7.1.2. all marketing information and intelligence

7.1.3. all trade secrets, processes and formulae.

7.2. For the proper protection of the confidential information the Master Franchisee will ensure that:

7.2.1. any employee or member of his staff, whether temporary or permanent, will at the commencement of their employment and no later be provided with a contract of employment or engagement which will include a like obligation to that of the Master Franchisee in respect of confidential information.

7.2.2. any [director *or* partner] of the Master Franchisee or any associated [company *or* firm] will be required to provide, in a form approved by the Master Franchisor, an undertaking in regard to confidential information in like form to that set out above in relation to the Master Franchisee before being given access to confidential information.

8. Third party agreements in relation to the Master Franchise

8.1. The Master Franchisor may not enter into any third party agreements or arrangements in relation to the Master Franchise which will have the effect of encumbrancing, charging or otherwise materially affecting the business of the Master Franchise or the receipts therefrom without the prior written consent of the Master Franchisor, the giving of which consent shall be at the absolute discretion of the Master Franchisor.

9. Goodwill

9.1. All goodwill in the Marks, the Master Franchise and the Franchise belongs to the Master Franchisor, whether generated by the Master Franchisee, the Franchisees or otherwise and the Master Franchisee agrees to make no claim in respect thereof.

10. Customers

10.1. All customers of the Master Franchisee and the Franchisees are customers of the Master Franchisor for all purposes except liability for defective [products *or* services].

10.2. The Master Franchisee will maintain an up-to-date record of all Franchisees in its [Territory *or* Territories] full details of which it will provide on demand to the Master Franchisor. The Master Franchisee will provide to the Master Franchisor a copy of the up-to-date list at least once every calendar month on the first day thereof or otherwise as detailed in the Manual.

11. Right of inspection

11.1. The Master Franchisee and/or its appointed agent will be entitled to inspect the operation of the Master Franchise at the Premises or at any other location used by the Master Franchisee in connection with the Master Franchise during any normal business hours in the [Territory *or* Territories] without further notice.

11.2. The Master Franchisee and/or its appointed agent will be entitled to inspect the operation of the Franchise at any premises used by a Franchisee in connection with the operation of the Franchise during any normal business hours in the [Territory *or* Territories] without further notice.

12. Market information

12.1. The Master Franchisee must at all times keep the Master Franchisor aware of developments in market conditions within the [Territory *or* Territories] including but not limited to:

12.1.1. actions by competitors or potential competitors of the Franchise

12.1.2. plans and proposals for business development by the Master Franchisee of the Master Franchise.

13. Compliance with laws of the [Territory *or* Territories]

13.1. The Master Franchisee will ensure that it complies at all material times with the laws of the [Territory *or* Territories] relevant to the Master Franchise including, but not limited to, those relating to:

13.1.1. date protection and freedom of information

13.1.2. taxes and tariffs

13.1.3. health and safety

13.1.4. equal opportunities

13.1.5. employment

13.1.6. insurance

13.1.7. occupiers' liability

13.1.8. business registration [and company returns]

13.1.9. the prevention of money laundering.

14. Indemnity

14.1. The Master Franchisee will indemnify the Master Franchisor in respect of any losses, damage or liability the Master Franchisor may incur as a result of the Master Franchisee's acts or omissions, whether deliberate, accidental, negligent or reckless, in the course of the performance or purported performance of its obligations or rights under this Agreement whether such acts or omissions amount to a breach of an express or implied obligation under this Agreement or a breach of any other legal requirement or obligation, code of practice, licence, consent, forbearance, approval, permission or rule.

14.2. For the avoidance of doubt losses, damage and liability shall include but not be limited to economic and commercial loss, loss of goodwill, legal and other costs associated with legal proceedings of any kind which the Master Franchisor has to bring or to which it has to respond, fines, penalties, damages and any financial consequence whatever flowing directly or indirectly from the matters set out in this Clause 14.

15. Organisation and supervision of Franchisees within the [Territory *or* Territories]

15.1. The Master Franchisee must ensure that it sets up and maintains such structure as will enable it to monitor and organise the Franchisees within the [Territory *or* Territories].

15.2. Each Franchisee's operation must be checked by the Master Franchisee at least once a month to ensure that it is complying with the terms of the Franchise including but not limited to that:

    15.2.1. correct systems are being followed and implemented

    15.2.2. adequate financial reporting to the Master Franchisor is taking place.

15.3. In the event that there is inadequate compliance with the terms of its Franchise the Master Franchisee must take all reasonable steps to ensure that a Franchisee does so comply.

15.4. If the Franchisee fails to comply after reasonable steps have been taken by the Master Franchisee to ensure compliance then the Franchise Agreement must be terminated.

15.5. Prior to any new Franchisee being provided with materials or information (other than that in the public domain) about the Franchise the Master Franchisor must ensure that it has signed a Franchise Agreement for each location from which it intends to operate.

15.6. The Master Franchisee will carry out an audit of each Franchisee at least once every calendar year at its own expense. The Master Franchisee may if it wishes seek to recover such cost from the Franchisee in accordance with the terms of the Franchise Agreement.

16. Appointment of Franchisees

16.1. The Master Franchisee is responsible for the selection and appointment of new Franchisees within the [Territory *or* Territories]. In doing so it must have due regard to the commercial well-being of existing Franchisees and those holding Franchises outside the [Territory *or* Territories].

16.2. No appointment may be made without the prior written approval of the Master Franchisor. Any appointment purportedly made in contravention of this requirement will be of no legal effect and in breach of this Agreement as the Master Franchisee will have no authority so to do. For the avoidance of doubt it is hereby agreed that nothing in this Clause 16 shall be taken to have the effect of constituting or implying any agency on the part of the Master Franchisee on behalf of the Master Franchisor.

17. Promotion of the Franchise

17.1. The Master Franchisee will impose a levy of [1%] of gross turnover ('the promotional levy') on each Franchisee to provide for the advertising, marketing and promotion of the Franchise within the [Territory *or* Territories].

17.2. The sums received in respect of the promotional levy shall be deposited in a separate bank account in the name of [*the Master Franchisee's name*].

17.3. The Master Franchisee will keep separate books of account in respect of the promotional levy which will be available for inspection by the Franchisees within the [Territory *or* Territories] and the Master Franchisor upon the giving of 7 days written notice to the Master Franchisee.

17.4. All promotional activities and material used in connection therewith are subject to the prior approval of the Master Franchisor and such activities should be undertaken only after reasonable consultation with the Franchisees.

18. Audit of Franchisees

18.1. The Master Franchisor may at its discretion undertake audits of the individual Franchisees as agent of the Master Franchisee in addition to or instead of any audit undertaken by the Master Franchisee. In such eventuality the Master Franchisee shall be responsible for the payment of the Master Franchisor's reasonable costs as if such audit were an audit of the Master Franchisee itself.

18.2. Save in exceptional circumstances the Master Franchisor will not undertake such audits as mentioned in this Clause 18 without prior consultation with the Master Franchisee.

19. Master Franchisor's supervision of the Master Franchisee

19.1. The Master Franchisor may undertake an audit of the Master Franchisee's business at any time during the currency of this Agreement and for a period of six months after termination for any reason. Such audit may consist of both financial and other matters connected with compliance with the terms of the Master Franchise.

19.2. The Master Franchisor will once every calendar year undertake an annual audit of the Master Franchise of not more than 5 days in length. Members of the Master Franchisor's staff or agents appointed by it will undertake the audit, the number of participants will be reasonable and subject to prior consultation with the Master Franchisee. The Master Franchisee will pay the reasonable costs of the audit including payroll, fees, travel and accommodation (if reasonably necessary) of the staff or agents involved.

19.3. The Master Franchisee undertakes to provide all reasonable assistance during any audit under this Clause 19 including the provision of and access to all documents, computer records and accounts reasonably required. The Master Franchisee also agrees to answer all questions and provide such information as is required by the Master Franchisor to carry out the audit.

20. Master Franchise fees and charges

20.1. Upon signing this Agreement the Master Franchisee will:

20.1.1. pay the Master Franchisor the Initial Franchise Fee of £[...]

20.1.2. provide an [irrevocable] [performance bond *or* standby letter of credit *or* bank guarantee *or* deposit] [in a form approved by the Master Franchisor] in the sum of £[...] to [remain in force *or* be retained by the Master Franchisor] until [*6 months*] after the termination of this Agreement

20.1.3. pay the Master Franchisor's legal fees as invoiced to it in respect of this Agreement

20.1.4. pay the cost of the Initial Training as invoiced.

20.2. [...]% of the initial franchise fees paid to the Master Franchisee by the Franchisees is to be paid within 1 month of their becoming due whether received by the Master Franchisee or not.

20.3. The Master Franchisee will pay the Monthly Service Fee on the first day of each month by [standing order *or* direct debit].

20.4. The Master Franchisee will pay for all materials and equipment provided by the Master Franchisor within [*14 days*] of the rendering of an invoice in respect thereof.

20.5. All costs connected with any audit visit and Training will be paid within [*14 days*] of the rendering of an invoice whether rendered in advance or otherwise.

20.6. Interest will be charged on all sums outstanding under this Agreement at [*4*]% above the minimum lending rate of [...] Bank or [*8%*] whichever is the greater, whether before or after any judgment entered in respect thereof.

20.7. All payments must be by direct bank transfer or such other means as the Master Franchisor may stipulate from time to time.

20.8. All payments must be made in full without any deductions whether by way of set off or any other reason unless previously expressly authorised by the Master Franchisor in writing.

21. Novation

21.1. No novation, assignment or delegation of the obligations and benefits of this Agreement by the Master Franchisee is permitted.

21.2. The Master Franchisor may novate, assign or delegate the benefits and obligations of this Agreement on giving [*21 days*] written notice to the Master Franchisee.

22. Termination of this Agreement

22.1. This Agreement may expire by effluxion of time or in accordance with the following provisions.

22.2. In the event that the Master Franchisee fails to remedy any remediable breach of which it has been notified in writing by the Master Franchisor within [*28 days*] the Master Franchisor may at its absolute discretion terminate forthwith this Agreement.

22.3. In the event that the Master Franchisee commits any irremediable material breach or persistently commits any remediable breach of this Agreement the Master Franchisor may terminate this Agreement forthwith.

22.4. The Master Franchisor may terminate this Agreement forthwith in the event that the Master Franchisee:

22.4.1. is [declared bankrupt *or* wound up due to insolvency]

22.4.2. makes or seeks a composition with its creditors

22.4.3. enters into or seeks an insolvent voluntary arrangement

22.4.4. becomes the subject of the appointment of a manager, receiver or liquidator

22.4.5. is the subject of an administration order

22.4.6. has its assets charged or seized for the satisfaction of a debt

22.4.7. seeks to challenge the Master Franchisor's Intellectual Property Rights in relation to the Intellectual Property connected with the Franchise or Master Franchise

22.4.8. behaves in a way which is likely to bring the Franchise into disrepute including but not limited to conviction for an indictable criminal offence

22.4.9. divulges confidential business information in connection with the Franchise to an unauthorised third party

22.4.10. fails to comply with the terms of any software licence connected with the Franchise or Master Franchise

22.4.11. misappropriates or permits, tolerates or facilitates the misappropriation of any funds in connection with the Franchise belonging to or lawfully withheld from any employee, agent, Franchisee, customer or any other person who has dealings with the Franchise

22.4.12. fails to provide adequate support to and supervision of the Franchisees within the [Territory *or* Territories] and/or fails to deal fairly with them

22.4.13. fails to comply with its obligations in respect of the Franchisees

22.4.14. fails to commence, carry on or terminate as appropriate its Master Franchise business

22.4.15. fails to pay any sum due under this Agreement for more than [*28 days*] after its due date

22.4.16. neglects to furnish any document or other information which the Master Franchisee is obliged to provide within [*28 days*] of its due date.

22.5. The Master Franchisor may terminate this Agreement if there is any material re-organisation of the Master Franchisee's business structure unless:

22.5.1. such re-organisation is not the result of insolvency

22.5.2. the resultant company or organisation is bound by the provisions of this Agreement

22.5.3. the beneficial ownership of the resultant entity is not in the hands of competitors of the Master Franchisor, the Master Franchisee or the Franchisees anywhere in the world except to the extent that such ownership does not exceed [*10%*] of the total.

22.6. In the event that there is a change in legislation which materially affects the legitimate interests of the Master Franchisor in respect of the Master Franchise or Franchise the Master Franchisor will be entitled to terminate this Agreement upon giving reasonable notice to the Master Franchisee which must be not less than [*28 days*] and in no instance more than [*56 days*].

23. Post termination rights and obligations

23.1. Termination of this Agreement for any reason shall not affect the rights of either Party in respect of the period after termination nor either Party's rights which may have arisen as a result of any breach pre-dating the termination.

23.2. In order to ensure the proper protection of the Franchise, including its Marks and Goodwill upon termination of the Master Franchise the Master Franchisee must:

23.2.1. assign, novate or transfer to the Master Franchisor or such party as the Master Franchisor shall require all agreements with Franchisees, third party suppliers and such other third parties as the Master Franchisor may reasonably require

23.2.2. cease operation of the Master Franchise including but not limited to the use of all Marks, telephone numbers and e-mail addresses associated with the Franchise/Master Franchise

23.2.3. remove all signage, Marks, names, advertisements and other material indicating that the Master Franchise was operated from the premises

23.2.4. return all copies of the Manual and all other literature and material supplied for or associated with the Franchise/Master Franchise other than that which is not branded or specific to the Franchise

23.2.5. return all copies of software, business information documentation and other materials containing business information connected with the Franchise/Master Franchise

23.2.6. remove or erase from all computers and other electronic equipment all copies and versions of any software specific to the Franchise/Master Franchise

23.2.7. not use any confidential business information received by it during the course of the operation of the Master Franchise and must not disclose such information to any third party including Franchisees whether within or without the [Territory *or* Territories]

23.2.8. not use any Know-how obtained through the Master Franchise save where the same is in the public domain unless such Know-how has come into the public domain through the breach of the Master Franchisee

23.2.9. provide all reasonable assistance to the Master Franchisor to achieve an orderly transfer of the Master Franchise to any party nominated by the Master Franchisor

23.2.10. The Master Franchisee hereby grants the Master Franchisor an irrevocable power of attorney to effect such of these acts as is necessary for any purpose contained in this Clause 23.

24. Post termination restrictions on the Master Franchisee

24.1. The Master Franchisee must not for a period of [12] months after termination of the Master Franchise for any reason be engaged in, involved or associated with, either by itself or in connection or association with any other entity, any business within the [Territory *or* Territories] which is similar to that of the Franchisor, whether as franchisee, agent, principal, adviser or in any other capacity. [Such limitation extends to the [directors *or* principal shareholders] of the Master Franchisee].

24.2. The Master Franchisee must not for a period of [12] months after termination either for itself or on behalf of any other entity, seek, solicit or obtain orders from any entity which was a customer within the [Territory *or* Territories] of any Franchisee and/or the Master Franchisee at the time of termination [or for a period of [2] years prior thereto]. Nor shall the Master Franchisee represent itself as having been formerly connected with the Franchise. [Such limitations extend to the [directors *or* principal shareholders] of the Master Franchisee].

24.3. The Master Franchisee shall not for a period of [12] months after termination seek to entice away or recruit any employee of either the Master Franchisor or any Franchisee who was so employed at the time of termination.

24.4. [In order to ensure the effectiveness of the provisions in this Clause 24 the Master Franchisee will obtain from its [directors *or* principal shareholders] a deed of agreement in a form approved by the Master Franchisor whereby each [director *or* principal shareholder] agrees to be bound by the provisions of this Clause 24].

24.5. The copyright and Intellectual Property in all Marks and materials (including but not limited to the Manual) shall remain the copyright and Intellectual Property of the Master Franchisor. The Master Franchisee agrees not to disclose the contents of the Manual or other material to any third party after the termination of the Master Franchise save where the material is in the pubic domain other than as a result of breach of this Agreement by the Master Franchisee or those acting on its behalf or with its agreement or sanction.

25. Severability

25.1. In the event that any of the restrictions in this Agreement are found by a court of competent jurisdiction to be unenforceable because they are unreasonable but which would be enforceable were specific words, phrases or clauses removed then the restrictions shall apply as if such words, phrases or clauses were removed.

25.2. In the event that any term of this Agreement is found to be invalid or otherwise unenforceable then such term shall be regarded and construed as severable from the Agreement so as not to affect the validity and enforceability of the remainder.

26. Whole agreement

26.1. This Agreement supersedes and replaces any previous agreement between the Parties whether oral or in writing in relation to the Master Franchise. The Master Franchisee hereby agrees that in entering into this Agreement it has not relied upon any warranty or representation made by or on behalf of the Master Franchisor save where expressly stated in this Agreement. The Parties hereby agree that this Agreement constitutes the whole agreement between the Parties in respect of the Master Franchise.

26.2. Nothing in this Clause 26 shall be construed as limiting or excluding either Party's liability to the other for fraud or deceit in inducing the making of this Agreement.

26.3. Without prejudice to the generality of the foregoing the following is agreed between the Parties:

26.3.1. all financial information provided by the Master Franchisor to the Master Franchisee is provided in good faith and is intended to be indicative only. The Master Franchisee hereby acknowledges that it accepts that the provision of such information is at the request of the Master Franchisee on the basis that it does not constitute a representation, warranty, or guarantee by the Master Franchisor and that the Master Franchisee has not placed reliance upon it for the purpose of entering into this Agreement or for any other purpose

26.3.2. the Master Franchisee accepts that the Master Franchisor does not and cannot predict how the Franchise or Master Franchise will perform in the [Territory *or* Territories] either under the Master Franchisee or at all

26.3.3. the Master Franchisee warrants that it has been advised by the Master Franchisor to seek independent legal and financial advice before entering into this Agreement and that its decision to make this Agreement is based solely upon its own judgement and assessment of the commerciality of the Master Franchise and Franchise in the [Territory *or* Territories].

27. Variation

27.1. Any variation of the terms of this Agreement must be in writing signed by the Parties.

28. Further action

28.1. The Parties agree that they will expeditiously carry out such further acts as may be necessary for the purpose of this Agreement including the execution and delivery of such instruments, deeds, licences, notifications as may be reasonably required by the other Party or by law.

29. Set off

29.1. Notwithstanding any other express or implied term of this Agreement the Master Franchisor reserves the right to set off against any sum payable or owed by it to the Master Franchisee any debt or other liability, whether absolute or contingent, owed by the Master Franchisee to the Master Franchisor, or any sum, debt or other liability, absolute or contingent, owed by the Master Franchisee to any third party for which the Master Franchisor is liable or may be liable in default of payment or discharge by the Master Franchisee. In the event of such set off the Master Franchisee irrevocably authorises the Master Franchisor to pay from such sum or sums held by the Master Franchisor for the Master Franchisee such sum as will discharge any such debt or liability to a third party or discharge the debt or sum owed to the Master Franchisor.

30. *Force majeure*

30.1. Neither Party shall have any liability to the other for any delay, omission, failure or inadequate performance of this Agreement which is the result of circumstances beyond its reasonable control. Where a Party is so affected in its performance of this Agreement it will notify the other Party in writing as soon as is reasonably practical.

31. Waiver

31.1. No failure, neglect or delay in enforcing any of the terms of this Agreement may be construed as a waiver of any of the Master Franchisor's rights in respect thereof nor such neglect, failure or delay a variation of the express terms of the Agreement.

32. Third party rights

32.1. The Parties to this Agreement agree that it is not hereby intended that any rights should be conferred upon or enforceable by any third party as defined in the Contracts (Rights of Third Parties) Act 1929.

33. Notices

33.1. All notices under this Agreement shall be in writing and shall be delivered personally [or by first class, registered or recorded post] [or by facsimile transmission] in every case to the other Party's Agreed Address. [In the case of first class post notice will be deemed to be received [3] business days after the date of posting].

34. Law and jurisdiction

34.1. This Agreement is governed by the law of England and Wales and is subject to the [exclusive] jurisdiction of the courts of England and Wales.

35. Schedules

35.1. The Schedules form part of this Agreement including any subsequent amendments made thereto.

Signed, etc.

SCHEDULE 1

The [Territory *or* Territories]

[*Set out details of the Territory/Territories*]

Signed, etc.

SCHEDULE 2

The Franchise

[*Set out details of the Franchise, business model, etc.*]

Signed, etc.

SCHEDULE 3

The Franchise Agreement

[*Attach a copy of the Franchise Agreement*]

Signed, etc.

SCHEDULE 4

The Target[s]

[*Set out details of the Target/Targets]*]
Signed, etc.

SCHEDULE 5

The Term

[*Define the Term*]
Signed, etc.

SCHEDULE 6

The Manual

[*Append a copy of the Manual*]
Signed, etc.

SCHEDULE 7

Initial Training and Training

[*Set out the details of the Initial Training and Training*]
Signed, etc.

SCHEDULE 8

Initial Franchise Fee and Monthly Service Fee

[*Set out details of the Initial and Monthly Service Fees*]
Signed, etc.

SCHEDULE 9

Parties' Agreed Addresses

[*Set out the Parties' Agreed Addresses*]
Signed, etc.

PRECEDENT 11B   Non-exclusive master franchise agreement

NON-EXCLUSIVE MASTER FRANCHISE AGREEMENT

THIS NON-EXCLUSIVE MASTER FRANCHISE AGREEMENT is dated [...] and is made BETWEEN:

1.   [*Name of Master Franchisor*] [of [*address*] *or* whose registered office is at [*address*]], [*company registration number*] ('the Master Franchisor'); and
2.   [*Name of Master Franchisee*] [of [*address*] *or* whose registered office is at [*address*]], [*company registration number*] ('the Master Franchisee').

RECITALS

1.   The Master Franchisor has developed the Franchise as defined herein [and has acquired a reputation for [*describe*]] and is the owner of the intellectual property including goodwill associated with the Franchise.
2.   By this Agreement the Master Franchisor wishes to appoint the Master Franchisee to [manage and] expand the franchise network for the Franchise within the [Territory *or* Territories] as defined below.
3.   The Master Franchisee [is an experienced Franchise developer and] wishes to [expand *or* maintain] the network for the Franchise in the [Territory *or* Territories].

DEFINITIONS

In this Agreement the following definitions apply:

'Franchise'	A business model and system as described in Schedule 2 to this Agreement.
'Franchise Agreement'	The agreement a copy of which is set out in Schedule 3 as amended from time to time.
'Franchisee'	Any entity holding a Franchise under the Master Franchise except where the context indicates that it also refers to franchisees who hold a Franchise under a different Master Franchise or directly from the Master Franchisor.
'Initial Franchise Fee'	A sum set out in Schedule 8 to be paid by the Master Franchisee at the commencement of the Master Franchise.
'Initial Training'	The initial training set out in Schedule 7.
'Know-how'	The knowledge and expertise of the Master Franchisor in creating [and running] the Franchise as set out in the Manual and any other literature or other media provided by the Master Franchisor in connection with the Franchise or Master Franchise.
'Manual'	An instruction manual which fully describes the operation of the Franchise, a copy of which is in Schedule 6.
'Marks'	The marks, trademarks and get-up associated with the Franchise.
'Master Franchise'	The master franchise granted by the Master Franchisor to the Master Franchisee under this Agreement.
'Materials'	Those materials, literature, computer software and other equipment of whatever nature needed for the operation of the Franchise and supplied by the Master Franchisor.

'Monthly Service Fee'	A monthly charge as set out in Schedule 8 as varied from time to time.
'Party' and 'Parties'	The Master Franchisor and the Master Franchisee.
'Parties' Agreed Addresses'	Addresses for service as set out in Schedule 9 and as varied from time to time.
'Premises'	The premises at [*Master Franchisee's address*].
'Target[s]'	Target or targets as set out in Schedule 4 or as varied by written agreement between the parties from time to time.
'Term'	The duration of this Agreement as defined in Schedule 5.
'[Territory *or* Territories]'	The territory or territories as set out in Schedule 1 to this Agreement.
'Training'	The training set out in Schedule 7.

INTERPRETATION

In this Agreement:

1. The singular includes the plural and one gender includes all.
2. References to Schedules and Clauses are to those in this Agreement.
3. Reference to a statutory provision includes any amendment or replacement provision relevant to the Agreement.
4. Reference to a document includes that document as amended, altered or replaced subsequent to the date of this Agreement.
5. Reference to writing includes facsimile transmission, e-mail, and similar media unless the context otherwise expressly provides.
6. Time expressed in days excludes the first day but includes the last day. If the last day does not fall on a normal business day in [both] England and Wales [and the [Territory *or* Territories]] then the last day will be deemed to be the first normal business day thereafter in [the [Territory *or* Territories] and] England and Wales.
7. The headings in this document do not form part of the Agreement.

OPERATIVE PROVISIONS

1. The Master Franchise

1.1. The Master Franchisor hereby grants to the Master Franchisee a Master Franchise for the Term subject to the terms and conditions of this Agreement to be carried on from the Premises, within the [Territory *or* Territories].

2. The Master Franchisor's obligations

2.1. At the commencement of the Term of the Master Franchise the Master Franchisor will provide the Master Franchisee with the following:

2.1.1. the Manual

2.1.2. the Training

2.1.3. the Materials.

2.2. During the Term the Master Franchisor will:

2.2.1. keep current and where necessary update the contents of the Manual

2.2.2. provide such further training as may be necessary for the exercise of the Master Franchise by the Master Franchisee. Such training shall be at the reasonable cost of the Master Franchisee

2.2.3. provide such further materials as are necessary for the operation of the Master Franchise at the reasonable cost of the Master Franchisee

2.2.4. provide market information, technical assistance and relevant additional Know-how as may be reasonably necessary

2.2.5. permit the Master Franchisee to use the Marks as set out below. For the avoidance of doubt the Master Franchisor gives no warranty as to the validity of the Marks.

3. The Master Franchisee's obligations

3.1. The Marks

3.1.1. The Marks are to be used by the Master Franchisee solely for purposes authorised by the Master Franchisor and connected with the Franchise and Master Franchise, for which sole purpose the Master Franchisee is hereby granted licence.

3.1.2. The Marks are to be used in ways stipulated from time to time by the Master Franchisor in connection with the Master Franchise and Franchise.

3.1.3. The Marks are not to be altered, abbreviated, modified or used in connection with any other marks, brands, or the like without the express prior written approval of the Master Franchisor, which permission is at the Master Franchisor's absolute discretion. The Master Franchisor may however at any time modify the Marks and/or substitute new Marks for those existing at the time of this Agreement and the new or modified Marks will be deemed to be the Marks as defined in this Agreement. For the avoidance of doubt the Master Franchisee will not be eligible for any compensation in such circumstances as those set out herein in this Clause 3.1.3.

3.1.4. No other marks are to be used by the Master Franchisee in connection with the Master Franchise or Franchise.

3.1.5. No copies or imitations of the Marks are to be used by the Master Franchisee for any purpose during the currency of this Agreement or thereafter. At no time is the Master Franchisee to register or attempt to register any Mark in connection with the Franchise or Master Franchise.

3.1.6. The Master Franchisee is not to commit any act or omission which is likely adversely to affect the Master Franchisor's goodwill in the Marks and/or Franchise and/or to damage the Master Franchisor's reputation.

3.1.7. The Master Franchisee is to report to the Master Franchisor any infringement of the Marks by any third party and to assist it in taking such steps as may be necessary.

3.1.8. In all uses of the Marks the Master Franchisee must include a clear and appropriate indication of whether the Mark is registered or unregistered.

3.1.9. If any recording of a Mark at a Trade Marks Registry is required the Master Franchisee will provide all reasonable assistance to the Master Franchisor during the currency of this Agreement.

3.1.10. The Master Franchisee may not use the name of the Franchise or any of the Marks as part of its own name. It may however trade under the Franchise name and Marks during the Term.

3.1.11. The Marks will remain at all times both during the Term and thereafter the property of the Master Franchisor and/or its successors or assignees.

3.2. Know-how

3.2.1. The Master Franchisee may not use the Know-how for any purpose other than the operation of the Master Franchise or Franchise nor permit third parties other than Franchisees to do so. During the Term the Master Franchisor must take all reasonable steps to prevent knowledge of the Know-how coming into the hands of third parties other than Franchisees (whether or not they are under the Master Franchise).

3.3. Training

3.3.1. The Master Franchisee will ensure that it [and its employees/staff] attend[s] the Initial Training provided by the Master Franchisor prior to the commencement of the operation of the Master Franchise. The course will be provided at the reasonable expense of the Master Franchisee. If the Master Franchisee [or its employees/staff] fail[s] to complete the course to the reasonable satisfaction of the Master Franchisor then the Master Franchisee's Initial Franchise Fee will be refunded subject to deduction to cover the costs of the Initial Training.

3.3.2. The Master Franchisee will have a continuing obligation to attend [and to ensure that its employees/staff attend] such further Training as the Master Franchisor requires as set out in Schedule 7.

3.3.3. If during the Term the Master Franchisor reasonably considers that [an employee *or* a member of staff] has not completed the Training to its satisfaction then it may require that the [employee *or* member of staff] is not employed to work in the operation of the Master Franchise.

3.4. Conduct of the Master Franchise

3.4.1. The Master Franchisee must at all times comply with any reasonable directions given by the Master Franchisor as to the conduct and management of the Master Franchise and the Franchisees including but not limited to:

3.4.1.1. the implementation of changes or updates to the operation of the Franchise

3.4.1.2. the addition and development of new Franchisees within the [Territory *or* Territories].

3.4.2. The Master Franchisee must at all times operate the Master Franchise to the highest business and ethical standards in full compliance with the Manual.

3.4.3. Without prejudice to the generality of the foregoing the Master Franchisee must ensure there is compliance with all relevant law and regulation including, whether national or supra-national, but not limited to, employment law and regulation, money laundering law and regulation, health and safety requirements and all other statutory and common law requirements relating to the operation of the Master Franchise.

3.4.4. The Master Franchisee must keep insured the premises and business of the Master Franchisee including but not limited to all appropriate third party liabilities as specified in the Manual. The Master Franchisee will provide copies of all insurance documents, including certificates and polices to the Master Franchisor upon demand.

3.4.5. The Master Franchisee must inform the Master Franchisor forthwith of proposed changes in its business arrangements and obtain its prior written approval before implementation including but not limited to:

3.4.5.1. changes in ownership of more than [5%] of the nominal share capital or equity of the Master Franchisee or any business, company or firm with which it is associated in the performance of the Master Franchise

3.4.5.2. material changes (in the case of a limited company) to the memorandum and/or articles of association

3.4.5.3. any share agreements between [shareholders *or* partners] in the Master Franchisee or its associated or connected companies or firms

3.4.5.4. changes in the [directors *or* partners] of the Master Franchisee.

3.5. Premises

3.5.1. The Master Franchise must at all times be carried out from the Premises or such other premises as have been approved in writing by the Master Franchisor prior to the use thereof.

3.6. Accounts and records

3.6.1. The Master Franchisee must maintain throughout the Term proper accounts, books and records in relation to the Master Franchise.

3.6.2. Copies of the accounts, books and records must be available to the Master Franchisor upon reasonable notice and audited details of gross annual turnover and annual profit and loss must be provided to the Master Franchisor within [72 *days*] of the conclusion of each financial year of the Master Franchise.

3.6.3. In the event that the Master Franchisor requires any supporting documentation in relation to the audited details of gross annual turnover and annual profit and loss the Master Franchisee agrees to provide the same within [14 *days*] of being notified in writing of such request.

3.6.4. The obligation to provide audited details of gross annual turnover and annual profit and loss and supporting documentation in this Clause 3.6 will remain if the Master Franchise has terminated but the audited details of gross annual turnover and annual profit and loss and/or supporting documentation have not been provided prior to the termination thereof. In such circumstances the time limits for compliance will be [72 *days*] and [14 *days*] respectively from the date of the end of the current financial year of the Master Franchise or [72 *days*] and [14 *days*] respectively from the date of termination of the Master Franchise, whichever is the sooner.

3.7. Targets

3.7.1. It shall be an express obligation of this Agreement that the Master Franchisee achieves the Target from year to year. Failure to so is a breach of this Agreement.

3.8. Marketing, advertising and promotion of the Franchise

3.8.1. The Master Franchisee is responsible at all times during the Term for the promotion of the Franchise within the [Territory *or* Territories]. This must be conducted as agreed from time to time with the Master Franchisor [and where considered appropriate by the Master Franchisor in consultation with the other master franchisors of the Franchise in the [Territory *or* Territories]] and in accordance where applicable with the provisions in the Manual. The marketing and advertising associated with the promotion of the Franchise is to be financed by a fund administered by the Master Franchisee and which is to be funded by the Master Franchisee and the Franchisees.

3.8.2. The Master Franchisee warrants that it will not make any warranties or representations to the Franchisees or any third parties regarding the Master Franchisee and the Franchise save those which have been expressly approved by the Master Franchisor in writing or which are included and approved in the Manual as modified from time to time.

3.9. Financial capability

3.9.1. The Master Franchisee must ensure that it has at all material times the financial means, including but not limited to working capital, to discharge its obligations under this Agreement and to maintain the integrity and reputation of the Franchise.

3.10. Sole business

3.10.1. During the Term the Master Franchisee will not carry on any other business, either directly or indirectly, save with the prior written consent of the Master Franchisor.

The Master Franchisor may at any time at its sole discretion withdraw such consent on the giving of not less than [3 *months*] written notice.

3.10.2. The Master Franchisee may not have any direct or indirect financial or other interest in any business which may be reasonably considered to be a competitor of the Franchise anywhere in the world other than the direct or indirect holding of shares in a public listed company where that shareholding amounts to less than [1%] of the total nominal share capital of the public listed company.

4. Audit of Master Franchisee's books by Master Franchisor

4.1. During the Term and for a period of [12 *months*] after its termination the Master Franchisor shall be entitled by itself or through auditors appointed by it to require, having given reasonable written notice, the production of the Master Franchisee's books of accounts for the purpose of auditing them at the premises of the Master Franchisee. Audits will take place during ordinary office hours.

4.2. In the event that any audit referred to in this Clause 4 should disclose an underpayment of more than [3%] of the sums properly payable to the Master Franchisor under this Agreement during any financial year or part thereof of the Master Franchise the Master Franchisee will be required to pay the Master Franchisor the reasonable cost of the audit in addition to the sums properly due under this Agreement. Any such shortfall as mentioned in this Clause 4.2 shall be paid within [7 *days*] of the figure being notified in writing to the Master Franchisee.

5. No agency

5.1. The Master Franchisee is not for any purpose the agent of the Master Franchisor. The Master Franchisee must ensure that a notice is displayed at the Premises in a prominent position stating that the business there carried on is carried on by an independent [company *or* firm] called [*specify*] which is the holder of a licence from the Master Franchisor to conduct business under its name but that the Master Franchisee is not in any way an agent of the Master Franchisor for any purpose whatever. A similar notice must be included in all correspondence and literature used in the operation of the Master Franchise.

6. Territory and other variations

6.1. The Master Franchisor reserves the right to require the Master Franchisee under this Agreement to operate differently from other Master Franchisees (whether within the [Territory *or* Territories] or outside) if the Master Franchisor considers that market and other conditions so require.

7. Confidential information

7.1. The Master Franchisee agrees not to disclose any confidential information provided by the Master Franchisor during the Term or at any time thereafter to any third party save where the law requires. The Master Franchisee also agrees not to use any such confidential information for any other purpose other than for the promotion and running of the Master Franchise and will not use the information for any business or other purpose of its own. For the avoidance of doubt such information includes but is not limited either in type, *genus* or subject to:

7.1.1. all business information supplied to the Master Franchisee by the Master Franchisor regarding the Franchise

7.1.2. all marketing information and intelligence

7.1.3. all trade secrets, processes and formulae.

7.2. For the proper protection of the confidential information the Master Franchisee will ensure that:

7.2.1. any employee or member of his staff, whether temporary or permanent, will at the commencement of their employment and no later be provided with a contract of employment or engagement which will include a like obligation to that of the Master Franchisee in respect of confidential information

7.2.2. any [director or partner] of the Master Franchisee or any associated [company or firm] will be required to provide, in a form approved by the Master Franchisor, an undertaking in regard to confidential information in like form to that set out above in relation to the Master Franchisee before being given access to confidential information.

8. Third party agreements in relation to the Master Franchise

8.1. The Master Franchisor may not enter into any third party agreements or arrangements in relation to the Master Franchise which will have the effect of encumbrancing, charging or otherwise materially affecting the business of the Master Franchise or the receipts therefrom without the prior written consent of the Master Franchisor, the giving of which consent shall be at the absolute discretion of the Master Franchisor.

9. Goodwill

9.1. All goodwill in the Marks, the Master Franchise and the Franchise belongs to the Master Franchisor, whether generated by the Master Franchisee, the Franchisees or otherwise and the Master Franchisee agrees to make no claim in respect thereof.

10. Customers

10.1. All customers of the Master Franchisee and the Franchisees are customers of the Master Franchisor for all purposes except liability for defective [products or services].

10.2. The Master Franchisee will maintain an up-to-date record of all Franchisees full details of which it will provide on demand to the Master Franchisor. The Master Franchisee will provide to the Master Franchisor a copy of the up-to-date list at least once every calendar month on the first day thereof or otherwise as detailed in the Manual.

11. Right of inspection

11.1. The Master Franchisee and/or its appointed agent will be entitled to inspect the operation of the Master Franchise at the Premises or at any other location used by the Master Franchisee in connection with the Master Franchise during any normal business hours in the [Territory or Territories] without further notice.

11.2. The Master Franchisee and/or its appointed agent will be entitled to inspect the operation of the Franchise at any premises used by a Franchisee in connection with the operation of the Franchise during any normal business hours in the [Territory or Territories] without further notice.

12. Market information

12.1. The Master Franchisee must at all times keep the Master Franchisor aware of developments in market conditions within the [Territory or Territories] including but not limited to:

12.1.1. actions by competitors or potential competitors of the Franchise

12.1.2. plans and proposals for business development by the Master Franchisee of the Master Franchise.

13. Compliance with laws of the [Territory or Territories]

13.1. The Master Franchisee will ensure that it complies at all material times with the laws of the [Territory or Territories] relevant to the Master Franchise including, but not limited to, those relating to:

13.1.1. data protection and freedom of information

13.1.2. taxes and tariffs

13.1.3. health and safety

13.1.4. equal opportunities

13.1.5. employment

13.1.6. insurance

13.1.7. occupiers' liability

13.1.8. business registration [and company returns]

13.1.9. prevention of money laundering.

14. Indemnity

14.1. The Master Franchisee will indemnify the Master Franchisor in respect of any losses, damage or liability the Master Franchisor may incur as a result of the Master Franchisee's acts or omissions, whether deliberate, accidental, negligent or reckless, in the course of the performance or purported performance of its obligations or rights under this Agreement whether such acts or omissions amount to a breach of an express or implied obligation under this Agreement or a breach of any other legal requirement or obligation, code of practice, licence, consent, forbearance, approval, permission or rule.

14.2. For the avoidance of doubt losses, damage and liability shall include but not be limited to economic and commercial loss, loss of goodwill, legal and other costs associated with legal proceedings of any kind which the Master Franchisor has to bring or to which it has to respond, fines, penalties, damages and any financial consequence whatever flowing directly or indirectly from the matters set out in this Clause 14.

15. Organisation and supervision of Franchisees

15.1. The Master Franchisee must ensure that it sets up and maintains such structure as will enable it to monitor and organise the Franchisees.

15.2. Each Franchisee's operation must be checked by the Master Franchisee at least once a month to ensure that it is complying with the terms of the Franchise including but not limited to that:

15.2.1. correct systems are being followed and implemented

15.2.2. adequate financial reporting to the Master Franchisor is taking place.

15.3. In the event that there is inadequate compliance with the terms of its Franchise the Master Franchisee must take all reasonable steps to ensure that a Franchisee does so comply.

15.4. If the Franchisee fails to comply after reasonable steps have been taken by the Master Franchisee to ensure compliance then the Franchise Agreement must be terminated.

15.5. Prior to any new Franchisee being provided with materials or information (other than that in the public domain) about the Franchise the Master Franchisor must ensure that it has signed a Franchise Agreement for each location from which it intends to operate.

15.6. The Master Franchisee will carry out an audit of each Franchisee at least once every calendar year at its own expense. The Master Franchisee may if it wishes seek to recover such cost from the Franchisee in accordance with the terms of the Franchise Agreement.

16. Appointment of Franchisees

16.1. The Master Franchisee is responsible for the selection and appointment of new Franchisees. In doing so it must have due regard to the commercial well-being of existing Franchisees whether under the Master Franchise or otherwise and whether within or outside the [Territory or Territories].

16.2. No appointment may be made without the prior written approval of the Master Franchisor. Any appointment purportedly made in contravention of this requirement will be of no legal effect and in breach of this Agreement as the Master Franchisee will have no authority so to do. For the avoidance of doubt it is hereby agreed that nothing in this Clause 16 shall be taken to have the effect of constituting or implying any agency on the part of the Master Franchisee on behalf of the Master Franchisor.

17. Promotion of the Franchise

17.1. The Master Franchisee will impose a levy of [*1%*] of gross turnover ('the promotional levy') on each Franchisee to provide for the advertising, marketing and promotion of the Franchise within the [Territory *or* Territories].

17.2. The sums received in respect of the promotional levy shall be deposited in a separate bank account in the name of [*the Master Franchisee*].

17.3. The Master Franchisee will keep separate books of account in respect of the promotional levy which will be available for inspection by the Franchisees within the [Territory *or* Territories] and the Master Franchisor upon the giving of 7 days written notice to the Master Franchisee.

17.4. All promotional activities and material used in connection therewith are subject to the prior approval of the Master Franchisor and such activities should be undertaken only after reasonable consultation with the Franchisees.

18. Audit of Franchisees

18.1. The Master Franchisor may at its discretion undertake audits of the individual Franchisees as agent of the Master Franchisee in addition to or instead of any audit undertaken by the Master Franchisee. In such eventuality the Master Franchisee shall be responsible for the payment of the Master Franchisor's reasonable costs as if such audit were an audit of the Master Franchisee itself.

18.2. Save in exceptional circumstances the Master Franchisor will not undertake such audits as mentioned in this Clause 18 without prior consultation with the Master Franchisee.

19. Master Franchisor's supervision of the Master Franchisee

19.1. The Master Franchisor may undertake an audit of the Master Franchisee's business at any time during the currency of this Agreement and for a period of six months after termination for any reason. Such audit may consist of both financial and other matters connected with compliance with the terms of the Master Franchise.

19.2. The Master Franchisor will once every calendar year undertake an annual audit of the Master Franchise of not more than 5 days in length. Members of the Master Franchisor's staff or agents appointed by it will undertake the audit. The number of participants will be reasonable and subject to prior consultation with the Master Franchisee. The Master Franchisee will pay the reasonable costs of the audit including payroll, fees, travel and accommodation (if reasonably necessary) of the staff or agents involved.

19.3. The Master Franchisee undertakes to provide all reasonable assistance during any audit under this Clause 19 including the provision of and access to all documents, computer records and accounts reasonably required. The Master Franchisee also agrees to answer all questions and provide such information as is required by the Master Franchisor to carry out the audit.

20. Master Franchise fees and charges

20.1. Upon signing this Agreement the Master Franchisee will:

20.1.1. pay the Master Franchisor the Initial Franchise Fee of £[...]

20.1.2. provide an [irrevocable] [performance bond *or* standby letter of credit *or* bank guarantee *or* deposit] [in a form approved by the Master Franchisor] in the sum of £[...] to [remain in force *or* be retained by the Master Franchisor] until [6 *months*] after the termination of this Agreement

20.1.3. pay the Master Franchisor's legal fees as invoiced to it in respect of this Agreement

20.1.4. pay the cost of the Initial Training as invoiced.

20.2. [...]% of the initial franchise fees paid to the Master Franchisee by the Franchisees is to be paid within 1 month of their becoming due whether received by the Master Franchisee or not.

20.3. The Master Franchisee will pay the Monthly Service Fee on the first day of each month by [standing order *or* direct debit].

20.4. The Master Franchisee will pay for all materials and equipment provided by the Master Franchisor within [14] days of the rendering of an invoice in respect thereof.

20.5. All costs connected with any audit visit and Training will be paid within [14] days of the rendering of an invoice whether rendered in advance or otherwise.

20.6. Interest will be charged on all sums outstanding under this Agreement at [4%] above the minimum lending rate of [...] Bank or [8%] whichever is the greater, whether before or after any judgment entered in respect thereof.

20.7. All payments must be by direct bank transfer or such other means as the Master Franchisor may stipulate from time to time.

20.8. All payments must be made in full without any deductions whether by way of set off or any other reason unless previously expressly authorised by the Master Franchisor in writing.

21. Novation

21.1. No novation, assignment or delegation of the obligations and benefits of this Agreement by the Master Franchisee is permitted.

21.2. The Master Franchisor may novate, assign or delegate the benefits and obligations of this Agreement on giving [21 *days*] written notice to the Master Franchisee.

22. Termination of this Agreement

22.1. This Agreement may expire by effluxion of time or in accordance with the following provisions.

22.2. In the event that the Master Franchisee fails to remedy any remediable breach of which it has been notified in writing by the Master Franchisor within [28 *days*] the Master Franchisor may at its absolute discretion terminate forthwith this Agreement.

22.3. In the event that the Master Franchisee commits any irremediable material breach or persistently commits any remediable breach of this Agreement the Master Franchisor may terminate this Agreement forthwith.

22.4. The Master Franchisor may terminate this Agreement forthwith in the event that the Master Franchisee:

22.4.1. is [declared bankrupt *or* wound up due to insolvency]

22.4.2. makes or seeks a composition with its creditors

22.4.3. enters into or seeks an insolvent voluntary arrangement

22.4.4. becomes the subject of the appointment of a manager, receiver or liquidator

22.4.5. is the subject of an administration order

22.4.6. has its assets charged or seized for the satisfaction of a debt

22.4.7. seeks to challenge the Master Franchisor's intellectual property rights in relation to the intellectual property connected with the Franchise or Master Franchise

22.4.8. behaves in a way which is likely to bring the Franchise into disrepute including but not limited to conviction for an indictable criminal offence

22.4.9. divulges confidential business information in connection with the Franchise to an unauthorised third party

22.4.10. fails to comply with the terms of any software licence connected with the Franchise or Master Franchise

22.4.11. misappropriates or permits, tolerates or facilitates the misappropriation of any funds in connection with the Franchise belonging to or lawfully withheld from any employee, agent, Franchisee, customer or any other person who has dealings with the Franchise

22.4.12. fails to provide adequate support to and supervision of the Franchisees and/or fails to deal fairly with them

22.4.13. fails to comply with its obligations in respect of the Franchisees

22.4.14. fails to commence, carry on or terminate as appropriate its Master Franchise business

22.4.15. fails to pay any sum due under this Agreement for more than [28 *days*] after its due date

22.4.16. neglects to furnish any document or other information which the Master Franchisee is obliged to provide within [28 *days*] of its due date.

22.5. The Master Franchisor may terminate this Agreement if there is any material re-organisation of the Master Franchisee's business structure unless:

22.5.1. such re-organisation is not the result of insolvency

22.5.2. the resultant company or organisation is bound by the provisions of this Agreement

22.5.3. the beneficial ownership of the resultant entity is not in the hands of competitors of the Master Franchisor, the Master Franchisee or the Franchisees anywhere in the world except to the extent that such ownership does not exceed [10%] of the total.

22.6. In the event that there is a change in legislation which materially affects the legitimate interests of the Master Franchisor in respect of the Master Franchise or Franchise the Master Franchisor will be entitled to terminate this Agreement upon giving reasonable notice to the Master Franchisee which must be not less than [28 *days*] and in no instance more than [56 *days*].

23. Post termination rights and obligations

23.1. Termination of this Agreement for any reason shall not affect the rights of either Party in respect of the period after termination nor either Party's rights which may have arisen as a result of any breach pre-dating the termination.

23.2. In order to ensure the proper protection of the Franchise, including its Marks and Goodwill upon termination of the Master Franchise the Master Franchisee must:

23.2.1. assign, novate or transfer to the Master Franchisor or such party as the Master Franchisor shall require all agreements with Franchisees, third party suppliers and such other third parties as the Master Franchisor may reasonably require

23.2.2. cease operation of the Master Franchise including but not limited to the use of all Marks, telephone numbers and e-mail addresses associated with the Franchise/Master Franchise

23.2.3. remove all signage, Marks, names, advertisements and other material indicating that the Master Franchise was operated from the premises

23.2.4. return all copies of the Manual and all other literature and material supplied for or associated with the Franchise/Master Franchise other than that which is not branded or specific to the Franchise

23.2.5. return all copies of software, business information documentation and other materials containing business information connected with the Franchise/Master Franchise

23.2.6. remove or erase from all computers and other electronic equipment all copies and versions of any software specific to the Franchise/Master Franchise

23.2.7. not use any confidential business information received by it during the course of the operation of the Master Franchise and must not disclose such information to any third party including Franchisees whether within or outside the [Territory *or* Territories]

23.2.8. not use any Know-how obtained through the Master Franchise save where the same is in the public domain unless such Know-how has come into the public domain through the breach of the Master Franchisee

23.2.9. provide all reasonable assistance to the Master Franchisor to achieve an orderly transfer of the Master Franchise to any party nominated by the Master Franchisor.

23.3. The Master Franchisee hereby grants the Master Franchisor an irrevocable power of attorney to effect such of these acts as is necessary for any purpose contained in this Clause 23.

24. Post termination restrictions on the Master Franchisee

24.1. The Master Franchisee must not for a period of [12] months after termination of the Master Franchise for any reason be engaged in, involved or associated with, either by itself or in connection or association with any other entity, any business within the [Territory *or* Territories] which is similar to that of the Franchisor, whether as franchisee, agent, principal, adviser or in any other capacity. [Such limitation extends to the [directors *or* principal shareholders] of the Master Franchisee].

24.2. The Master Franchisee must not for a period of [12] months after termination either for itself or on behalf of any other entity, seek, solicit or obtain orders from any entity which was a customer within the [Territory *or* Territories] of any Franchisee and/or the Master Franchisee at the time of termination [or for a period of [2] years prior thereto]. Nor shall the Master Franchisee represent itself as having been formerly connected with the Franchise. [Such limitations extend to the [directors *or* principal shareholders] of the Master Franchisee].

24.3. The Master Franchisee shall not for a period of [12] months after termination seek to entice away or recruit any employee of either the Master Franchisor or any Franchisee who was so employed at the time of termination.

24.4. [In order to ensure the effectiveness of the provisions in this Clause 24 the Master Franchisee will obtain from its [directors *or* principal shareholders] a deed of agreement in a form approved by the Master Franchisor whereby each [director *or* principal shareholder] agrees to be bound by the provisions of this Clause 24].

24.5. The copyright and intellectual property in all Marks and materials (including but not limited to the Manual) shall remain the copyright and intellectual property of the Master Franchisor. The Master Franchisee agrees not to disclose the contents of the Manual or other material to any third party after the termination of the Master Franchise save where the material is in the pubic domain other than as a result of breach of this Agreement by the Master Franchisee or those acting on its behalf or with its agreement or sanction.

25. Severability

25.1. In the event that any of the restrictions in this Agreement are found by a court of competent jurisdiction to be unenforceable because they are unreasonable but which would be enforceable were specific words, phrases or clauses removed then the restrictions shall apply as if such words, phrases or clauses were removed.

25.2. In the event that any term of this Agreement is found to be invalid or otherwise unenforceable then such term shall be regarded and construed as severable from the Agreement so as not to affect the validity and enforceability of the remainder.

26. Whole agreement

26.1. This Agreement supersedes and replaces any previous agreement between the Parties whether oral or in writing in relation to the Master Franchise. The Master Franchisee hereby agrees that in entering into this Agreement it has not relied upon any warranty or representation made by or on behalf of the Master Franchisor save where expressly stated in this Agreement. The Parties hereby agree that this Agreement constitutes the whole agreement between the Parties in respect of the Master Franchise.

26.2. Nothing in this Clause 26 shall be construed as limiting or excluding either Party's liability to the other for fraud or deceit in inducing the making of this Agreement.

26.3. Without prejudice to the generality of the foregoing the following is agreed between the Parties:

26.3.1. all financial information provided by the Master Franchisor to the Master Franchisee is provided in good faith and is intended to be indicative only. The Master Franchisee hereby acknowledges that it accepts that the provision of such information is at the request of the Master Franchisee on the basis that it does not constitute a representation, warranty, or guarantee by the Master Franchisor and that the Master Franchisee has not placed reliance upon it for the purpose of entering into this Agreement or for any other purpose

26.3.2. the Master Franchisee accepts that the Master Franchisor does not and cannot predict how the Franchise or Master Franchise will perform in the [Territory or Territories] either under the Master Franchisee or at all

26.3.3. the Master Franchisee warrants that it has been advised by the Master Franchisor to seek independent legal and financial advice before entering into this Agreement and that its decision to make this Agreement is based solely upon its own judgement and assessment of the commerciality of the Master Franchise and Franchise in the [Territory or Territories].

27. Variation

27.1. Any variation of the terms of this Agreement must be in writing signed by the Parties.

28. Further action

28.1. The Parties agree that they will expeditiously carry out such further acts as may be necessary for the purpose of this Agreement including the execution and delivery of such instruments, deeds, licences, notifications as may be reasonably required by the other Party or by law.

29. Set off

29.1. Notwithstanding any other express or implied term of this Agreement the Master Franchisor reserves the right to set off against any sum payable or owed by it to the Master Franchisee any debt or other liability, whether absolute or contingent, owed by the Master Franchisee to the Master Franchisor, or any sum, debt or other liability, absolute or contingent, owed by the Master Franchisee to any third party for which the Master Franchisor is liable or may be liable in default of payment or discharge by the Master Franchisee. In the event of such set off the Master Franchisee irrevocably authorises the Master Franchisor to pay from such sum or sums held by the Master Franchisor for the Master Franchisee such sum as will discharge any such debt or liability to a third party or discharge the debt or sum owed to the Master Franchisor.

30. *Force majeure*

30.1. Neither Party shall have any liability to the other for any delay, omission, failure or inadequate performance of this Agreement which is the result of circumstances beyond its reasonable control. Where a Party is so affected in its performance of this Agreement it will notify the other Party in writing as soon as is reasonably practical.

31. Waiver

31.1. No failure, neglect or delay in enforcing any of the terms of this Agreement may be construed as a waiver of any of the Master Franchisor's rights in respect thereof nor such neglect, failure or delay a variation of the express terms of the Agreement.

32. Third party rights

32.1. The Parties to this Agreement agree that it is not hereby intended that any rights should be conferred upon or enforceable by any third party as defined in the Contracts (Rights of Third Parties) Act 1929.

33. Notices

33.1. All notices under this Agreement shall be in writing and shall be delivered personally [or by first class, registered or recorded post] [or by facsimile transmission] in every case to the other Party's Agreed Address. [In the case of first class post notice will be deemed to be received [3] business days after the date of posting].

34. Law and jurisdiction

34.1. This Agreement is governed by the law of England and Wales and is subject to the [exclusive] jurisdiction of the courts of England and Wales.

35. Schedules

35.1. The Schedules form part of this Agreement including any subsequent amendments made thereto.

Signed, etc.

SCHEDULE 1

The [Territory *or* Territories]

[*Set out details of the Territory/Territories*]

Signed, etc.

SCHEDULE 2

The Franchise

[*Set out details of the Franchise, business model, etc.*]

Signed, etc.

SCHEDULE 3

The Franchise Agreement

[*Attach a copy of the Franchise Agreement*]

Signed, etc.

SCHEDULE 4

The Target[s]

[*Set out details of the Target/Targets*]

Signed, etc.

SCHEDULE 5

The Term

[*Define the Term*]

Signed, etc.

SCHEDULE 6

The Manual

[*Append a copy of the Manual*]

Signed, etc.

SCHEDULE 7

Initial Training and Training

[*Set out the details of the Initial Training and Training*]

Signed, etc.

SCHEDULE 8

Initial Franchise Fee and Monthly Service Fee

[*Set out details of the Initial and Monthly Service Fees*]

Signed, etc.

SCHEDULE 9

Parties' Agreed Addresses

[*Set out the Parties' Agreed Addresses*]

Signed, etc.

PRECEDENT 11C   Non-exclusive franchise agreement

FRANCHISE AGREEMENT

Non-exclusive

THIS FRANCHISE AGREEMENT is dated [...] and is made BETWEEN:

1. [*Name of Franchisor*] [of [*address*] *or* whose registered office is at [*address*]], [*company registration number*] ('the Franchisor'); and
2. [*Name of Franchisee*] [of [*address*] *or* whose registered office is at [*address*]], [*company registration number*] ('the Franchisee').

RECITALS

1. [The Franchisor has developed the Franchise as defined herein [and has acquired a reputation for [*describe*]] and is the owner of the intellectual property including goodwill associated with the Franchise *or* The Franchisor has the rights within the Territory to the Franchise as defined herein].
2. By this Agreement the Franchisor wishes to appoint the Franchisee to operate the Franchise from the Premises as defined below.

DEFINITIONS

In this Agreement the following definitions apply:

'Franchise'	A business model and system as described in Schedule 2 to this Agreement.
'Initial Franchise Fee'	A sum set out in Schedule 7 to be paid by the Franchisee at the commencement of the Franchise.
'Initial Training'	The initial training set out in Schedule 6.
'Know-how'	The knowledge and expertise of the Franchisor connected with the Franchise as set out in the Manual and any other literature or other media provided by the Franchisor in connection with the Franchise.
'Manual'	An instruction manual which fully describes the operation of the Franchise, a copy of which is in Schedule 5.
'Marks'	The marks, trademarks and get-up associated with the Franchise.
['The Master Franchisor']	[The holder of the Master Franchise from whom the Franchisor's rights in respect of the Franchise devolve].
'Materials'	Those materials, literature, computer software and other equipment of whatever nature needed for the operation of the Franchise and supplied by the Master Franchisor.

'Monthly Service Fee'	A monthly charge as set out in Schedule 7 as varied from time to time.
'Party' and 'Parties'	The Franchisor and the Franchisee.
'Parties' Agreed Addresses'	Addresses for service as set out in Schedule 8 and as varied from time to time.
'Premises'	The premises at [*Franchisee's address*].
['Target *or* Targets]'	Target or targets as set out in Schedule 3 or as varied by written agreement between the Parties from time to time.
'Term'	The duration of this Agreement as defined in Schedule 4.
'[Territory *or* Territories]'	The territory or territories as set out in Schedule 1 to this Agreement.
'Training'	The training set out in Schedule 6.

INTERPRETATION

In this Agreement:

1. The singular includes the plural and one gender includes all.
2. References to Schedules and Clauses are to those in this Agreement.
3. Reference to a statutory provision includes any amendment or replacement provision relevant to the Agreement.
4. Reference to a document includes that document as amended, altered or replaced subsequent to the date of this Agreement.
5. Reference to writing includes facsimile transmission, e-mail, and similar media unless the context otherwise expressly provides.
6. Time expressed in days excludes the first day but includes the last day. If the last day does not fall on a normal business day in [both] England and Wales [and the [Territory *or* Territories] then the last day will be deemed to be the first normal business day thereafter in [the Territory *or* Territories] and] England and Wales.
7. The headings in this document do not form part of the Agreement.

OPERATIVE PROVISIONS

1. The Franchise

1.1. The Franchisor hereby grants to the Franchisee a non-exclusive Franchise for the Term subject to the terms and conditions of this Agreement, to be carried on from the Premises, within the [Territory *or* Territories].

2. The Franchisor's obligations

2.1. At the commencement of the Term of the Franchise the Franchisor will provide the Franchisee with the following:

2.1.1. the Manual

2.1.2. the Training

2.1.3. the Materials.

2.2. During the Term of this Agreement the Franchisor will:

2.2.1. keep current and where necessary update the contents of the Manual

2.2.2. provide such further training as may be necessary for the exercise of the Franchise by the Franchisee. Such training shall be at the reasonable cost of the Franchisee

2.2.3. provide such further materials as are necessary for the operation of the Franchisee at the reasonable cost of the Franchisee

2.2.4. provide market information, technical assistance and relevant additional Know-how as may be reasonably necessary

2.2.5. permit the Franchisee to use the Marks as set out below. For the avoidance of doubt the Franchisor gives no warranty as to the validity of the Marks.

3. Setting up the Franchise business

3.1. The Premises must be decorated and fitted out in a manner consistent with the requirements of the Manual and as expressly specified by the Franchisor. The Franchisee may not begin trading from the Premises until they have been approved by the Franchisor and such approval is confirmed in writing.

4. The Franchisee's obligations

4.1. The Marks

4.1.1. The Marks are to be used by the Franchisee solely for purposes authorised by the Franchisor and connected with the Franchise and Franchisee, for which sole purpose the Franchisee is hereby granted licence.

4.1.2. The Marks are to be used in ways stipulated from time to time by the Franchisor in connection with the Franchise.

4.1.3. The Marks are not to be altered, abbreviated, modified or used in connection with any other marks, brands, or the like without the express prior written approval of the Franchisor, which permission is at the Franchisor's absolute discretion. The Franchisor may however at any time modify the Marks and/or substitute new Marks for those existing at the time of this Agreement and the new or modified Marks will be deemed to be the Marks as defined in this Agreement. For the avoidance of doubt the Franchisee will not be eligible for any compensation in such circumstances as those set out herein in this Clause 4.1.3.

4.1.4. No other marks are to be used by the Franchisee in connection with the Franchise.

4.1.5. No copies or imitations of the Marks are to be used by the Franchisee for any purpose during the currency of this Agreement or thereafter. At no time is the Franchisee to register or attempt to register any Mark in connection with the Franchise.

4.1.6. The Franchisee is not to commit any act or omission which is likely adversely to affect the [Master] Franchisor's goodwill in the Marks and/or Franchise and/or to damage the [Master] Franchisor's reputation.

4.1.7. The Franchisee is to report to the Franchisor any infringement of the Marks by any third party and to assist it in taking such steps as may be necessary.

4.1.8. In all uses of the Marks the Franchisee must include a clear and appropriate indication of whether the Mark is registered or unregistered.

4.1.9. If any recording of a Mark at a Trade Marks Registry is required the Franchisee will provide all reasonable assistance to the Franchisor during the Term.

4.1.10. The Franchisee may not use the name of the Franchise or any of the Marks as part of its own name. It may however trade under the Franchise name and Marks during the Term.

4.1.11. The Marks will remain at all times both during the Term and thereafter the property of the [Master] Franchisor and/or its successors or assignees.

4.2. Know-how

4.2.1. The Franchisee may not use the Know-how for any purpose other than the operation of the Franchise nor permit third parties to do so. During the Term the Franchisor must take all reasonable steps to prevent knowledge of the Know-how coming into the hands of third parties.

4.3. Training

4.3.1. The Franchisee will ensure that it [or its employees/staff] attend[s] the Initial Training provided by the Franchisor prior to the commencement of the operation of the Franchise. The course will be provided at the reasonable expense of the Franchisee. If the Franchisee [or its employees/staff] fail[s] to complete the course to the reasonable satisfaction of the Franchisor then the Franchisee's Initial Franchise Fee will be refunded subject to deduction to cover the costs of the Initial Training.

4.3.2. The Franchisee will have a continuing obligation to attend [or to ensure that its employees/staff attend] such further Training as the Franchisor requires [as set out in Schedule 6].

4.3.3. If during the Term the Franchisor reasonably considers that [an employee *or* a member of staff] has not completed the Training to its satisfaction then it may require that the [employee *or* member of staff] is not employed to work in the operation of the Franchise.

4.4. Conduct of the Franchisee

4.4.1. The Franchisee must at all times comply with any reasonable directions given by the Franchisor as to the conduct and management of the Franchise including but not limited to the implementation of changes or updates to the operation of the Franchise.

4.4.2. The Franchisee must at all times operate the Franchise to the highest business and ethical standards in full compliance with the Manual.

4.4.3. Without prejudice to the generality of the foregoing the Franchisee must ensure there is compliance with all relevant law and regulation whether national or supra-national including, but not limited to, employment law and regulation, money laundering law and regulation, health and safety requirements and all other statutory and common law requirements relating to the operation of the Franchise.

4.4.4. The Franchisee must keep insured the premises and business of the Franchisee including but not limited to all appropriate third party liabilities as specified in the Manual. The Franchisee will provide copies of all insurance documents, including certificates and polices to the Franchisor upon demand.

4.4.5. The Franchisee must inform the Franchisor forthwith of proposed changes in its business arrangements and obtain its prior written approval before implementation including but not limited to:

4.4.5.1. changes in ownership of more than [5%] of the nominal share capital or equity of the Franchisee or any business, company or firm with which it is associated in the performance of the Franchise

4.4.5.2. material changes (in the case of a limited company) to the memorandum and/or articles of association

4.4.5.3. any share agreements between [shareholders *or* partners] in the Franchisee or its associated or connected companies or firms

4.4.5.4. changes in the [directors *or* partners] of the Franchisee.

4.5. Premises

4.5.1. The Franchise must at all times be carried out from the Premises or such other premises as have been approved in writing by the Franchisor prior to the use thereof.

4.6. Accounts and records

4.6.1. The Franchisee must maintain throughout the Term proper accounts, books and records in relation to the Franchise.

4.6.2. Copies of the accounts, books and records must be available to the Franchisor [and Master Franchisor] upon reasonable notice and audited details of gross annual turnover and annual profit and loss must be provided to the Franchisor [and Master Franchisor] within [72] days of the conclusion of each financial year of the Franchisee.

4.6.3. In the event that the Franchisor [and/or the Master Franchisor] requires any supporting documentation in relation to the audited details of gross annual turnover and annual profit and loss the Franchisee agrees to provide the same within [14] days of being notified in writing of such request.

4.6.4. The obligation to provide audited details of gross annual turnover and annual profit and loss and supporting documentation in this Clause 4.6 will remain if the Franchise has terminated but the audited details of gross annual turnover and annual profit and loss and/or supporting documentation have not been provided prior to the termination thereof. In such circumstances the time limits for compliance will be [72] days and [14] days respectively from the date of the end of the current financial year of the Franchisee or [72] days and [14] days respectively from the date of termination of the Franchise, whichever is the sooner.

4.7. Targets

4.7.1. It shall be an express obligation of this Agreement that the Franchisee achieves the Target[s] from year to year. Failure to do so is a breach of this Agreement.

4.8. Marketing, advertising and promotion of the Franchise

4.8.1. The Franchisee is responsible at all times during the Term for the local promotion, marketing and advertising of the Franchise within the [Territory *or* Territories]. This must be conducted as agreed from time to time with the Franchisor and in accordance where applicable with the provisions in the Manual.

4.8.2. The wider marketing and advertising associated with the promotion of the Franchise is to be financed by a fund administered by the Franchisor and which is to be funded by the Franchisees within the Territory.

4.8.3. The Franchisee warrants that it will not make any warranties or representations to any third parties regarding the Franchise save those which have been expressly approved by the Franchisor in writing or which are included and approved in the Manual as modified from time to time.

4.9. Financial capability

4.9.1. The Franchisee must ensure that it has at all material times the financial means, including but not limited to working capital, to discharge its obligations under this Agreement and to maintain the integrity and reputation of the Franchise.

4.10. Sole business

4.10.1. During the Term the Franchisee will not carry on any other business, either directly or indirectly, save with the prior written consent of the Franchisor. The Franchisor may at any time at its sole discretion withdraw such consent on the giving of not less than [3] months written notice.

4.10.2. The Franchisee may not have any direct or indirect financial or other interest in any business which may be reasonably considered to be a competitor of the Franchise anywhere in the world other than the direct or indirect holding of shares in a public listed company where that shareholding amounts to less than [1]% of the total nominal share capital of the public listed company.

4.11. No agency

4.11.1. The Franchisee is not for any purpose the agent of the Franchisor [or Master Franchisor]. The Franchisee must ensure that a notice is displayed at the Premises in a prominent position stating that the business there carried on is carried on by an independent [company *or* firm] called [*specify*] which is the holder of a licence from the Franchisor to conduct business under its name but that the Franchisee is not in any way an agent of the Franchisor for any purpose whatever. A similar notice must be included in all correspondence and literature used in the operation of the Franchise.

5. Audit of the Franchisee's books by Franchisor

5.1. During the Term and for a period of [12] months after its termination the Franchisor [and/or the Master Franchisor] shall be entitled by itself or through auditors appointed by it to require, having given reasonable written notice, the production of the Franchisee's books of accounts for the purpose of auditing them at the premises of the Franchisee. Audits will take place during ordinary office hours.

5.2. In the event that any audit referred to in this Clause 5 should disclose an under-payment of more than [3]% of the sums properly payable to the Franchisor under this Agreement during any financial year or part thereof of the Franchisee the Franchisee will be required to pay the Franchisor [and/or the Master Franchisor] the reasonable cost of the audit in addition to the sums properly due under this Agreement. Any such shortfall as mentioned in this Clause 5.2 shall be paid within [7] days of the figure being notified in writing to the Franchisee.

6. Variations of mode of operation

6.1. The Franchisor reserves the right to require the Franchisee under this Agreement to operate differently from other Franchisees if the Franchisor considers that market and other conditions so require.

7. Confidential information

7.1. The Franchisee agrees not to disclose any confidential information provided by the Franchisor during the Term or at any time thereafter to any third party save where the law requires. The Franchisee also agrees not to use any such confidential information for any other purpose other than for the promotion and running of the Franchise and will not use the information for any business or other purpose of its own. For the avoidance of doubt such information includes but is not limited either in type, *genus* or subject to:

7.1.1. all business information supplied to the Franchisee by the Franchisor regarding the Franchise

7.1.2. all marketing information and intelligence

7.1.3. all trade secrets, processes and formulae.

7.2. For the proper protection of the confidential information the Franchisee will ensure that:

7.2.1. any employee or member of his staff, whether temporary or permanent, will at the commencement of their employment and no later be provided with a contract of employment or engagement which will include a like obligation to that of the Franchisee in respect of confidential information

7.2.2. any [director *or* partner] of the Franchisee or any associated [company *or* firm] will be required to provide, in a form approved by the Franchisor, an undertaking in regard to confidential information in like form to that set out above in relation to the Franchisee before being given access to confidential information.

8. Third party agreements in relation to the Franchisee

8.1. The Franchisee may not enter into any third party agreements or arrangements in relation to the Franchise which will have the effect of encumbrancing, charging or otherwise materially affecting the business of the Franchisee or the receipts therefrom without the prior written consent of the Franchisor, the giving of which consent shall be at the absolute discretion of the Franchisor.

9. Goodwill

9.1. All goodwill in the Marks and the Franchise belongs to the [Master] Franchisor, whether generated by the Franchisee or otherwise and the Franchisee agrees to make no claim in respect thereof.

10. Customers

10.1. All customers of the Franchisee are customers of the Franchisor for all purposes except liability for defective [products *or* services].

11. Right of inspection

11.1. The Franchisor [and/or the Master Franchisor] and/or its appointed agent will be entitled to inspect the operation of the Franchise at the Premises or at any other location used by the Franchisee in connection with the Franchise during any normal business hours in the [Territory *or* Territories] without further notice.

12. Market information

12.1. The Franchisee must at all times keep the Franchisor aware of developments in market conditions within the [Territory *or* Territories] including but not limited to:

12.1.1. actions by competitors or potential competitors of the Franchise

12.1.2. plans and proposals for business development by the Franchisee.

13. Compliance with laws of the [Territory *or* Territories]

13.1. The Franchisee will ensure that it complies at all material times with the laws of the [Territory *or* Territories] relevant to the Franchise including, but not limited to, those relating to:

13.1.1. data protection and freedom of information

13.1.2. taxes and tariffs

13.1.3. health and safety

13.1.4. equal opportunities

13.1.5. employment

13.1.6. insurance

13.1.7. occupiers' liability

13.1.8. business registration [and company returns]

13.1.9. the prevention of money laundering.

14. Indemnity

14.1. The Franchisee will indemnify the Franchisor [and the Master Franchisor] in respect of any losses, damage or liability the Franchisor may incur as a result of the Franchisee's acts or omissions, whether deliberate, accidental, negligent or reckless, in the course of the performance or purported performance of its obligations or rights under this Agreement whether such acts or omissions amount to a breach of an express or implied obligation under this Agreement or a breach of any other legal requirement or obligation, code of practice, licence, consent, forbearance, approval, permission or rule.

14.2. For the avoidance of doubt losses, damage and liability shall include but not be limited to economic and commercial loss, loss of goodwill, legal and other costs associated with legal proceedings of any kind which the Franchisor [and/or the Master Franchisor] has to bring or to which it has to respond, fines, penalties, damages and any financial consequence whatever flowing directly or indirectly from the matters set out in this Clause 14.2.

15. Operation of the Franchise

15.1. The Franchisor will check at least once a month to ensure that the Franchisee is complying with the terms of the Franchise including but not limited to that:

15.1.1. correct systems are being followed and implemented

15.1.2. adequate financial reporting to the Franchisor is taking place.

15.2. In the event that there is inadequate compliance with the terms of its Franchise the Franchisee must take all reasonable steps to ensure that it does so comply.

15.3. If the Franchisee fails to comply after reasonable steps have been taken by the Franchisor to ensure compliance then the Franchise Agreement will be terminated.

15.4. The Franchisor will carry out an audit of the Franchisee at least once every calendar year at the Franchisee's reasonable expense.

16. Appointment of Franchisees

16.1. In selecting and appointing new franchisees the Franchisor will have due regard to the commercial well-being of the Franchisee.

16.2. [No appointment of a new franchisee will be made without the prior written approval of the Master Franchisor. For the avoidance of doubt it is hereby agreed that nothing in this Clause 16 shall be taken to have the effect of constituting or implying any agency on the part of the Franchisor on behalf of the Master Franchisor].

17. Promotion of the Franchise

17.1. The Franchisor will levy a fee of [...]% of gross turnover ('the promotional levy') on the Franchisee to provide for the advertising, marketing and promotion of the Franchise within the Territory.

17.2. The sums received in respect of the promotional levy shall be deposited in a separate bank account in the name of the Franchisor.

17.3. The Franchisor will keep separate books of accounts in respect of the promotional levy which will be available for inspection by the Franchisee upon the giving of 7 days written notice to the Franchisor.

17.4. All promotional activities (and material used in connection therewith) will only be undertaken or used after reasonable consultation with the Franchisees in the Territory.

18. Franchisor's supervision of the Franchisee

18.1. The Franchisor may undertake an audit of the Franchisee's business at any time during the Term and for a period of six months after termination for any reason. Such audit may consist of both financial and other matters connected with compliance with the terms of the Franchise.

18.2. The Franchisor will once every calendar year undertake an audit of the Franchisee of not more than 5 days in length. Members of the Franchisor's staff or agents appointed by it will undertake the audit, the number of participants being reasonable and subject to prior consultation with the Franchisee. The Franchisee will pay the reasonable costs of the audit including payroll, fees, travel and accommodation (if reasonably necessary) of the staff or agents involved.

18.3. The Franchisee undertakes to provide all reasonable assistance during any audit under this Clause 18.3 including the provision of and access to all documents, computer records and accounts reasonably required. The Franchisee also agrees to answer all questions and provide such information as is required by the Franchisor to carry out the audit.

18.4. [The Master Franchisor may at its discretion undertake audits of the Franchisee in addition to or instead of any audit undertaken by the Franchisor. In such eventuality the Franchisee shall be responsible for the payment of the Master Franchisor's reasonable costs].

19. Franchisee fees and charges

19.1. Upon signing this Agreement the Franchisee will:

19.1.1. pay the Franchisor the Initial Franchise Fee of £[...]

19.1.2. provide an [irrevocable] [performance bond *or* standby letter of credit *or* bank guarantee *or* deposit] in the sum of £[...] to [remain in force *or* be retained by the Franchisor] until [6] months after the termination of this Agreement

19.1.3. pay the Franchisor's legal fees as invoiced to it in respect of this Agreement

19.1.4. pay the cost of the Initial Training as invoiced.

19.2. The Franchisee will pay the Monthly Service Fee on the first day of each month by [standing order *or* direct debit].

19.3. The Franchisee will pay for all materials and equipment provided by the Franchisor within [14] days of the rendering of an invoice in respect thereof.

19.4. All costs connected with any audit visit and Training will be paid within [14] days of the rendering of an invoice whether rendered in advance or otherwise.

19.5. Interest will be charged on all sums outstanding under this Agreement at [4]% above the minimum lending rate of [...] Bank or [8]% whichever is the greater, whether before or after any judgment entered in respect thereof.

19.6. All payments must be by direct bank transfer or such other means as the Franchisor may stipulate from time to time.

19.7. All payments must be made in full without any deductions whether by way of set off or any other reason unless previously expressly authorised by the Franchisor in writing.

20. Sale of the Franchisee's business

20.1. No novation, assignment or delegation of the obligations and benefits of this Agreement by the Franchisee is permitted.

20.2. The Franchisee may sell its Franchise business subject to the conditions set out in this Clause 20. In the event that an authorised sale takes place the Franchisor will grant a new Franchise to the purchaser for a minimum period of [5] years subject to the purchaser signing an agreement in like form to this or in such form as is then the standard form of agreement for the Franchise.

20.3. For a purchaser to be approved the following conditions must be met:

20.3.1. the period for the Franchisor to exercise its right of pre-emption must have expired or the Franchisor must have notified the Franchisee in writing that it did not intend to exercise it

20.3.2. the purchaser must be a bona fide arm's length purchaser whose experience, competence and financial standing meet the Franchisor's requirements. The Franchisee must provide all information regarding these matters which the Franchisor may reasonably require

20.3.3. the purchaser must complete satisfactorily the Initial Training

20.3.4. there must be a transfer of the Franchisee's interest in the Premises to the purchaser, where required with the lessor's or other superior title holder's consent

20.3.5. there will be a transfer fee payable to the [Master] Franchisor on completion of [10]% of the sale price of the Franchisee's Franchise business unless the purchaser is not introduced to the Franchisee by the Franchisor in which case the transfer fee will be [5]% of the sale price. The fee will cover the administration costs and all external costs and charges of the Franchisor in connection with the sale

20.3.6. for the purpose of the sale the Franchisee will appoint an independent valuer to be agreed with the Franchisor who must be a member or fellow of the Institute of Chartered Accountants in England and Wales or such other body as may have succeeded it. In the absence of agreement on an appointment within [14] days of the Franchisor being notified of the proposed sale the Franchisor will request the President of the Institute to make an appointment. In either case the valuer will act as an expert not as an arbitrator or adjudicator. The fees and costs of the valuer will be borne by the Franchisee. The valuer will value the Franchise business at a fair market value as a going concern assuming a willing purchaser and seller and will include the consideration to be paid for all fixtures, fittings and stock. The Franchise business must be sold at the price certified by the valuer

20.3.7. any sale of the Franchise business to a third party must be completed in time for the Franchisor to enter into a replacement Franchise Agreement before the expiry of this Agreement

20.3.8. upon exchange of contracts for the sale of the business the purchaser shall deposit [10]% of the sale price with the solicitors appointed by the Franchisor. Upon completion of the sale the purchaser shall pay to the solicitors appointed by the Franchisor the balance of the purchase price to be held by the solicitors as agent for the Franchisee subject to a lien in favour of the Franchisor for any sums due to the Franchisor from the Franchisee.

20.4. **Franchisor's pre-emption right**

20.4.1. The Franchisor has a right of pre-emption in the event of a proposed sale of the Franchisee's Franchise business. The Franchisor must notify the Franchisee of its intention to exercise this right within [14] days of receipt by it of both an offer from a third party and the valuation referred to above together with any supporting documentation reasonably required by the Franchisor in relation to the offer. The price to be paid by the Franchisor will be the value certified by the valuer less any sums owed at that time to the Franchisor by the Franchisee in connection with the Franchisee's obligation under this Agreement.

20.4.2. The Franchisee must not be or have been in persistent breach of any obligation under this Agreement.

20.4.3. The Franchisee must execute at the time of the sale a discharge in favour of the Franchisor from all claims against the Franchisor and indemnify it against any claim arising from the period of operation of the Franchise by the Franchisee.

20.4.4. The lease or freehold of the Premises shall be assigned or transferred to the Franchisor under the terms of the then current edition of the National Conditions of Sale and the following conditions shall apply:

20.4.4.1. no deposit shall be payable by the Franchisor

20.4.4.2. the Franchisee must deduce title:

20.4.4.2.1. in the case of registered land pursuant to the provisions of Section 110 of the Land Registration Act 1925

20.4.4.2.2. in the case of unregistered land commencing with the lease under which the Premises are held by the Franchisee

20.4.4.3. vacant possession must be provided on completion

20.4.4.4. the Franchisee must sell with full title guarantee.

20.5. The Franchisee must take all reasonable steps whether under the provisions of Section 38(4) of the Landlord and Tenant Act 1954 or otherwise to give effect to the provisions of this Clause 20.

20.6. The Franchisor may novate, assign or delegate the benefits and obligations of this Agreement on giving [21] days written notice to the Franchisee.

21. Termination of this Agreement

21.1. This Agreement may expire by effluxion of time or in accordance with the following provisions.

21.2. In the event that the Franchisee fails to remedy any remediable breach of which it has been notified in writing by the Franchisor within [28] days the Franchisor may at its absolute discretion terminate forthwith this Agreement.

21.3. In the event that the Franchisee commits any irremediable material breach or persistently commits any remediable breach of this Agreement the Franchisor may terminate this Agreement forthwith.

21.4. The Franchisor may terminate this Agreement forthwith in the event that the Franchisee:

21.4.1. is [declared bankrupt *or* wound up due to insolvency]

21.4.2. makes or seeks a composition with its creditors

21.4.3. enters into or seeks an insolvent voluntary arrangement

21.4.4. becomes the subject of the appointment of a manager, receiver or liquidator

21.4.5. is the subject of an administration order

21.4.6. has its assets charged or seized for the satisfaction of a debt

21.4.7. seeks to challenge the [Master] Franchisor's intellectual property rights in relation to the intellectual property connected with the Franchise

21.4.8. behaves in a way which is likely to bring the Franchise into disrepute including but not limited to conviction for an indictable criminal offence

21.4.9. divulges confidential business information in connection with the Franchise to an unauthorised third party

21.4.10. fails to comply with the terms of any software licence connected with the Franchise

21.4.11. misappropriates or permits, tolerates or facilitates the misappropriation of any funds in connection with the Franchise belonging to or lawfully withheld from any employee, agent, Franchisee, customer or any other person who has dealings with the Franchise

21.4.12. fails to commence, carry on or terminate as appropriate its Franchise business

21.4.13. fails to pay any sum due under this Agreement for more than [28] days after its due date

21.4.14. neglects to furnish any document or other information which the Franchisee is obliged to provide within [28] days of its due date.

21.5. The Franchisor may terminate this Agreement if there is any material re-organisation of the Franchisee's business structure unless:

21.5.1. such re-organisation is not the result of insolvency

21.5.2. the resultant company or organisation is bound by the provisions of this Agreement

21.5.3. the beneficial ownership of the resultant entity is not in the hands of competitors of the Franchisor, the Franchisee or the Franchisees anywhere in the world except to the extent that such ownership does not exceed [10%] of the total.

21.6. In the event that there is a change in legislation which materially affects the legitimate interests of the Franchisor in respect of the Franchisee or Franchise the Franchisor will be entitled to terminate this Agreement upon giving reasonable notice to the Franchisee which must be not less than [28] days and in no instance more than [56] days.

22. Post termination rights and obligations

22.1. Termination of this Agreement for any reason shall not affect the rights of either Party in respect of the period after termination nor either Party's rights which may have arisen as a result of any breach pre-dating the termination.

22.2. In order to ensure the proper protection of the Franchise, including its Marks and Goodwill upon termination of the Franchise the Franchisee must:

22.2.1. assign, novate or transfer to the Franchisor or such party as the Franchisor shall require all agreements with third party suppliers and such other third parties as the Franchisor may reasonably require

22.2.2. cease operation of the Franchise including but not limited to the use of all Marks, telephone numbers and e-mail addresses associated with the Franchise/Franchisee

22.2.3. remove all signage, Marks, names, advertisements and other material indicating that the Franchisee has operated from the premises

22.2.4. return all copies of the Manual and all other literature and material supplied for or associated with the Franchise/Franchisee other than that which is not branded or specific to the Franchise

22.2.5. return all copies of software, business information documentation and other materials containing business information connected with the Franchise

22.2.6. remove or erase from all computers and other electronic equipment all copies and versions of any software specific to the Franchise

22.2.7. not use any confidential business information received by it during the course of the operation of the Franchise and must not disclose such information to any third party whether within or without the [Territory *or* Territories]

22.2.8. not use any Know-how obtained through the Franchise save where the same is in the public domain unless such Know-how has come into the public domain through the breach of the Franchisee

22.2.9. provide all reasonable assistance to the Franchisor to achieve an orderly transfer of the Franchise to any party nominated by the Franchisor

22.3. The Franchisee hereby grants the Franchisor an irrevocable power of attorney to effect such of these acts as is necessary for any purpose contained in this Clause 22.

23. Post termination restrictions on the Franchisee

23.1. The Franchisee must not for a period of [12] months after termination of the Franchise for any reason be engaged in, involved or associated with, either by itself or in connection or association with any other entity, any business within the [Territory or Territories] which is similar to that of the Franchise, whether as franchisee, agent, principal, adviser or in any other capacity. [Such limitation extends to the [directors or principal shareholders] of the Franchisee].

23.2. The Franchisee must not for a period of [12] months after termination either for itself or on behalf of any other entity, seek, solicit or obtain orders from any entity which was a customer of the Franchisee at the time of termination [or for a period of [2] years prior thereto]. Nor shall the Franchisee represent itself as having been formerly connected with the Franchise. [Such limitations extend to the [directors or principal shareholders] of the Franchisee].

23.3. The Franchisee shall not for a period of [12] months after termination seek to entice away or recruit any employee of either the Franchisor or any Franchisee who was so employed at the time of termination.

23.4. [In order to ensure the effectiveness of the provisions in this Clause 23 the Franchisee will obtain from its [directors or principal shareholders] a deed of agreement in a form approved by the Franchisor whereby each [director or principal shareholder] agrees to be bound by the provisions of this Clause 23].

23.5. The copyright and intellectual property in all Marks and materials (including but not limited to the Manual) shall remain the copyright and intellectual property of the [Master] Franchisor. The Franchisee agrees not to disclose the contents of the Manual or other material to any third party after the termination of the Franchise save where the material is in the pubic domain other than as a result of breach of this Agreement by the Franchisee or those acting on its behalf or with its agreement or sanction.

24. Severability

24.1. In the event that any of the restrictions in this Agreement are found by a court of competent jurisdiction to be unenforceable because they are unreasonable but which would be enforceable were specific words, phrases or clauses removed then the restrictions shall apply as if such words, phrases or clauses were removed.

24.2. In the event that any term of this Agreement is found to be invalid or otherwise unenforceable then such term shall be regarded and construed as severable from the Agreement so as not to affect the validity and enforceability of the remainder.

25. Whole agreement

25.1. This Agreement supersedes and replaces any previous agreement between the Parties whether oral or in writing in relation to the Franchise. The Franchisee hereby agrees that in entering into this Agreement it has not relied upon any warranty or representation made by or on behalf of the Franchisor save where expressly stated in this Agreement. The Parties hereby agree that this Agreement constitutes the whole agreement between the Parties in respect of the Franchise.

25.2. Nothing in this Clause 25 shall be construed as limiting or excluding either Party's liability to the other for fraud or deceit in inducing the making of this Agreement.

25.3. Without prejudice to the generality of the foregoing the following is agreed between the Parties:

25.3.1. all financial information provided by the Franchisor to the Franchisee is provided in good faith and is intended to be indicative only. The Franchisee hereby acknowledges that it accepts that the provision of such information is at the request of the Franchisee on the basis that it does not constitute a representation, warranty, or guarantee by the Franchisor and that the Franchisee has not placed reliance upon it for the purpose of entering into this Agreement or for any other purpose

25.3.2. the Franchisee accepts that the Franchisor does not and cannot predict how the Franchise will perform in the [Territory *or* Territories] either under the Franchisee or at all

25.3.3. the Franchisee warrants that it has been advised by the Franchisor to seek independent legal and financial advice before entering into this Agreement and that its decision to make this Agreement is based solely upon its own judgement and assessment of the commerciality of the Franchise in the [Territory *or* Territories].

26. Variation

26.1. Any variation of the terms of this Agreement must be in writing signed by the Parties.

27. Further action

27.1. The Parties agree that they will expeditiously carry out such further acts as may be necessary for the purpose of this Agreement including the execution and delivery of such instruments, deeds, licences, notifications as may be reasonably required by the other Party or by law.

28. Set off

28.1. Notwithstanding any other express or implied term of this Agreement the Franchisor reserves the right to set off against any sum payable or owed by it to the Franchisee any debt or other liability, whether absolute or contingent, owed by the Franchisee to the Franchisor, or any sum, debt or other liability, absolute or contingent, owed by the Franchisee to any third party for which the Franchisor is liable or may be liable in default of payment or discharge by the Franchisee. In the event of such set off the Franchisee irrevocably authorises the Franchisor to pay from such sum or sums held by the Franchisor for the Franchisee such sum as will discharge any such debt or liability to a third party or discharge the debt or sum owed to the Franchisor.

29. *Force majeure*

29.1. Neither Party shall have any liability to the other for any delay, omission, failure or inadequate performance of this Agreement which is the result of circumstances beyond its reasonable control. Where a Party is so affected in its performance of this Agreement it will notify the other Party in writing as soon as is reasonably practical.

30. Waiver

30.1. No failure, neglect or delay in enforcing any of the terms of this Agreement may be construed as a waiver of any of the Franchisor's rights in respect thereof nor such neglect, failure or delay a variation of the express terms of the Agreement.

31. Third party rights

31.1. The Parties to this Agreement agree that it is not hereby intended that any rights should be conferred upon or enforceable by any third party as defined in the Contracts (Rights of Third Parties) Act 1999 [save in respect of rights of the Master Franchisor conferred by and arising from this Agreement].

32. Notices

32.1. All notices under this Agreement shall be in writing and shall be delivered personally [or by first class, registered or recorded post] [or by facsimile transmission] in every case to the other Party's Agreed Address. [In the case of first class post notice will be deemed to be received [3] business days after the date of posting.]

33. Law and jurisdiction

33.1. This Agreement is governed by the law of England and Wales and is subject to the [exclusive] jurisdiction of the courts of England and Wales.

34. Schedules

34.1. The Schedules form part of this Agreement including any subsequent amendments made thereto.

Signed, etc.

SCHEDULE 1

The [Territory *or* Territories]

[*Set out details of the Territory/Territories*]

Signed, etc.

SCHEDULE 2

The Franchise

[*Set out details of the Franchise, business model, etc.*]

Signed, etc.

SCHEDULE 3

The Target[s]

[*Set out details of the Target/Targets*]

Signed, etc.

SCHEDULE 4

The Term

[*Define the Term*]

Signed, etc.

SCHEDULE 5

The Manual

[*Append a copy of the Manual*]

Signed, etc.

SCHEDULE 6

Initial Training and Training

[*Set out the details of the Initial Training and Training*]

Signed, etc.

SCHEDULE 7

Initial Franchise Fee and Monthly Service Fee

[*Set out details of the Initial and Monthly Service Fees*]

Signed, etc,

SCHEDULE 8

Parties' Agreed Addresses

[*Set out the Parties' Agreed Addresses*]

Signed, etc.

12

Guarantees and indemnities

12.1   Introduction

The law relating to guarantees and indemnities is both technical and well established and so it is not intended to attempt a summary in this chapter.

Three precedents have been included which are easily adaptable to various commercial situations.

First, there is a trade guarantee relating to the guaranteeing of a contract. This is in full form (**Precedent 12A**).

Second, there is a guarantee for the supply of goods. Again this is in full form (**Precedent 12B**).

Third, to complement the two guarantees there is a short form of indemnity which may be adapted and matched with either of the above (**Precedent 12C**).

PRECEDENT 12A   Guarantee for performance of a contract

GUARANTEE FOR PERFORMANCE OF A CONTRACT

THIS AGREEMENT is dated [...] and is made

BETWEEN:

1.   [*Name of guarantor*] of [*address*] ('the Guarantor'); and
2.   [*Name of beneficiary of guarantee*] [of [*address*] *or* whose registered office is at [*address*]], [*company registration number*] ('the Beneficiary').

RECITALS

1.   This Agreement is intended to guarantee performance of a contract ('the Contract') between the Beneficiary and [*name of other contracting party*] ('the Contractor').
2.   Under the Contract the Contractor undertook to carry out certain works set out in Schedule 1 hereto for the price of £[...].

OPERATIVE PROVISIONS

1. The Guarantor hereby guarantees the performance of the Contract by the Contractor.

2. If the Contractor shall be in breach of any term or condition of the Contract or fail in

any way to fulfil his obligations under it which results in loss, damage, costs or expense to the Beneficiary then the Guarantor shall indemnify the Beneficiary [and his personal representatives] in respect thereof.

3. The Contractor shall not be in breach of the Contract if the Contract is annulled or set aside by the parties thereto or by a court or tribunal having jurisdiction to do so.

4. In the event that there is any dispute as to the amount of the loss, damage, costs or expense then the amount shall be determined by [name of expert] ('the Expert'), or if he is unable to carry out such task for whatever reason by an expert chosen by him or his personal representatives.

5. The Expert shall act as an expert not as an arbitrator.

6. The fees of the Expert shall be borne equally by the Beneficiary and the Guarantor.

7. The Guarantor shall not be released or discharged from this Guarantee by any agreement or arrangement between the Contactor and Beneficiary without the Guarantor's agreement.

8. The Guarantor will not be released from this Guarantee:

8.1. in the event that there is an alteration in the obligations of the Contractor under the Contract

8.2. if there is a forbearance on the part of the Beneficiary as to payment, time, performance or otherwise.

[Signatures of both parties.]

PRECEDENT 12B   Continuing limited guarantee for the supply of goods

CONTINUING LIMITED GUARANTEE FOR THE SUPPLY OF GOODS

THIS AGREEMENT is dated [...] and is made

BETWEEN:

1. [Name of guarantor] of [address] ('the Guarantor'); and
2. [Name of supplier] [of [address] or whose registered office is at [address]], [company registration number] ('the Supplier').

RECITALS

1. This agreement ('the Guarantee') is intended to guarantee payment for goods ('the Goods') continuing to be supplied by the Supplier to [name of buyer] ('the Buyer').
2. The Goods are to be supplied under the Supplier's standard terms and conditions from time to time ('the Standard Terms').

OPERATIVE PROVISIONS

1. In consideration of the Supplier having agreed at the Guarantor's request to supply the Buyer with the Goods for his trade and business the Guarantor guarantees to be answerable and responsible to the Supplier for the payment by the Buyer of the price of the Goods that the Buyer may from time to time request be supplied [and delivered] to him by the Supplier notwithstanding that the Guarantor may not have notice or knowledge of any act

or omission on the Buyer's part to pay the Supplier for any Goods supplied by the Supplier to the Buyer in accordance with the Standard Terms up to a limit of £[...] ('the Limit') being the total aggregate sum for which the Guarantor shall be liable under this Guarantee.

2. This Guarantee is to constitute a continuing guarantee for the whole debt up to the Limit that is contracted with the Supplier by the Buyer in respect of Goods which are to be supplied [and delivered] to the Buyer.

3. This Guarantee is to be treated as a security for the whole debt owed to the Supplier by the Buyer in respect of the Goods and not limited to so much of it as equates to the Limit.

4. If the Supplier receives any dividend, composition or payment from the Buyer or from his estate it is to be taken and applied by the Supplier as a payment without any deduction from any claim arising from this Guarantee.

5. The Guarantor's right to be subrogated to the Supplier in respect of such dividend, composition or payment shall not arise until the Supplier has been paid in full the amount of his claim against the Buyer.

6. The Supplier may without notice to the Guarantor and without discharging or impairing the Guarantor's liability under this Guarantee:

6.1. refuse to supply further Goods to the Buyer

6.2. grant the Buyer or any acceptors, endorsers or drawers of promissory notes, bills of exchange or other securities received by the Supplier from the Buyer or on which the Buyer may be liable to the Supplier time or other indulgence, compound with him or them (as appropriate).

7. The Supplier may enforce this Guarantee even if at the time when any proceedings are being taken against the Guarantor negotiable or other securities referable to this Guarantee are outstanding or in circulation.

8. [No changes in the members or constitution of the Supplier shall affect the enforceability of this Guarantee notwithstanding Section 18 of the Partnership Act 1890].

9. This Guarantee shall be revocable at any time on the Guarantor giving [...] months written notice to the Supplier in respect of future transactions only, such notice to be sent by [state method of service of notice] to [state address for service of notice].

10. The Guarantor waives all rights as guarantor which would prevent the Supplier treating him as if he were the principal debtor, to which he hereby consents, including but not limited to any variation of the Standard Terms and the method of performance thereof which the Supplier and the Buyer may agree to be bound by.

Dated:

[Signature of guarantor]

PRECEDENT 12C   Indemnity by principal debtor to a guarantor liable under a guarantee

INDEMNITY BY PRINCIPAL DEBTOR TO A GUARANTOR LIABLE UNDER A GUARANTEE

THIS DEED OF INDEMNITY is made the [... day of ...]

BETWEEN:

1.   [Name of principal debtor] of [address] ('the Principal'); and
2.   [Name of guarantor] of [address] ('the Guarantor').

RECITALS

1. This Deed supplements a guarantee ('the Guarantee') of [*date*] a copy of which is set
    out in Schedule 1 hereto made between the Guarantor and [*name of party guaranteed*]
    ('the Supplier').
2. The Principal has agreed to make this Deed in consideration of the Guarantor's having
    entered into the Guarantee.

OPERATIVE PROVISION

The Principal, in consideration of the Guarantor's having entered into the Guarantee, hereby
agrees that he or his personal representatives will keep the Guarantor and his personal
representatives, together with their estates indemnified against all actions, proceedings,
liability, claims, damages, costs and expenses in relation to or arising out of the Guarantee.

SIGNED AS A DEED

[*Signature of principal debtor*]

[*Signatures of witnesses*]

13

Information technology

13.1 Introduction

This chapter provides two basic agreements and a licence.

The first agreement is for the provision of data to users such as, for example, financial information sourced from a provider's personal researches and/or from restricted sources such as contemporaneous information on the prices of listed securities (**Precedent 13A**). In such a contract, apart from service levels and pricing which reflect the desirability of automatic result and review, the protection of copyright in the data is of key importance.

The second agreement is intended as generic for support and maintenance services with the possibility of the supplier writing some of his own software (**Precedent 13B**).

Both contracts are focused on the needs of small or medium-size suppliers and clients/customers. They are intended to be flexible so that a variety of services can be provided, changed, modified or discontinued without the need each time for a further contract. In all cases, however, proper order is maintained through the use of variable or bolt-on schedules to the overarching agreement.

The intellectual property rights of the supplier are carefully safeguarded and very often the rights to software supplied will be held by a third party supplier. This reflects the commercial fact that, except in the case of very large-scale development and implementation projects for new systems, much if not all of the software will be bought 'off the peg' which will provide the customer with better long-term commercial security, albeit sometimes compromising bespoke requirements.

The licence provides for numerous variations and is multi-purpose (**Precedent 13C**). It is a signed agreement rather than shrink wrap or cling wrap (which are more akin to standard terms and conditions). It is most likely to be useful for small and medium-scale software developers producing code for mainframe applications and networks.

PRECEDENT 13A   Contract covering the provision of data services

GENERIC INFORMATION TECHNOLOGY CONTRACT SERVICES CONTRACT COVERING THE PROVISION OF DATA SERVICES

THIS AGREEMENT dated [*date*] is made by and between:

1. [*Name*] a company incorporated in England and Wales under company number [*number*] and whose registered office is at [*address*] ('the Supplier'); and
2. [*Name*] a company incorporated in England and Wales under company number [*number*] and whose registered office is at [*address*] ('the Client').

RECITALS

1. The Supplier supplies a range of services connected with the provision of information technology.
2. The Supplier is willing to provide the Services (as defined below) and the Client is willing to appoint the Supplier to provide the Services in accordance with the provisions of this Agreement.

DEFINITIONS

In this Agreement and the Schedules, the following words shall have the following meaning:

'Agreed Addresses'	Supplier: [*address*]; Client: [*address*].
'Client Data'	Data provided by the Client as described in the Schedules hereto and as varied from time to time.
'Commencement Date'	The date on which a Service is commenced as set out in the Schedules.
'Customer'	Customer of the Client who is permitted to receive the data as specified in this Agreement.
'Fee'	The amounts set out in the Schedules to this Agreement in respect of each of the Services as may be varied from time to time.
'Party' and 'Parties'	The Supplier and the Client, and 'Party' shall mean either one of them.
'Review Date'	Any date from which the Supplier is entitled to increase the Fees for a Service as set out in the Schedules to this Agreement.
'Review Period'	A period beginning on any Review Date and ending on the day before the next Review Date, and qualified uses of the term are to be construed accordingly.
['RPI']	[The Retail Price Index maintained and published by the Office for National Statistics.]
'Schedules'	The Schedules attached to this Agreement and as varied or added to from time to time by written agreement.

'Service' and 'Services'	The service or services set out in the Schedules which the Client has agreed from time to time to receive from the Supplier and as may be varied or added to by the Parties by written agreement from time to time.
'Supplier Data'	All information and data of the Supplier which are to be provided to the Client under this Agreement.
'Term'	The minimum initial or renewal period that the Client agrees to receive a Service pursuant to this Agreement as set out in the Schedules and as varied from time to time.

INTERPRETATION

In this Agreement:

1. The singular includes the plural and one gender includes all.
2. References to Schedules and Clauses are to those in this Agreement.
3. Reference to a statutory provision includes any amendment or replacement provision relevant to the Agreement.
4. Reference to a document includes that document as amended, altered or replaced subsequent to the date of this Agreement.
5. Reference to writing includes facsimile transmission, e-mail, and similar media unless the context otherwise expressly provides.
6. Time expressed in days excludes the first day but includes the last day. If the last day does not fall on a normal business day in both England and Wales then the last day will be deemed to be the first normal business day.
7. The headings in this document do not form part of the Agreement.

OPERATIVE PROVISIONS

1. Duration of this Agreement

1.1. This Agreement shall continue from the date of its signing [until the ... of ... 20... *or* for a period of [...] years *or* until terminated by either Party under the provisions of Clause 18].

2. Services

2.1. The Supplier will provide the Service as set out in the Schedules as may be varied from time to time from the Commencement Date relevant to each Service for the relevant Term.

3. Consideration

3.1. In consideration for the Supplier providing the Service the Client shall pay the Fee as set out in the Schedules for each Service provided.

4. Provision of the Service

4.1. The Supplier shall use its best endeavours to provide the Service. If it is unable to do so for any reason it will notify the Client as soon as practically possible and inform the Client of:

4.1.1. the reason for its being unable to provide the Service

4.1.2. when the Service will be resumed.

4.2. If the Supplier fails to provide a Service for a continuous period of more than [1 *month*] the Client shall be entitled to serve written notice of termination upon the Supplier in relation to the Service affected.

4.3. Failure to provide a Service will not arise if the reason for the failure is a breach of this Agreement by the Client or a *force majeure* event.

5. Services to be provided

5.1. The Services which the Supplier can provide are set out in the Schedules. The Client and the Supplier shall agree the provision of an individual Service including service levels, specification, details of delivery, the Term and the Fee payable and their agreement shall be signified by the signing of a copy of the relevant Schedule as varied from time to time.

5.2. The Supplier and the Client may agree to include more than one Service in the same Schedule.

5.3. A Schedule may be varied or added to as agreed by the Parties from time to time, in writing. Any variation or addition to a Schedule shall be clearly indicated (including the additional or different Fee to be paid by the Client) and a like procedure followed to that set out in sub-paragraph 5.1.

6. Obligations of the Supplier

6.1. While the Supplier is performing the Service the Supplier will only supply the Supplier Data to the Client in the formats and by the means specified in the relevant Schedule or as the Parties agree from time to time.

7. Obligations of the Client

7.1. During the currency of this Agreement the Client will ensure that the Client's staff and agents cooperate and assist the Supplier.

7.2. In the event that the Client receives any notice, decision, notification or is the object of any enforcement action by a governmental or regulatory agency or body which is likely to affect the delivery of the Service by the Supplier, it will immediately inform the Supplier in writing indicating what action it is proposing to take in respect thereof.

8. Payment of Fee

8.1. A Fee shall be paid upon invoicing by the Supplier for each Service. [If the Client wishes to raise a purchase order to the Supplier prior to its being invoiced then it must do so and supply the order to the Supplier at least [1 *month*] before the Fee for the relevant Term is payable. For the avoidance of doubt the Fee will be due and payable on the relevant payment date whether any purchase order has been provided as set out herein and absent the timeous provision of a purchase order the Client will be invoiced prior to the beginning of a Term and required to pay as set out in the relevant Schedule].

8.2. If the Client does not make a payment by the date stated in an invoice or as otherwise provided for in this Agreement then the Supplier shall be entitled to:

8.2.1. charge interest on the outstanding amount at the rate of [5%] a year above the base lending rate of [...] Bank plc

8.2.2. require the Client to pay, in advance, for any Service (both including and in addition to the Service in respect of which it is in default) which has not yet been performed and

8.2.3. not perform any further Service.

9. Determination of revised Fees

9.1. The Fee for any Review Period is to be determined by the Supplier and notified in writing to the Client not less than [3 *months*] prior to the relevant Review Date. [A Fee for any Review Period may not increase by a greater percentage than any percentage increase in the RPI between the beginning and end of the previous Review Period (or in the case of the first Review Period between the Commencement date for a Service and its first Review date)].

9.2. [The Parties may agree a different figure from that set out in Clause 9.1, but in default of such agreement prior to the Review Date, the Fee payable shall be that set out in Clause 9.1].

10. Confidentiality

10.1. Each Party agrees not to disclose any confidential information provided by the other Party during the Term or at any time thereafter to any third party save where the law requires. Each Party also agrees not to use any such confidential information for any other purpose other than in connection with the provision of the Service and will not use the information for any business or other purpose of its own.

10.2. Each Party undertakes to procure that its employees, directors, agents and advisers and any other persons to whom it makes available confidential information shall also keep confidential the information the subject of this Clause 10.

11. Intellectual property

11.1. The Supplier owns the copyright, database and computer software rights and all other intellectual property rights ('IPR') in [the Supplier Data] [and the contents of any website provided by the Supplier as part of or the whole of the Service subject to the provisions of Clause 13.5 in relation to any data sourced from a third party supplier and provided by the Supplier to the Client as part of the Service] [and any software it supplies to or develops for the Client as part of the Service unless specific express written provision is made to the contrary].

11.2. The Client is licensed only to use the Supplier Data as part of the Service and does not thereby acquire any IPR in the Supplier Data. If this Agreement terminates for any reason, the Supplier Data must be returned and all rights cease. For the avoidance of doubt, upon termination the Supplier Data can no longer be used by the Client or the Customers of the Client for any purpose.

11.3. [Where the Supplier provides a Service incorporating the Client's logo, trademarks, marks, get-up or other branding associated with the Client ('Client's IPR') nothing in this Clause 11 shall have the effect of transferring such Client's IPR to the Supplier].

12. Acknowledgments

12.1. The Client shall acknowledge the source of the Supplier Data in any document (whether hardcopy, electronic or of any type) produced by the Client which uses the Supplier Data in any form in a format to be agreed with the Supplier and if required by the Supplier include a copy of the Supplier's logo alongside or adjacent to such acknowledgment.

13. Right to redistribute

13.1. The Supplier grants the Client the non-exclusive right to redistribute the Supplier Data to Customers as set out in this Clause 13.

13.2. The Service and the Supplier Data may only be used by the Client as specified in the Schedules to this Agreement.

13.3. Customers may not redistribute or extract the Supplier Data for any other purpose, and Supplier Data may not be used under this Agreement in any specialist value-added services of the Client or its Customers other than as specified in the Schedules hereto.

13.4. The Client agrees to ensure that any Customer agrees:

13.4.1. to comply with the requirements of Clause 11.2 and this Clause 13

13.4.2. not to infringe the Supplier's IPR or adversely affect them by its actions or inactions.

13.5. In the event that a third party's data, which is supplied to the Client by the Supplier and is not at the time of the Agreement subject to any licence fee payable by or on behalf of the Client and/or the Customer, becomes subject to such a charge or similar charge, then the Client agrees to ensure that all relevant licences and permissions are obtained from all the relevant data sources and that all fees and other charges due to any data source are paid by the Client upon demand.

13.6. The Client agrees to monitor the actions of its Customers in order to ensure compliance with the terms of this Agreement and to report timeously to the Supplier any infringement thereof.

13.7. The Supplier may, on [14] days written notice to the Client, examine the relevant books and records of the Client to ensure that there has been adherence to the terms and conditions of this Agreement.

14. Use of sub-suppliers

14.1. The Supplier may employ the services of a sub-supplier in order to deliver the Service to the Client. The Supplier shall in such case be responsible for ensuring that the Service provided by the sub-supplier is to the same or a comparable standard to that delivered or intended to be delivered by the Supplier.

15. Liability of the Supplier

15.1. The Supplier will use all reasonable endeavours to ensure that the Supplier Data is accurate. However the Supplier does not warrant the accuracy of Supplier Data provided either from its own resources or obtained from a third party and supplied by it under the terms of this Agreement.

15.2. The liability of the Supplier under or in connection with this Agreement for the provision of the Service whether arising in contract, tort, negligence, breach of statutory duty or otherwise howsoever shall not exceed a refund of that part of the annual fee for that Service paid by the Client to the Supplier or for such shorter period for which it had been agreed the Service would be provided, under this Agreement. The relevant Fee for the purpose of this Clause 15 will be that which relates to the particular Service in respect of which a successful claim is brought by the Client.

15.3. The Supplier shall not be liable to the Client for any indirect, consequential or economic loss including but not limited to damage, costs or expenses of any description, loss of profit, business, goodwill, turnover or any other loss arising from its performance or non-performance of its obligations in connection with this Agreement whether arising from breach of contract, tort, breach of duty, negligence or any other cause of action.

15.4. Nothing in this Clause 15 shall limit or remove the Supplier's liability for causing personal injury or death.

16. Indemnity

16.1. The Client will indemnify the Supplier in respect of any losses, damage or liability the Supplier may incur as a result of the Client's acts or omissions, whether deliberate, accidental, negligent or reckless, in the course of the provision by the Supplier of the Service to the Client under this Agreement whether such acts or omissions amount to a breach of an express or implied obligation under this Agreement or a breach of any other legal requirement or obligation, code of practice, licence, consent, forbearance, approval, permission or rule.

16.2. For the avoidance of doubt losses, damage and liability shall include but not be limited to economic and commercial loss, loss of goodwill, legal and other costs associated with legal proceedings of any kind which the Supplier has to bring or to which it has to respond, fines, penalties, damages and any financial consequence whatever flowing directly or indirectly from the matters set out in this Clause 16.

17. Whole agreement and previous agreements

17.1. This Agreement supersedes and replaces any previous agreement between the Parties whether oral or in writing in relation to the provision of the Service. The Parties hereby agree that in entering into this Agreement they have not relied upon any warranty or representation made by or on behalf of the other Party save where expressly stated in this Agreement. The Parties hereby agree that this Agreement including the Schedules constitutes the whole agreement between the Parties in relation to the provision of the Service.

17.2. Nothing in this Clause 17 shall be construed as limiting or excluding either Party's liability to the other for fraud or deceit in inducing the making of this Agreement.

18. Termination

18.1. The Service will start on the Commencement Date set out in the Schedules for each Service and will continue until terminated by either Party giving at least [3 *months*] written notice in respect of each Service, such notice to expire at the end of the Term for that Service, as initially set or renewed, as the case may be. Otherwise, the Service will be renewed for a further Term equivalent in duration to the initial Term for that Service or as provided for under this Clause 18.

18.2. In the event that all Services have been terminated for whatever reason this Agreement shall itself lapse within [28 *days*] of the end of the provision of the last remaining Service.

18.3. Without prejudice to the other remedies or rights a Party may have, the Supplier may terminate the provision of any Service at any time, on written notice to the Client, if the Client:

18.3.1. is [declared bankrupt *or* wound up due to insolvency]

18.3.2. makes or seeks a composition with its creditors

18.3.3. enters into or seeks an insolvent voluntary arrangement

18.3.4. becomes the subject of the appointment of a manager, receiver or liquidator

18.3.5. is the subject of an administration order

18.3.6. has its assets charged or seized for the satisfaction of a debt

18.3.7. seeks to challenge the Supplier's IPR

18.3.8. divulges confidential business information obtained from the Supplier

18.3.9. fails to comply with the terms of any software or data licence in connection with the Service

18.3.10. has any sum due under this Agreement remaining unpaid for more than [28 *days*]

18.3.11. does not furnish any document or other information which the Client is obliged to provide within [28 *days*] of its due date

18.3.12. is in breach of its obligations under this Agreement and in the case of a breach capable of remedy fails to remedy the same within [21 *days*] after receipt of the notice giving full particulars of the breach and requiring it to be remedied.

19. Consequences of termination of the Service and/or this Agreement

19.1. Upon termination of the Service the Client must pay for the Service provided prior to the date of termination as well as any further expenditure incurred by the Supplier after the date of termination arising from commitments reasonably entered into by the Supplier prior to the date of termination but payable by the Supplier afterwards.

19.2. Upon termination of the Service for any reason the Client shall cease to use or deal with any Supplier Data supplied in connection with that Service and shall destroy or return it together with any copies thereof as the Supplier shall reasonably direct.

19.3. Upon termination of the last of the Services provided to the Client and consequently the termination of this Agreement, the Client shall return or destroy (as reasonably required by the Supplier) all documents, materials or other information, whether in hard copy or electronic form, in its possession or control which constitute or include any confidential information of the Supplier.

20. *Force majeure*

20.1. The Supplier shall not have any liability to the Client for any delay, omission, failure or inadequate performance of this Agreement which is the result of circumstances beyond the reasonable control of the Supplier. Where the Supplier is so affected in its performance of this Agreement it will notify the Client as soon as is reasonably possible in writing.

21. Amendments

21.1. This Agreement may only be amended or varied in writing signed by the Parties or their duly authorised representatives.

22. Assignment

22.1. Neither Party may assign, charge, mortgage, sub-contract, delegate or otherwise assign or transfer its rights or obligations under this Agreement save where express provision is made for the same in this Agreement, without the prior written consent of the other Party.

22.2. A Party may assign or transfer its rights under this Agreement if such assignment or transfer takes place in the context of the disposal of all of its business to which the Service is related provided that the proposed assignee or transferee undertakes to the Supplier directly in a form reasonably required by the Supplier to be bound by the obligations of the proposed assignor.

23. Waiver

23.1. No failure, neglect or delay in enforcing any of the terms of this Agreement by one Party may be construed as a waiver of any of that Party's rights in respect thereof nor such neglect, failure or delay a variation of the express terms of the Agreement.

24. No agency, partnership, etc.

24.1. Neither Party is for any purpose the agent or partner of the other as a result of anything arising from this Agreement and each Party hereby undertakes not to represent to any third party that it has any authority to act on that other Party's behalf.

25. Further action

25.1. The Parties agree that they will expeditiously carry out such further acts as may be necessary for the purpose of this Agreement including the execution and delivery of such instruments, deeds, licences, notifications as may be reasonably required by the other Party or by law.

26. Severance

26.1. In the event that any term of this Agreement is found to be invalid or otherwise unenforceable then such term shall be regarded and construed as severable from the Agreement so as not to affect the validity and enforceability of the remainder.

27. Notices

27.1. All notices under this Agreement shall be in writing and shall be delivered personally [or by first class, registered or recorded post] [or by facsimile transmission] in every case to the other Party's Agreed Address. [In the case of first class post notice will be deemed to be received [3] business days after the date of posting.]

28. Non-solicitation

28.1. [Neither of the Parties shall during the currency of this Agreement and for a period of [12] months after its termination seek to entice away or recruit any employee of the other Party [or its associated companies] who is or was so employed during the currency of this Agreement].

29. Law and jurisdiction

29.1. This Agreement is governed by the law of England and Wales and is subject to the [exclusive] jurisdiction of the courts of England and Wales.

30. Third party rights

30.1. The Parties to this Agreement agree that it is not hereby intended that any rights should be conferred upon or enforceable by any third party as defined in the Contracts (Rights of Third Parties) Act 1999.

31. Schedules

31.1. The Schedules form part of this Agreement including any subsequent amendments made thereto.

Signed, etc.

SCHEDULE 1

Fund Fact Sheet Production and Fund Centre

1. The Service

1.1. The Service will consist of the usage of the Supplier's Fund Fact Sheet Production Platform for the production of Fund Fact Sheets and a web-based fund centre displaying fund-price, fund-performance, performance charts and hosting the Fund Factsheets.

1.2. Client Data

1.2.1. The Client will provide the Client Data that the Supplier will combine with the Supplier Data within the Fund Fact Sheet Production Platform. This will consist of all data other than that supplied by the Supplier. The Supplier will construct a series of Microsoft Excel workbooks for the Client Data to be collated into and then loaded into the Fund Fact Sheet Production Platform.

1.2.2. The Supplier will provide:

1.2.2.1. price (last working day's closing price at month end)

1.2.2.2. performance charts

1.2.2.3. performance numbers

1.2.2.4. rankings data

1.2.2.5. sector averages

1.2.2.6. benchmark data.

1.3. Usage and frequency

1.3.1. The Client will use the Fund Fact Sheet Production Platform to upload the Client Data. The Fund Fact Sheet Production Platform will combine the Client Data with the Supplier Data supplied by the Supplier and enable the Client to generate the Fund Fact Sheets.

1.3.2. The Client may use the Fund Fact Sheet Production Platform to produce Fund Fact Sheets on a monthly basis and as required to produce draft Fund Fact Sheets.

1.4. Format and design

1.4.1. The output format(s) and design(s) of the Fund Fact Sheets will be agreed between the Client and the Supplier at the outset of this contract. Subsequent alterations or additions to either the format or the design of the Fund Fact Sheets are not covered by this contract.

1.4.2. The output file format of the Fund Fact Sheets will be Portable Document Format ('PDF'), using the RGB colour space. Full colour PDFs will be provided, but there is no requirement for any professional print quality PDFs.

1.4.3. The design(s) of the Fund Facts Sheets is to follow as closely as possible the design(s) of the Client's existing Fund Fact Sheets as supplied to the Supplier.

1.5. Number of Fund Fact Sheets

1.5.1. A Fund Fact Sheet will be produced for each of the following funds:

1.5.1.1. ....

1.5.1.2. ....

1.6. Fund Centre

1.6.1. The Supplier shall deliver a series of web pages containing daily updating price and performance tables for all the Funds, with links to the Fact Sheets and a charting tool. The charting tool will allow the user to select funds, compare to sector averages and vary timescales.

2. Commencement Date

2.1. The Commencement date for this Service shall be [...].

3. Term

3.1. The Term for this Service shall be [...].

4. Fees

4.1. The Fee for this service shall be:

4.1.1. A one-off setup fee of £[...]

4.1.2. An annual fee of £[...]

4.2. Additional Funds can be added to the system at a cost of £[...] per fund per annum.

4.3. Costs for additional Fund Fact Sheets are based on the assumption that they fit the existing design templates. New design templates can be created as required, on a time and materials basis.

4.4. The Supplier charges development for new build at £[...] per day.

4.5. Fees shall be paid, with the addition of VAT, annually in advance upon invoicing by the Supplier in accordance with the following schedule: [...]

4.6. [The Fees will be subject to review on the Review Date. The Review Date for this Service will be the anniversary of the Commencement Date of this Service and each anniversary thereafter. From each Review Date for the period of 12 months thereafter the Fee will be the greater of the Fee payable immediately before the relevant Review Date and the revised Fee that is ascertained in accordance with the provisions set out in Clause 9 of the main Agreement].

Signed, etc.

PRECEDENT 13B   Information technology development, maintenance and support services contract

INFORMATION TECHNOLOGY DEVELOPMENT, MAINTENANCE AND SUPPORT SERVICES CONTRACT

THIS AGREEMENT dated [*date*] is made by and between:

1. [*Name*] a company incorporated in England and Wales under company number [*number*] and whose registered office is at [*address*] ('the Consultant'); and
2. [*Name*] a company incorporated in England and Wales under company number [*number*] and whose registered office is at [*address*] ('the Client').

RECITALS

1. The Consultant supplies a range of development, maintenance and support services connected with the provision and maintenance of information technology.
2. The Consultant is willing to provide the Services (as defined below) and the Client is willing to appoint the Consultant to provide the Services in accordance with the provisions of this Agreement.

DEFINITIONS

In this Agreement and the Schedules, the following words shall have the following meaning:

'Agreed Addresses'	Consultant: [*address*]; Client: [*address*].
['Anytime Support'	Urgent out of Standard Support Hours support cover as set out in Schedule 1 available [*24 hours a day* [except Christmas Day, Boxing Day and New Year's Day]].]
'Commencement Date'	The date on which a Service is commenced as set out in the Schedule 1.
'Delivery Date'	The delivery date for a Service or phase of a Service under Schedule 2.
'Fee'	The amounts set out in the Schedules to this Agreement in respect of each of the Services as may be varied from time to time.
'Party' and 'Parties'	The Consultant and the Client, and 'Party' shall mean either one of them.
'Review Date'	Any date from which the Consultant is entitled to increase the Fees for a Service as set out in Schedule 1 to this Agreement.
'Review Period'	A period beginning on any Review Date and ending on the day before the next Review Date, and qualified uses of the term are to be construed accordingly.
['RPI']	[The Retail Price Index maintained and published by the Office for National Statistics.]
'Schedules'	The Schedules attached to this Agreement and as varied or added to from time to time by written agreement.

'Service' and 'Support'	The service or services set out in the Schedules which the Client has agreed from time to time to receive from the Consultant and as may be varied or added to by the Parties by written agreement from time to time.
'Site[s]'	The location[s] of the System as specified in Schedule 3 and as varied from time to time.
'Standard Support'	Maintenance and support during Standard Support Hours.
'Standard Support Hours'	Monday to Friday 8am–6pm excluding bank holidays.
'System'	The Client's computer system, network and other components of the Client's information technology infrastructure as specified in Schedule 3.
'Term'	The minimum initial or renewal period that the Client agrees to receive a Service pursuant to this Agreement as set out in Schedule 1 and as varied from time to time.

INTERPRETATION

In this Agreement:

1. The singular includes the plural and one gender includes all.
2. References to Schedules and Clauses are to those in this Agreement.
3. Reference to a statutory provision includes any amendment or replacement provision relevant to the Agreement.
4. Reference to a document includes that document as amended, altered or replaced subsequent to the date of this Agreement.
5. Reference to writing includes facsimile transmission, e-mail, and similar media unless the context otherwise expressly provides.
6. Time expressed in days excludes the first day but includes the last day. If the last day does not fall on a normal business day in both England and Wales then the last day will be deemed to be the first normal business day.
7. The headings in this document do not form part of the Agreement.

OPERATIVE PROVISIONS

1. Duration of this Agreement

1.1. This Agreement shall continue from the date of its signing [until the ... of ... 20... *or* for a period of [...] years *or* until terminated by either Party under the provisions of Clause 16].

2. Services

2.1. The Consultant will provide the Service as set out in the Schedules as may be varied from time to time.

2.2. In the case of a Service set out in Schedule 1 the Consultant shall provide the Service from the Commencement Date.

2.3. In the case of a Service set out in Schedule 2 the Consultant shall deliver the Service as set out in the Schedule.

3. Consideration

3.1. In consideration for the Consultant providing the Service the Client shall pay the Fee as set out in the Schedules for each Service provided.

4. Provision of the Service

4.1. The Consultant shall use its best endeavours to provide the Service within the time limits set out in the Schedules. If it is unable to do so for any reason it will notify the Client as soon as practically possible and inform the Client of:

4.1.1. the reason for its being unable to provide the Service

4.1.2. when the Service will be resumed.

4.2. If the Consultant fails to respond within the time limits in Schedule 1 in relation to a Service set out in that Schedule on more than [6] successive occasions within the Term the Client shall be entitled to serve written notice of termination upon the Consultant in relation to the Service affected.

4.3. Failure to provide a Service will not arise if the reason for the failure is a breach of this Agreement by the Client or a *force majeure* event.

5. Services to be provided

5.1. The Services which the Consultant can provide are set out in the Schedules. The Client and the Consultant shall agree the provision of an individual Service including service levels, specification, Delivery Date (if applicable), details of delivery, the Term (if applicable) and the Fee payable and their agreement shall be signified by the signing of a copy of the relevant Schedule as varied from time to time.

5.2. A Schedule may be varied or added to as agreed by the Parties from time to time, in writing. Any variation or addition to a Schedule shall be clearly indicated (including the additional or different Fee to be paid by the Client) and a like procedure followed to that set out in Clause 5.1.

6. Obligations of the Client

6.1. During the currency of this Agreement the Client will ensure that the Client's staff and agents cooperate and assist the Consultant.

6.2. Where required the Client shall provide:

6.2.1. prompt and accurate information to the Consultant if and when a problem arises which requires support

6.2.2. access to its computers, computer network and other hardware to the Consultant and its agents and employees

6.2.3. all passwords, codes, keys and the like necessary for the carrying out of the Service by the Consultant whether on site or online

6.2.4. [temporary use during the Term of the Service of such computer and other equipment as the Consultant shall reasonably require]

6.2.5. [facilities for the [temporary] installation of such computer and other equipment as shall be necessary for the Consultant's provision of the Service]

6.2.6. [reasonable canteen and refreshment facilities [at its own expense] for the use of the Consultant's employees whilst providing a Service on site]

6.2.7. access to the Client's premises at all times reasonably necessary [including where appropriate outside normal office hours] for the purpose of carrying out a Service on site

6.2.8. such information as the Consultant reasonably requires for the performance of the Service.

6.3. In the event that the Client receives any notice, decision, notification or is the object of any enforcement action by a governmental or regulatory agency or body which is likely to affect the delivery of the Service by the Consultant, it will immediately inform the Consultant in writing indicating what action it is proposing to take in respect thereof.

7. Payment of Fee

7.1. A Fee shall be paid upon invoicing by the Consultant for each Service. [If the Client wishes to raise a purchase order to the Consultant prior to its being invoiced then it must do so and supply the order to the Consultant at least [1 month] before the Fee for the relevant Term is payable. For the avoidance of doubt the Fee will be due and payable on the relevant payment date whether any purchase order has been provided as set out herein and absent the timeous provision of a purchase order the Client will be invoiced prior to the beginning of a Term and required to pay as set out in the relevant Schedule].

7.2. If the Client does not make a payment by the date stated in an invoice or as otherwise provided for in this Agreement then the Consultant shall be entitled to:

7.2.1. charge interest on the outstanding amount at the rate of [5%] a year above the base lending rate of [...] Bank plc

7.2.2. require the Client to pay, in advance, for any Service (both including and in addition to the Service in respect of which it is in default) which has not yet been performed and

7.2.3. not perform any further Service.

8. Determination of revised Fees

8.1. The Fee for any Review Period is to be determined by the Consultant and notified in writing to the Client not less than [1] month prior to the relevant Review Date. [A Fee for any Review Period may not increase by a greater percentage than any percentage increase in the RPI between the beginning and end of the previous Review Period (or in the case of the first Review Period between the Commencement Date for a Service and its first Review date)].

8.2. [The Parties may agree a different figure from that set out in Clause 8.1, but in default of such agreement prior to the Review Date, the Fee payable shall be that set out in Clause 8.1].

8.3. Where the relevant Schedule provides for charging for the Service on an hourly or other time basis then the references in this Clause 8 to the Fee shall be construed as a reference to the hourly or other time rate.

9. Confidentiality

9.1. Each Party agrees not to disclose any confidential information provided by the other Party during the Term or prior to the Delivery Date (whichever is applicable) or at any time thereafter to any third party save where the law requires. Each Party also agrees not to use any such confidential information for any other purpose other than in connection with the provision of the Service and will not use the information for any business or other purpose of its own.

9.2. Each Party undertakes to procure that its employees, directors, agents and advisers and any other persons to whom it makes available confidential information shall also keep confidential the information the subject of this Clause 9.

9.3. The obligations in this Clause 9 shall continue after the termination of this Agreement.

10. Intellectual property

10.1. The Consultant owns all the intellectual property rights ('IPR') in any software it supplies to and/or develops for the Client in connection with the Service unless:

10.1.1. it belongs to a third party supplier in which case the Consultant will duly inform the Client

10.1.2. specific express written provision is made in the relevant Schedule or by amendment to this Agreement to the contrary.

10.2. In the case of software provided by the Consultant to which it owns the IPR absent any written agreement to the contrary any licence granted to the Client for its use shall continue only as long as the relevant Service is provided by the Consultant to the Client and all copies thereof must be either returned or destroyed at the direction of the Consultant when the Service is terminated.

11. Client's warranty

11.1. The Client warrants that it has all proper licences, permissions and where appropriate other IPR in all software installed on the System or to which it has access in the course of the operation of the System.

12. Use of sub-contractor

12.1. The Consultant may employ the services of a sub-contractor in order to deliver the Service to the Client. The Consultant shall in such case be responsible for ensuring that the Service provided by the sub-contractor is to the same or a comparable standard to that delivered or intended to be delivered by the Consultant.

13. Liability of the Consultant

13.1. The liability of the Consultant (and of any sub-contractor) under or in connection with this Agreement for the provision of the Service whether arising in contract, tort, negligence, breach of statutory duty or otherwise howsoever shall not exceed [a refund of that part of the Fee for that Service which has been paid by the Client to the Consultant under this Agreement]. The relevant Fee for the purpose of this Clause 13 will be that which relates to the particular Service in respect of which a successful claim is brought by the Client *or* the amount of professional negligence insurance cover carried by the Consultant which shall not be less than £[...]].

13.2. [The Consultant shall not be liable to the Client for any indirect, consequential or economic loss including but not limited to damage, costs or expenses of any description, loss of profit, business, goodwill, turnover or any other loss arising from its performance or non-performance of its obligations in connection with this Agreement whether arising from breach of contract, tort, breach of duty, negligence or any other cause of action].

13.3. Nothing in this Clause 13 shall limit or remove the Consultant's liability for causing personal injury or death.

14. Indemnity

14.1. The Client will indemnify the Consultant in respect of any losses, damage or liability the Consultant may incur as a result of the Client's acts or omissions, whether deliberate, accidental, negligent or reckless, in the course of the provision by the Consultant of the Service to the Client under this Agreement whether such acts or omissions amount to a breach of an express or implied obligation under this Agreement or a breach of any other legal requirement or obligation, code of practice, licence, consent, forbearance, approval, permission or rule.

14.2. For the avoidance of doubt losses, damage and liability shall include but not be limited to economic and commercial loss, loss of goodwill, legal and other costs associated with legal proceedings of any kind which the Consultant has to bring or to which it has to respond, fines, penalties, damages and any financial consequence whatever flowing directly or indirectly from the matters set out in this Clause 14.

15. Whole agreement and previous agreements

15.1. This Agreement supersedes and replaces any previous agreement between the Parties whether oral or in writing in relation to the provision of the Service. The Parties hereby agree that in entering into this Agreement they have not relied upon any warranty or representation made by or on behalf of the other Party save where expressly stated in this Agreement. The Parties hereby agree that this Agreement including the Schedules constitutes the whole agreement between the Parties in relation to the provision of the Service.

15.2. Nothing in this Clause 15 shall be construed as limiting or excluding either Party's liability to the other for fraud or deceit in inducing the making of this Agreement.

16. Termination of maintenance and support services

16.1. In the case of a Service set out in Schedule 1 the Service will start on the Commencement Date set out in the Schedule for each Service and will continue until terminated by either Party giving at least [3] months written notice in respect of each Service, such notice to expire at the end of the Term for that Service, as initially set or renewed, as the case may be. Otherwise, the Service will be renewed for a further Term equivalent in duration to the initial Term for that Service or as provided for under this Clause 16.

16.2. In the event that all Services under all Schedules have been terminated for whatever reason this Agreement shall itself lapse within [28] days of the end of the provision of the last remaining Service.

16.3. Without prejudice to the other remedies or rights a Party may have, the Consultant may terminate the provision of any Service at any time, on written notice to the Client, if the Client:

16.3.1. is [declared bankrupt *or* wound up due to insolvency]

16.3.2. makes or seeks a composition with its creditors

16.3.3. enters into or seeks an insolvent voluntary arrangement

16.3.4. becomes the subject of the appointment of a manager, receiver or liquidator

16.3.5. is the subject of an administration order

16.3.6. has its assets charged or seized for the satisfaction of a debt

16.3.7. seeks to challenge the Consultant's IPR

16.3.8. divulges confidential business information obtained from the Consultant

16.3.9. fails to comply with the terms of any software or data licence in connection with the Service

16.3.10. fails to pay any sum due under this Agreement for more than [28] days after the due date

16.3.11. fails to furnish any document or other information which the Client is obliged to provide within [28] days of its due date

16.3.12. is in breach of its obligations under this Agreement and in the case of a breach capable of remedy fails to remedy the same within [21] days after receipt of a notice giving full particulars of the breach and requiring it to be remedied.

17. Consequences of termination of the Service and/or this Agreement

17.1. Upon termination of the Service the Client must pay for the Service provided prior to the date of termination as well as any further expenditure incurred by the Consultant after the date of termination arising from commitments reasonably entered into by the Consultant prior to the date of termination but payable by the Consultant afterwards.

17.2. Upon termination of the last of the Services provided to the Client and consequently the termination of this Agreement, the Client shall return or destroy (as reasonably required by the Consultant) all documents, materials or other information, whether in hard copy or electronic form, in its possession or control which constitute or include any confidential information of the Consultant.

18. *Force majeure*

18.1. The Consultant shall not have any liability to the Client for any delay, omission, failure or inadequate performance of this Agreement which is the result of circumstances beyond the reasonable control of the Consultant. Where the Consultant is so affected in its performance of this Agreement it will notify the Client as soon as is reasonably possible in writing.

19. Amendments

19.1. This Agreement may only be amended or varied in writing signed by the Parties or their duly authorised representatives.

20. Assignment

20.1. Neither Party may assign, charge, mortgage, sub-contract, delegate or otherwise assign or transfer its rights or obligations under this Agreement save where express provision is made for the same in this Agreement, without the prior written consent of the other Party.

20.2. A Party may assign or transfer its rights under this Agreement if such assignment or transfer takes place in the context of the disposal of all of its business to which the Service is related provided that the proposed assignee or transferee undertakes to the Consultant directly in a form reasonably required by the Consultant to be bound by the obligations of the proposed assignor.

21. Waiver

21.1. No failure, neglect or delay in enforcing any of the terms of this Agreement by one Party may be construed as a waiver of any of that Party's rights in respect thereof nor such neglect, failure or delay a variation of the express terms of the Agreement.

22. No agency, partnership, etc.

22.1. Neither Party is for any purpose the agent or partner of the other as a result of anything arising from this Agreement and each Party hereby undertakes not to represent to any third party that it has any authority to act on that other Party's behalf.

23. Further action

23.1. The Parties agree that they will expeditiously carry out such further acts as may be necessary for the purpose of this Agreement including the execution and delivery of such instruments, deeds, licences, notifications as may be reasonably required by the other Party or by law.

24. Severance

24.1. In the event that any term of this Agreement is found to be invalid or otherwise unenforceable then such term shall be regarded and construed as severable from the Agreement so as not to affect the validity and enforceability of the remainder.

25. Notices

25.1. All notices under this Agreement shall be in writing and shall be delivered personally [or by first class, registered or recorded post] [or by facsimile transmission] in every case to the other Party's Agreed Address. [In the case of first class post notice will be deemed to be received [3] business days after the date of posting.]

26. Non-solicitation

26.1. [Neither of the Parties shall during the currency of this Agreement and for a period of [12] months after its termination seek to entice away or recruit any employee of the other Party [or its associated companies] who is or was so employed during the currency of this Agreement].

27. Law and jurisdiction

27.1. This Agreement is governed by the law of England and Wales and is subject to the [exclusive] jurisdiction of the courts of England and Wales.

28. Third party rights

28.1. The Parties to this Agreement agree that it is not hereby intended that any rights should be conferred upon or enforceable by any third party as defined in the Contracts (Rights of Third Parties) Act 1999.

29. Schedules

29.1. The Schedules form part of this Agreement including any subsequent amendments made thereto.

Signed, etc.

SCHEDULE 1
Support and Maintenance Service

1. Standard Support

1.1. The Commencement Date for Standard Support is [...].

1.2. The Review Date is [...] [and the anniversary of that date in each year thereafter].

1.3. The following Services are included in the support and maintenance Agreement and are available during Standard Support Hours.

1.3.1. Annual maintenance check

1.3.1.1. The annual maintenance check will cover those matters set out in the specification agreed and provided by the Consultant prior to the beginning of the Term and as varied or modified from time to time thereafter.

1.3.2. Telephone support

1.3.2.1. During Standard Support Hours the Client can contact the Consultant on one of the telephone numbers supplied and the Consultant will endeavour to provide, where possible, diagnosis and advice. If the problem cannot be adequately addressed on the telephone or online the Consultant will attend the relevant Site as soon as practically possible and in any event within 24 hours.

1.3.3. Online support

1.3.3.1. The Consultant will provide support by internet link where appropriate.

1.3.4. On-site support

1.3.4.1. On-site support at the Site in the event that telephone support and online support does not resolve a problem in the System.

2. [Anytime Support

2.1. [Telephone] [on-site] [and] [online] support is available at any time [excluding Christmas Day, Boxing Day and New Year's Day].

2.2. Anytime Support is intended only to be used for urgent problems which seriously compromise the operation of the System or an essential part thereof.

2.3. The Consultant in his reasonable discretion will decide what form of support is required on an incident by incident basis].

3. Response times

3.1. For telephone and online support the Consultant will, upon being fully notified of the problem, endeavour to provide immediate response during Standard Support Hours, [and within [...] hours during other times if the Client has agreed to have Anytime Support].

3.2. For on-site support a visit will be arranged as soon as practically possible for urgent matters and in any event within [...] hours. For routine maintenance or other non-urgent support the Consultant will arrange a visit at a time mutually convenient to both Parties.

4. Fee

4.1. Standard Support

4.1.1. There is an annual charge of £[...] payable [at the beginning of each Term] *or* [by [...] monthly instalments].

4.1.2. In the event of the System being materially modified, extended, changed or developed during the Term the Consultant reserves the right to amend the annual charge in whole or in part for the current Term and/or thereafter. Such variation shall be agreed in writing. In the event that the Parties are unable to agree a variation the Consultant shall be at liberty to serve a notice terminating the Service in not less than 30 days from the date of service thereof. In such event any annual fee already paid shall be refunded in respect of each complete calendar month remaining from the date of termination (not the date of the notice).

4.1.3. Standard Support includes:

4.1.3.1. [[...] hours per month of telephone support

4.1.3.2. [...] hours per month of online support

4.1.3.3. [...] hours per month of on-site support].

4.2. Additional support will be provided at the following hourly rates:

4.2.1. £[...] per hour for telephone support

4.2.2. £[...] per hour for online support

4.2.3. £[...] per hour for on-site.

4.3. [On-site hourly times exclude travel to and from the site for which no charge is made [subject to fair usage]].

4.4. [Anytime Support

4.4.1. There is an annual charge of £[...] payable [at the beginning of each Term *or* by [...] monthly instalments]. Anytime Support includes Standard Support and the Fee for additional work done during Standard Support Hours will be in accordance with the prices for additional Standard Support.

4.4.2. In the event of the System being materially modified, extended, changed or developed during the Term the Consultant reserves the right to amend the annual charge in whole or in part for the current Term and/or thereafter. Such variation shall be agreed in writing. In the event that the Parties are unable to agree a variation the Consultant shall be at liberty to serve a notice terminating the Service in not less than 30 days from the date of service thereof. In such event any annual fee already paid shall be refunded in respect of each complete calendar month remaining from the date of termination (not the date of the notice).

4.4.3. Anytime Support includes:

4.4.3.1. [...] hours per month of telephone support

4.4.3.2. [...] hours per month of online support

4.4.3.3. [...] hours per month of on-site support].

4.5. Additional Anytime Support will be charged at the following rates:

4.5.1. £[...] per hour for telephone support

4.5.2. £[...] per hour for online support

4.5.3. £[...] per hour for on-site support.]

4.6. Wherever reasonably possible the Consultant will provide an estimate of the likely cost of carrying out work. The Consultant will attempt to keep the Client appraised of progress and the likely completion time of any work being carried out.

5. Materials

5.1. The Fee for Standard [and Anytime] Support does not include materials of any kind including software, hardware or consumables. These will invoiced for as extras at the Consultant's standard prices, details of which will be provided on request.

Signed, etc.

SCHEDULE 2

Development and Project Service

1. Scope of Service

1.1. The Consultant will provide advice on:

1.1.1. software needs and where appropriate development, enhancement and modifications

1.1.2. system development and improvement

1.1.3. hardware modification, development and improvement.

1.2. The Consultant will provide where required:

1.2.1. written estimates and where appropriate quotes for implementing any of the above

1.2.2. full specification including prices of individual components.

1.3. Where required the Consultant will write or procure software. For the avoidance of doubt, the IPR in any software, other than that sourced from third parties, shall belong exclusively to the Consultant unless otherwise expressly agreed in writing. Where software is written by or produced from a sub-contractor the IPR in the software shall belong exclusively to the Consultant unless otherwise expressly agreed in writing.

1.4. [Where software other than that of a third party is supplied by the Consultant during the course of the provision of the Service the Client will first enter into a separate licence agreement with the Consultant as a condition of use of such software. Such licence agreement will provide, inter alia, for:

1.4.1. the period of the licence

1.4.2. a commitment by the Consultant to provide updates (where appropriate) and support for the software during the period of the licence].

1.5. The details of the Service to be provided are set out in the appendix to this Schedule.

2. Fee

2.1. The Fee for this Service shall be as follows:

2.1.1. [*Set out details of cost including where appropriate hourly rate, fixed price etc., consumables, etc.*].

3. Delivery date

3.1. The Delivery date for this Service shall be [*Set out details of phases, etc.*].

Signed, etc.

SCHEDULE 3

The System

[*Set out details and specification of the Client's computer network, installations and equipment and details of the Site[s]*]

Signed, etc.

PRECEDENT 13C   Software licence agreement

SOFTWARE LICENCE AGREEMENT

THIS AGREEMENT dated [*date*] is made by and between:

1. [*Name*] a company incorporated in England and Wales under company number [*number*] and whose registered office is at [*address*] ('the Licensor'); and
2. [*Name*] a company incorporated in England and Wales under company number [*number*] and whose registered office is at [*address*] ('the Licensee').

RECITALS

1. The Licensor has developed certain computer software programs and applications.
2. The Licensor has agreed to grant the Licensee a non-exclusive licence to use certain software program[s] on its computer system.

DEFINITIONS

In this Agreement and the Schedules, the following words shall have the following meaning:

'Agreed Address'	The address of each Party as set out in Schedule 4.
'Fee'	The sum[s] payable under this Agreement for the non-exclusive use of the Software by the Licensee as set out in Schedule 2 and as varied from time to time.
'Intellectual Property Rights' ('IPR')	All rights relating to the protection by law of any process, discovery, design, formula, invention, drawing, specification, mark, trade mark, get-up or other work including but not limited to those rights which may be protected by any form of registration including where applicable the right to seek such registration available for the protection of any discovery, invention, name, design, process or works in which copyright or any rights in the nature of copyright subsist and all patents, copyrights, registered designs, design rights, trade marks, service marks and other forms of protection from time to time subsisting in relation to the same, including the right to apply for any such registration.
'Licence'	The licence granted by the Licensor to the Licensee pursuant to this Agreement.
'Party and Parties'	The Licensor and the Licensee.
'Site[s]'	The location[s] of the System.
'Software'	The software the subject matter of this Licence details of which are set out in Schedule 1. The Software includes all written materials in connection therewith.
'Specification'	The specification of the Software set out in Schedule 1.
'System'	The Client's computer system, network, and other components of the Client's information technology infrastructure as specified in Schedule 3 and as may be amended from time to time.
'Term'	The period for which the Licence is valid as set out in Schedule 2.

INTERPRETATION

In this Agreement:

1. The singular includes the plural and one gender includes all.
2. References to Schedules and Clauses are to those in this Agreement.
3. Reference to a statutory provision includes any amendment or replacement provision relevant to the Agreement.
4. Reference to a document includes that document as amended, altered or replaced subsequent to the date of this Agreement.
5. Reference to writing includes facsimile transmission, e-mail, and similar media unless the context otherwise expressly provides.
6. Time expressed in days excludes the first day but includes the last day. If the last day does not fall on a normal business day in both England and Wales then the last day will be deemed to be the first normal business day.
7. The headings in this document do not form part of the Agreement.

OPERATIVE PROVISIONS

1. Grant of Licence

1.1. The Licensor hereby grants to the Licensee the Licence to use the Software for the duration of the Term on the System on the terms and conditions set out in this Agreement.

1.2. The Licensee may use the Software only for its own internal business use and may not make it available to third parties [nor use it for any outsourcing purposes or services].

1.3. The Software may only be used on the System at the Site[s]. Any additions or material variations to either the System or the Site[s] must be notified to the Licensor in writing. Additions or material variations to the System shall invalidate this Licence unless prior written consent is obtained from the Licensor for the continued use of the Software (which may be subject to an additional or increased Fee).

1.4. Mere replacement of the System or parts thereof with new but comparable equipment or substitution of a new Site for the old shall not necessarily count as an addition or material variation for the purpose of this Licence but prior notification must still be given to the Licensor as a condition of grant of this Licence.

1.5. The Licensee acknowledges that it is licensed to use the Software only in accordance with the express terms of this Agreement.

2. The Term

2.1. The Term of the licence shall be as set out in Schedule 2 unless terminated under the provisions of Clause 17 or any other Clause.

3. Payment

3.1. The Licence Fee shall be paid by the Licensee as provided in Schedule 2 and is exclusive of VAT and any other sales tax or duty.

3.2. The Fee or any part thereof or any subsequent charge in respect of the Software shall be payable by the Licensee within [14] days of receipt of an invoice in respect thereof.

3.3. The Licensor shall be entitled to charge interest on late payments at the yearly rate of [...]% per annum above the lending rate of [...] Bank plc calculated daily whether before or after judgment.

4. Deliverables

4.1. Unless expressly agreed otherwise delivery of the Software will be effected by the delivery of one copy in an appropriate machine readable electronic format to the Licensee.

5. Installation

5.1. Where appropriate the Licensor will install the Software in accordance with the specification in Schedule 1.

6. Replacement copies

6.1. In the event that the Software delivered is subsequently lost, damaged or corrupted the Licensor will deliver a replacement copy provided such loss, damage or corruption occurs during the Term. The Licensor reserves the right to make a reasonable charge for the cost of a replacement including the cost of re-installation.

7. Provision of test data

7.1. During or after installation the Licensee agrees to provide suitable test data where required by the Licensor.

8. Acceptance of the Software

8.1. The Licensee shall be deemed to accept the Software once the Licensor has demonstrated to the Licensee's reasonable satisfaction that it is operating correctly and in accordance with the specification set out in Schedule 1.

8.2. In the event that the Licensor is unable to demonstrate within [7] days of its installation that the Software is operating correctly and in accordance with the specification set out in Schedule 1 the Licensee shall be entitled to reject it and receive a full refund of any Fee it has already paid. Alternatively the Licensee may allow the Licensor a further [7] days to enable the Licensor to correct any errors. Failure to demonstrate by the end of the further [7] day period that the Software is operating correctly and in accordance with the specification set out in Schedule 1 will entitle the Licensee to reject the Software as set out above.

8.3. The Licensee will not be entitled to reject the Software if the reason for the inability of the Licensor to demonstrate that the Software is operating correctly and in accordance with the specification set out in Schedule 1 is that there is a defect in the System in whole or in part which was not reasonably apparent at the time the Licence was ordered and which is not reasonably remediable. In such eventuality the Licensee may rescind this Agreement on condition that it pays the reasonable costs and expenses of the Licensor including but not limited to:

8.3.1. installation costs calculated [*on the normal hourly rate charged by the Licensor for maintenance and support as set out in its normal terms and conditions*]

8.3.2. reasonable development costs relating specifically to the Licensor's intended use of the Software.

9. Making copies

9.1. The Licensee may make copies of the Software to the extent reasonably necessary for its installation, operation and maintenance only with the prior written consent of the Licensor. Such copies will be the property of the Licensor and may only be used in accordance with the terms of this Licence. The Licensee shall ensure that all such copies bear the Licensor's proprietary notice.

10. Modifications to the Software

10.1. No modification or adaption of the Software is permissible without the prior written consent of the Licensor. Prior to seeking any such consent the Licensee shall request the Licensor to make such modification or adaption itself.

10.2. Subject to such consent being obtained the Licensee may modify the Software only for the purpose of its internal use and in accordance with the intended use as set out in Schedule 1. Such modified Software, and any information relating to it which the Licensee may have obtained as a result of any decompiling, reverse engineering, disassembling or analysis may not be transferred to, supplied to or in any way made available for, the use of third parties. All such modified versions of the Software shall be subject to this Licence as if the same had not been modified.

10.3. Subject to this Clause 10, the Licensee undertakes not to translate, adapt, vary, modify, disassemble, decompile, reverse engineer or correct the Software save as is permitted by the Copyright, Designs and Patent Act 1988.

11. Security

11.1. During the Term and until all copies of the Software have been destroyed or returned to the Licensor thereafter the Licensee shall be responsible for ensuring the safety of the Software and the prevention of any breach by a third party of the Licensor's IPR in relation thereto.

11.2. The Licensee shall undertake to keep a complete record of all copies made of the Software and to make such record available to the Licensor upon reasonable notice.

12. Intellectual Property Rights

12.1. The Licensee acknowledges that the IPR and all other proprietary rights in the Software belong exclusively to the Licensor. The Licensee undertakes to notify the Licensor in writing forthwith of any infringement or other unauthorised use of the Software of which it becomes aware.

12.2. In the event that any claim is made against the Licensee by any third party arising from or related to any claim by the third party of infringement of its alleged IPR or any other proprietary right in the Software by the Licensee then the Licensee shall forthwith inform the Licensor in writing and the Licensor shall at its own expense take such action as is necessary to resist or otherwise address such claim. The Licensee hereby undertakes in such circumstances to allow and permit the Licensor to have sole conduct of any negotiation or litigation in relation thereto insofar as the same is consistent with law.

12.3. If any claim of infringement of IPR or other proprietary right in the Software is for whatever reason successful against the Licensee (other than where such claim is successful because the Licensee has acted in a way inconsistent with its obligations under this Agreement) then the Licensee shall be indemnified by the Licensor provided that it has acted at all times with the knowledge and consent of the Licensor and/or as is required by law.

12.4. If at any time during the Term it comes to the attention of the Licensor that use of the Software by the Licensee as permitted under this Licence would or is likely to constitute an infringement of a third party's IPR or other proprietary rights in the Software then it may:

12.4.1. obtain if possible a licence for the Licensee to use the Software

12.4.2. replace or modify the Software so as to avoid such infringement but so as to render the same or comparable function as the Software. Such replacement or modification shall be at the Licensor's expense.

12.5. If neither of the above courses of action is in the opinion of the Licensor reasonable (including but not limited to on grounds of cost) then the Licensee shall return the Software, this Agreement will be terminated and any sums expended by it for the acquisition of this Licence will be refunded within [14] days.

12.6. The Licensor shall not be liable in respect of any claim for infringement of a third party's property rights arising from the use of the Software:

12.6.1. in any way other than that contained within the specification in Schedule 1

12.6.2. on any equipment other than that contained within the System as set out in Schedule 3

12.6.3. in any place other than the Site[s]

12.6.4. in a form modified without the consent of the Licensor.

13. Warranties

13.1. The Licensor warrants that:

13.1.1. the Software will conform to the Specification and provide the functionality described therein for a minimum of [...] months

13.1.2. the Licensor will provide the necessary training and reference manuals to use the Software effectively

13.1.3. the Software is compatible with the licensed programs set out in Schedule 1

13.1.4. it has taken all reasonable precautions to ensure that no known viruses or damaging agents are present in the Software when delivered.

13.2. The Licensor will remedy any defect within [4] weeks of written notification of such defect or will replace the Software if more appropriate.

13.3. The following events shall render the warranties void and unenforceable:

13.3.1. incorrect use, operation or corruption of the Software by the Licensee or anyone authorised by it to use the Software

13.3.2. unauthorised modifications to the Software

13.3.3. use or attempted use of the Software in equipment or with programs not included in Schedule 1.

13.4. To the extent permitted by law, the Licensor:

13.4.1. provides no warranty in respect of any third party programs. The Licensor will however, whenever possible, pass on to the Licensee the benefit of any warranty attaching to a third party program supplied by the Licensee in connection with the Software

13.4.2. provides no warranty that the Software is free from error nor that the Licensee shall enjoy use of the Software without interruption due to error or defect

13.4.3. excludes all warranties in respect of the Software regarding quality and fitness for purpose save where expressly included in this Agreement.

14. Insurance

14.1. The Licensor will maintain professional negligence, employers' liability, third party liability and product liability insurance cover during the Term of this Agreement to the minimum sum of £[...] and will on written request provide appropriate certificates to the Licensee within [14] days if receiving such notice.

15. Indemnities and limitation of liability

15.1. The Licensor shall indemnify the Licensee:

15.1.1. in an unlimited sum in relation to death or injury caused by the Licensor and its employees in the course of performance of this Agreement

15.1.2. up to a limit of £[...] for damage to property (other than intangible property) caused by the negligence of the Licensor or its employees or by any defect in the Software. This limit shall apply to a single event or series of connected events.

15.2. The Licensor shall not be liable to the Licensee for any indirect, consequential or economic loss including but not limited to damage, costs or expenses of any description, loss of data, loss of profit, business, goodwill, turnover or any other loss arising from its performance or non-performance of its obligations in connection with this Agreement whether arising from breach of contract, tort, breach of duty, negligence or any other cause of action save in respect of personal injury or death.

15.3. The Licensor's liability for direct loss or damage, except for personal injury, death or damage to non-tangible property shall be limited to [the sum of £[...] or the maximum sum for which the Licensor carries professional negligence insurance whichever is the lesser *or* a sum representing the Fee for one year of the Licence].

15.4. It is hereby agreed by the Parties that the limitations and exclusions in this Clause 15 shall be for the benefit also of the employees, sub-contractors and suppliers of the Licensor.

15.5. The Parties hereby agree and acknowledge that the limitations and exclusions contained in this Clause 15 are reasonable in the context of this Agreement.

16. Confidential information

16.1. The Licensee agrees not to disclose any confidential information provided by the Licensor during the Term or at any time thereafter to any third party save where the law requires. The Licensee also agrees not to use any such confidential information for any other purpose other than in connection with the use of the Software for the purpose set out in the Specification and will not use the information for any other business or other purpose of its own. For the avoidance of doubt such information includes but is not limited either in type, *genus* or subject to:

16.1.1. all business information supplied to the Licensee by the Licensor regarding the Software

16.1.2. all trade secrets, processes, formulae and code.

16.2. [For the proper protection of the confidential information the Licensee will ensure that:

16.2.1. any employee or member of its staff, whether temporary or permanent, will at the commencement of their employment and no later be provided with a contract of employment or engagement which will include a like obligation to that of the Licensee in respect of confidential information

16.2.2. any [director *or* partner] of the Licensee or any associated [company *or* firm] will be required to provide, in a form approved by the Licensor, an undertaking in regard to confidential information in like form to that set out above in relation to the Licensee before being given access to confidential information].

16.3. The Licensee hereby undertakes promptly to inform the Licensor of any unauthorised disclosure of confidential information by or to any third party and to assist the Licensor in any appropriate remedial action the Licensor should take.

16.4. This Clause 16 shall remain in full force and effect notwithstanding any termination of the Licence or this Agreement.

17. Termination

17.1. [The Licensee may terminate the Licence at any time by giving at least [...] days notice in writing to the Licensor during the Term].

17.2. In the event that the Licensee:

17.2.1. fails to remedy any remediable breach of this Agreement of which it has been notified in writing by the other Party within [...] days

17.2.2. commits any irremediable material breach or persistently commits any remediable breach of this Agreement

17.2.3. permanently discontinues the use of the Software

the Licensor may terminate this Agreement forthwith.

17.3. [In the event that the Licensee fails to make any payment on time as required by this Agreement the Licensor may terminate this Agreement upon giving [...] days notice of its intention to do so].

18. Effect of termination

18.1. Upon termination of the Licence the Licensee shall return or destroy (as reasonably required by the Licensor) all copies of the Software in its possession or control and certify to the Licensor that it has done the same.

18.2. Termination of the Licence shall not bring to an end obligations under this Agreement expressed to continue after its termination.

19. Data protection

19.1. Both Parties undertake to comply with the provisions of the Data Protection Act 1998 and other comparable or related legislation insofar as it relates to the provisions and obligations of the Parties under this Agreement.

20. No agency, partnership, etc.

20.1. Neither Party is for any purpose the agent or partner of the other as a result of anything arising from this Agreement and each Party hereby undertakes not to represent to any third party that it has any authority to act on that other Party's behalf.

21. Notices

21.1. All notices under this Agreement shall be in writing and shall be delivered personally [or by first class, registered or recorded post] [or by facsimile transmission] in every case to the other Party's Agreed Address. [In the case of first class post notice will be deemed to be received [3] business days after the date of posting.]

22. Amendments

22.1. Any variation of the terms of this Agreement must be in writing signed by both Parties.

23. Assignment

23.1. Neither Party may assign, charge, mortgage, sub-contract, delegate or otherwise assign or transfer its rights or obligations under this Agreement and Licence save where express provision is made for the same in this Agreement, without the prior written consent of the other Party.

23.2. A Party may assign or transfer its rights under this Agreement and Licence if such assignment or transfer takes place in the context of the disposal of:

    23.2.1. in the case of the Licensee that part of the business which uses the Software

    23.2.2. in the case of the Licensor that part of its business which will be responsible for the Licensor's continuing obligations under this Agreement

provided that the proposed assignee or transferee undertakes to the other Party directly in a form reasonably required by that other Party to be bound by the obligations of the proposed assignor.

24. Whole agreement and previous agreements

24.1. This Agreement supersedes and replaces any previous agreement between the Licensor and the Licensee whether oral or in writing in relation to the Licence. The Parties hereby agree that in entering into this Agreement they have not relied upon any warranty or representation made by or on behalf of the other Party save where expressly stated in this Agreement. The Parties hereby agree that this Agreement constitutes the whole agreement between the Parties in respect of the Licence.

25. *Force majeure*

25.1. The Licensor shall not have any liability to the Licensee for any delay, omission, failure or inadequate performance of this Agreement which is the result of circumstances beyond the reasonable control of the Licensor. Where the Licensor is so affected in its performance of this Agreement it will notify the Licensee as soon as is reasonably possible in writing.

26. Waiver

26.1. No failure or delay on the part of either Party to exercise the whole or any part of any right or remedy under this Agreement shall be construed or operate as a waiver of that right in whole or in part.

27. Invalid clauses

27.1. In the event that any term of this Agreement is found to be invalid or otherwise unenforceable then such term shall be regarded and construed as severable from the Agreement so as not to affect the validity and enforceability of the remainder.

28. Time of the essence

28.1. Time shall be of the essence in this Agreement in respect of any time limit, date, period or term whether as originally set out herein or by any subsequent variation or agreement.

29. Use of sub-contractor

29.1. The Licensor may employ the services of a sub-contractor to perform its obligations under this Agreement. The Licensor shall in such case be responsible for ensuring that the service provided by the sub-contractor is to the same or a comparable standard to that delivered or intended to be delivered by the Licensor.

30. Set off

30.1. The Licensor may set off against any liability it may have to the Licensee whether liquidated or unliquidated any sum it is due from the Licensee.

31. Third party rights

31.1. The Parties to this Agreement agree that it is not hereby intended that any rights should be conferred upon or enforceable by any third party as defined in the Contracts (Rights of Third Parties) Act 1999.

32. Law and jurisdiction

32.1. This Agreement is governed by the law of England and Wales and is subject to the [exclusive] jurisdiction of the courts of England and Wales subject to the following.

32.2. If the dispute between the parties is one regarding the functions or capabilities of the Software then such dispute shall be referred to the President of the British Computer Society or its successor who shall be requested to nominate an expert to act as expert not arbitrator. The costs of the expert shall be borne by both parties in equal measure subject to the expert's determination otherwise. His decision shall be binding and final on both parties subject to his being in manifest error.

33. Non-solicitation

33.1. [Neither of the Parties shall during the currency of this Agreement and for a period of [12] months after its termination seek to entice away or recruit any employee of the other Party [or its associated companies] who is or was so employed during the currency of this Agreement].

34. Schedules

34.1. The Schedules form part of this Agreement including any subsequent amendments made thereto.

SCHEDULE 1

Details and Specification of the Software

[Insert details and specification of the Software]

Signed, etc.

SCHEDULE 2

The Term and the Fee

[*Insert details of the Term and the Fee*]

Signed, etc.

SCHEDULE 3

The System

[*Insert details of the System*]

Signed, etc.

SCHEDULE 4

Parties' Agreed Addresses

[*Insert the Agreed Addresses of the Parties*]

Signed, etc.

14

Joint ventures

14.1 Introduction

A joint venture (JV) is essentially an arrangement between two or more commercial entities whereby they agree to pool resources and/or cooperate with a view to achieving a profit from a specific enterprise or undertaking.

This chapter is intended to assist the practitioner in drawing up simple JV agreements where the relationship is governed purely by contract and falls short of any corporate merger or partnership. The participating entities remain strictly distinct.

There are relative merits and demerits of contractual JVs. The principal advantages are:

(a) they are comparatively simple to set up as there are no structural changes to the entities themselves;

(b) they are very flexible and can usually be terminated without undue difficulty;

(c) their tax affairs are very straightforward as, not being a distinct legal entity, the JV does not itself have a tax liability;

(d) the possibility of liability being incurred by one entity which will also be a liability of the other, is usually less than in the case of a partnership;

(e) little or no transferring of assets is involved which minimises costs and potential tax liabilities to the parties.

The principal disadvantages are essentially the obverse of the advantages, i.e.:

(a) the lack of structural re-enforcement may militate against long-term involvement and investment;

(b) keeping the tax affairs of the participating entities separate may not always be advantageous;

(c) there is no limitation of liability per se (although the participants may shield themselves individually).

Contractual JVs are therefore best suited to one-off projects or cooperation in a specific area for a defined time period. Typically this would occur when different entities wish to bid together for a specific contract.

The precedent provides a flexible contract for a contract based joint venture (**Precedent 14A**).

PRECEDENT 14A   Agreement between two parties to develop a product

AGREEMENT BETWEEN TWO PARTIES TO DEVELOP A PRODUCT

THIS AGREEMENT is made the [... day of ...] ('the Commencement Date') BETWEEN:

1. [*Name of company*] a company incorporated in England under number [*registration number*] whose registered office is at [*address*] ('the Designer'); and
2. [*Name of company*] a company incorporated in England under number [*registration number*] whose registered office is at [*address*] ('the Manufacturer').

RECITALS

1. The Designer is [*a designer of industrial vacuum cleaners*].
2. The Manufacturer is a manufacturer of, inter alia, [*industrial vacuum cleaners*].
3. The Designer and Manufacturer have agreed to design and manufacture together [*a new industrial vacuum cleaner*] ('the Product') and thereafter to market and sell it in the United Kingdom and abroad [under the designer's name].
4. Accordingly the Designer and the Manufacturer have agreed to enter into various mutual commitments and obligations as set out in this Agreement [for the time specified herein].

DEFINITIONS

In this Agreement the following definitions apply:

'Agreed Addresses'	The agreed addresses of the Parties as set out in Schedule 1.
'IPR'	All intellectual property rights relating to the protection by law of any process, discovery, design, formula, invention, drawing, specification, mark, trade mark, get-up or other work including but not limited to those rights which may be protected by any form of registration including where applicable the right to seek such registration available for the protection of any discovery, invention, name, design, process or works in which copyright or any rights in the nature of copyright subsist and all patents, copyrights, registered designs, design rights, trade marks, service marks and other forms of protection from time to time subsisting in relation to the same, including the right to apply for any such registration.
'Material[s]'	Designs, drawings, calculations, recorded data, papers, reports, specifications, notes, whether in hard copy or electronic format, models, mock-ups and any other information relating to the Product.
'Party' and 'Parties'	The Designer and the Manufacturer.
'Premises'	The factory at [...] belonging to the Manufacturer.
'Project'	The designing, manufacturing, marketing and selling of the Product.
'RPI'	The Retail Price Index maintained and published by the United Kingdom Office for National Statistics.

['Royalty']	[A royalty payable to the Designer in respect of each unit of Product sold to a third party by the Manufacturer under the provisions of this Agreement and as set out in Schedule 3].
'Term'	The period that this Agreement remains in force including any extension or renewal of the original Term.
'Tooling'	The equipment and tooling necessary for the manufacture of the Product.

INTERPRETATION

In this Agreement:

1. The singular includes the plural and one gender includes all.
2. References to Schedules and Clauses are to those in this Agreement.
3. Reference to a statutory provision includes any amendment or replacement provision relevant to the Agreement.
4. Reference to a document includes that document as amended, altered or replaced subsequent to the date of this Agreement.
5. Reference to writing includes facsimile transmission, e-mail, and similar media unless the context otherwise expressly provides.
6. Time expressed in days excludes the first day but includes the last day. If the last day does not fall on a normal business day in both England and Wales then the last day will be deemed to be the first normal business day.
7. The headings in this document do not form part of the Agreement.

OPERATIVE PROVISIONS

1. Nature of this Agreement

1.1. This Agreement relates only to the Project as a joint venture. It does not constitute either Party the agent of the other nor a partnership between the Parties.

2. Term of this Agreement

2.1. The Term of this Agreement will be [...] years. The Term may be extended or renewed by written agreement between the Parties. In the absence of agreement this Agreement will expire by effluxion of time on the [...] anniversary of its commencement date.

3. Timetable for pre-production work

3.1. The Parties agree to carry out pre-production design and implementation work on the Project in accordance with the details set out in Schedule 2 to this Agreement.

4. Manufacture and sale of the Product

4.1. It is agreed by the Parties that [the Product will be exclusively marketed under the Designer's name and sold only by it *or* the Product will be sold by the Designer and by the Manufacturer to third parties for resale under the third party's own name].

4.2. [The Tooling will be used only for the manufacture of the Product].

4.3. Sales to the Designer

4.3.1. The Manufacturer will manufacture and supply the Product to the Designer at the prices set out in Schedule 4 during the Term. [The resale price shall be at the discretion of the Designer after consulting with the Manufacturer].

4.3.2. The Manufacturer undertakes to use its best endeavours to provide a minimum of [...] units of the Product per month for purchase by the Designer from the conclusion of the design stage [and will use its best endeavours to supply the full number of units of the Product whatever the size of the order from the Designer].

4.3.3. [The Designer will order units of the Product in batches of not less than [... *thousand units*]].

4.3.4. [The Designer undertakes to purchase a minimum of [...] units per month].

4.3.5. Sales to the Designer of the Product will be on [the Manufacturer's standard terms and conditions as varied from time to time. Where those terms and conditions are inconsistent with the terms of this Agreement, this Agreement shall prevail].

4.3.6. [The Designer undertakes not to purchase a similar product to the Product from any other manufacturer [for sale inside the United Kingdom]].

4.4. [**Sales to third parties**

4.4.1. [The Product shall not be supplied to any third party for sale in the [*United Kingdom*].

4.4.2. The Manufacturer will pay a Royalty to the Designer in respect of each unit of Product sold in accordance with the provisions of Schedule 3].

4.5. Conformity with pre-production samples

4.5.1. Unless expressly agreed to the contrary all units of the Product whether supplied to the Designer or third parties shall conform to the standard and specification of the approved pre-production samples.

5. Termination

5.1. Prior to completion of the Tooling

5.1.1. In the event that the Parties cannot agree all of the matters set out Schedule 2 prior to preparation of the Tooling either Party may terminate this Agreement by giving [...] days notice in writing to the other Party. If this Agreement is terminated under the provisions of this Clause then no liabilities shall accrue to either Party in respect of it as a result of termination. Nothing in this Clause shall affect the liability of either Party for any breaches which pre-date such termination.

5.2. After completion of the Tooling

5.2.1. This Agreement will expire by effluxion of time unless renewed or extended on the [...] anniversary of the Commencement Date.

5.2.2. After completion in full or in part of the Tooling either Party may terminate this Agreement by serving written notice on the other Party if:

5.2.2.1. the Party upon whom notice is served has committed a material breach of this Agreement which is incapable of remedy or

5.2.2.2. the Party upon whom notice is served has committed a remediable material breach but has failed to remedy it within [...] days of being served with notice to effect such remedy.

5.2.3. For the avoidance of doubt any such termination as is envisaged in this Clause 5.2 is without prejudice to the right of either Party to seek to rely upon rights already accrued under this Agreement and to any rights of either Party which are deemed to survive its termination.

5.2.4. The Agreement shall in any event terminate when the Tooling is no longer capable of producing the Product to approved pre-production standard.

5.3. Termination due to insolvency

5.3.1. Either Party may terminate this Agreement forthwith in the event that the other Party:

5.3.1.1. is [declared bankrupt *or* wound up due to insolvency]

5.3.1.2. makes or seeks a composition with its creditors

5.3.1.3. enters into or seeks an insolvent voluntary arrangement

5.3.1.4. becomes the subject of the appointment of a manager, receiver or liquidator

5.3.1.5. is the subject of an administration order

5.3.1.6. has its assets charged or seized for the satisfaction of a debt.

6. Intellectual property rights

6.1. Each Party shall retain IPR in all Materials it has created or has had created prior to or outside of this Agreement.

6.2. The IPR in the Materials created jointly by the Parties in pursuance of this Agreement shall be treated by the Parties as belonging to them jointly.

6.3. Where the Materials incorporate Material the IPR of which was the property of one Party the IPR of the incorporated Material shall remain with that Party.

6.4. Where new joint IPR are created both Parties shall cooperate to ensure that appropriate protection is obtained for those IPR by registration or such other legal means as are available [both in the UK and abroad].

6.5. Where any infringement is threatened or takes place to the joint IPR the Parties shall cooperate together to take such legal and other action as is reasonably prudent. In the event that one Party fails or refuses to take such action the other Party may take action on behalf of both Parties provided that it has:

6.5.1. informed the other Party that it intends to do so

6.5.2. obtained the written opinion of counsel:

6.5.2.1. as to what action should be taken and acts in accordance with that opinion

6.5.2.2. that such action stands a reasonable prospect of success and that it is proportionate to the risk.

6.6. If no agreement can be reached between the Parties as to the choice of counsel the Parties will jointly request the Chairman of the Bar to recommend counsel which recommendation shall be binding on the Parties.

6.7. In that event that action is taken by one or both Parties the costs thereof shall be borne equally by them (including those resulting from any adverse costs orders) and any damages recovered shall be divided equally between them after the deduction of costs and expenses.

6.8. Each Party grants to the other a licence to use its IPR as included in or created in the Materials for the purposes of this Agreement only and the other Party undertakes not to use it for any other purpose.

6.9. Upon termination of this Agreement each Party undertakes to return to the other that part of the Materials the IPR of which belongs to the other Party and to destroy forthwith all copies whether physical or electronic which it has not returned to the other Party.

7. Tooling

7.1. Upon termination of this Agreement the Tooling shall be destroyed unless either Party wishes to purchase the other Party's interest therein. In the event that one Party wishes to purchase the other's interest it shall pay to the other 50% of the agreed costs of the Tooling as set out in Schedule 2. In the event that both Parties wish to purchase the other's interest the Tooling shall go to the higher bidder. If the Designer purchases the Tooling it shall be responsible at its own cost for its removal from the Premises.

7.2. If either Party continues to use the Tooling to manufacture the Product then it shall pay a Royalty to the other Party as set out in Schedule 3.

8. Taxation

8.1. Each Party shall be liable for tax and duty due from it arising from its participation in the Project.

8.2. Each Party will indemnify the other in the event one Party is assessed and has to pay tax properly payable by the other.

8.3. Payments obliged to be made under this Agreement will be made without deduction by way of withholdings, set offs or counterclaims of any type except where a withholding or deduction is required by law. In the event that a withholding or deduction is made as required by law the Party making the withholding or deduction shall:

8.3.1. ensure that it withholds or deducts no more than the minimum the law requires

8.3.2. provide the other Party with a receipt, confirmation, certificate or such other document (whether electronic or physical) which will satisfy proper audit requirements

8.3.3. [make up to the other Party the sum deducted or withheld]

8.3.4. pay to the other Party promptly any refund or abatement it receives or is entitled to in relation to the sum deducted or withheld.

8.4. Each Party will use its best endeavours to minimise or avoid unnecessary tax liabilities being incurred by the other in respect of the Project.

8.5. All sums set out in this Agreement are exclusive of such VAT if any which may be payable.

9. *Force majeure*

9.1. In this Clause 9 *force majeure* includes but is not limited to civil commotion, war and terrorist action, state action, industrial action whether lawful or otherwise, non-availability of raw materials, components and labour at commercially viable prices, unavoidable accident, fire, flood, earthquake, subsidence, epidemic and other natural or physical disasters.

9.2. In the event that a Party is prevented by a *force majeure* event or happening from fulfilling any obligations under this Agreement it shall promptly so notify the other Party in writing [(for which purpose an acknowledged e-mail will suffice)]. The notifying Party shall thereafter be relieved from liability under this Agreement caused by the *force majeure* event or happening subject to its using its best endeavours to resume full performance as soon as possible.

9.3. In the event that a Party is informed of a *force majeure* event's preventing performance by the other Party and performance by that other Party does not recommence in full within [...] months then the Party not affected by the *force majeure* event or happening may give written notice to the other Party to terminate this Agreement in not less than 30 days from the date of receipt of the notice.

9.4. Such notice will have no effect if performance in full recommences within the 30 days or such greater period as the notice specifies.

9.5. If the Party affected by the *force majeure* event or happening is the Manufacturer and production or delivery is being delayed or prevented then the Designer may, if it has not served notice of termination under this Clause 9, serve a written notice on the Manufacturer that it will seek to obtain the Product from another source and the obligation under Clause 4.3.6 will be modified so as to permit such action by the Designer unless and until the Manufacturer is able to perform in full its obligations under this Agreement.

9.6. For the avoidance of doubt the Designer may serve notice of termination after it has served notice that it will seek to obtain the Product or a similar product from another source in the event that the Manufacturer has not been able to perform its obligations of supplying the Product for a period of [...] months.

10. Warranties

10.1. Each Party warrants to the other:

10.1.1. that it is the beneficial owner, free from encumbrances, of the IPR relating to that part of the Materials which it has contributed

10.1.2. that is has the requisite skill, knowledge, expertise, experience and resources, both material and financial, to perform its obligations under this Agreement.

11. Confidentiality

11.1. Each Party agrees not to disclose any confidential information provided by the other Party during the Term or at any time thereafter to any third party save where the law requires. Each Party also agrees not to use any such confidential information for any other purpose other than for the Project and will not use the information for any business or other purpose of its own. For the avoidance of doubt such information includes but is not limited either in type, *genus* or subject to:

11.1.1. all marketing information and intelligence

11.1.2. all costings and prices

11.1.3. all trade secrets, processes and formulae.

11.2. Each Party undertakes to procure that its employees, directors, agents and advisers and any other persons to whom it makes available confidential information shall also keep confidential the information the subject of this Clause 11.

12. Indemnity and limitation of liability

12.1. Each Party shall keep the other indemnified in respect of any loss, damage, penalty, surcharge, fine, confiscation, claim or demand of any kind the other shall suffer as a result of the former's negligence, breach of contract or other wrongful act or omission.

12.2. Neither Party shall be liable to the other for any economic, consequential or other losses including loss of reputation, profit or goodwill whether resulting from misrepresentation, misdescription, breach of contract, breach of duty or other act or omission (unless fraudulent) however caused.

12.3. Nothing in this Agreement shall limit the right of either Party to seek to recover damages for personal injury or death occasioned by breach of contract or breach of duty by the other Party, its employees or agents.

13. Invalid clauses

13.1. In the event that any term of this Agreement is found to be invalid or otherwise unenforceable then such term shall be regarded and construed as severable from the Agreement so as not to affect the validity and enforceability of the remainder.

14. Further action

14.1. The Parties agree that they will expeditiously carry out such further acts as may be necessary for the purpose of this Agreement including the execution and delivery of such instruments, deeds, licences, notifications as may be reasonably required by the other Party or by law.

15. Waiver

15.1. No failure, neglect or delay in enforcing any of the terms of this Agreement may be construed as a waiver by a Party of any of its rights in respect thereof nor such neglect, failure or delay constitute a variation of the express terms of the Agreement.

16. Law and jurisdiction

16.1. This Agreement is governed by the law of England and Wales and is subject to the [exclusive] jurisdiction of the courts of England and Wales.

17. Whole agreement

17.1. This Agreement supersedes and replaces any previous agreement between the Parties whether oral or in writing in relation to the Project. The Parties hereby agree that in entering into this Agreement neither has relied upon any warranty or representation made by or on behalf of the other Party save where expressly stated in this Agreement. The Parties hereby agree that this Agreement constitutes the whole agreement between the Parties in respect of the Project. The Parties agree that no variation may be made to it unless such variation is in writing and signed by both Parties.

18. Third party rights

18.1. The Parties to this Agreement agree that it is not hereby intended that any rights should be conferred upon or enforceable by any third party as defined in the Contracts (Rights of Third Parties) Act 1999.

19. Assignment

19.1. This Agreement is binding upon the Parties and their successors. Neither Party may assign the benefits or burdens of this Agreement without the prior written consent of the other Party [which it may in its absolute discretion withhold *or* which it will not unreasonably withhold].

19.2. [Either Party may sub-contract its obligations under this Agreement provided that it remains primary liable to the other Party and without prejudice to any rights it may have against its sub-contractor].

20. [Time of the essence

20.1. Time shall be of the essence for each obligation in this Agreement for which there is a stipulation as to the time of performance or for which a notice is required to be given].

21. Notices

21.1. All notices under this Agreement (unless specific and express provision is made otherwise) shall be in writing and shall be delivered personally [or by first class, registered or recorded post] [or by facsimile transmission] in every case to the other Party's Agreed Address. [In the case of first class post notice will be deemed to be received [3] business days after the date of posting.]

22. Schedules

22.1. The Schedules form part of this Agreement including any subsequent amendments made thereto.

Signed, etc.

SCHEDULE 1

Agreed Addresses

[*Insert Agreed Addresses of the parties*]

Signed, etc.

SCHEDULE 2

1. Pre-production timetable

1.1. The pre-production timetable will be as set out in the table below:

[*Design/test/production of prototype/ discussion/ evaluation, etc.*]	[*Date of completion*]

1.2. The Parties shall carry out the [*design and test, etc.*] as set out above.

1.3. [At the same time as delivery takes place of the first prototype] the Manufacturer shall inform the Designer of the cost of [producing the Tooling [which price shall include a [...%] of overhead cost] *or* purchasing the Tooling].

1.4. If the Parties agree the cost of the Tooling ('the Tooling Cost') then the Parties shall also agree the price ('the Purchase Price') at which the Products are to be sold by the Manufacturer to the Designer which shall be based upon [*an uplift of* [...]% *upon the manufacturing cost excluding fixed overheads*].

1.5. If the Parties have agreed the Tooling Cost and the Purchase Price then [*each Party*] shall bear [50%] of the Tooling Cost. The Manufacturer will thereafter [manufacture *or* procure] the Tooling.

1.6. After the [procurement *or* completion] of the Tooling the Manufacturer shall produce [...] pre-production samples of the Product [within ...] for the purpose of evaluation and conformity to agreed design and quality standards. The Designer shall notify the Manufacturer of any defect in the pre-production samples within [...] days of their being [delivered to the Designer *or* available for inspection].

1.7. Once the Designer agrees that the pre-production samples conform to the agreed standard for the Product the Parties shall agree a price at which the Product is to be sold ('the Resale Price'). In the absence of agreement the Resale Price shall be fixed at the Purchase Price plus [...]%.

1.8. The Designer will within [...] days place an order for at least the minimum number of the Products and the Manufacturer shall commence supplying them in accordance with the relevant terms and conditions of sale.

1.9. The Purchase Price and the Resale Price may be revised from time to time by agreement between the Parties. In the absence of agreement the revised Purchase Price and the revised Resale Price is to be determined at each anniversary of this Agreement by an increase representing the percentage increase in the RPI from the last anniversary (or in the case of the first year, the Commencement Date).

Signed, etc.

SCHEDULE 3

Royalties

1. Royalties payable on sales by the Manufacturer to third parties of the Product

1.1. The Manufacturer shall pay to the Designer a Royalty on each Product sold to a third party [in the sum of £[...] *or* a figure representing [...]% of the retail unit sale price] [less any packaging, shipping, insurance and other additional costs and nett of any taxation or duty payable by the Manufacturer].

1.2. [The Royalty shall be reviewed on each anniversary of this Agreement and in the absence of agreement shall increase by a figure representing the percentage increase in the RPI from the last anniversary (or in the case of the first year, the Commencement Date)].

1.3. The Manufacturer will keep accurate and complete records of all Products sold to third parties together with copies of all supporting documentation and make such records available to the Designer or its agents on the Designer giving [7] days written notice of its intention to inspect.

1.4. The Manufacturer will provide a monthly account to the Designer of Royalties due by it to the Designer by the last day of each calendar month and will pay such Royalties within [7] days of the end of each calendar month.

2. Post termination Royalty payments

2.1. The Party which retains and uses the Tooling as provided for in Clause [...] of the main Agreement shall pay to the Party a Royalty on each unit of the [...] [at the rate of £[...] *or* a figure representing [...]% of the retail unit sale price [less any packaging, shipping, insurance and other additional costs and nett of any taxation or duty payable by the retaining Party]].

2.2. The retaining Party will keep accurate and complete records of all Products sold to third parties together with copies of all supporting documentation and make such records available to the other Party or its agents on the other Party giving [7] days written notice of its intention to inspect.

2.3. The retaining Party will provide a monthly account to the other Party of Royalties due by it to the other Party by the last day of each calendar month and will pay such Royalties within [7] days of the end of each calendar month.

Signed, etc.

SCHEDULE 4

Agreed Prices

[Set out Schedule of Agreed Prices]

Signed, etc.

15

Leasing of equipment

15.1 Introduction

There are various ways in which equipment may be leased to a hirer.

On the one hand, there are those agreements which are intended to provide the hirer with some form of proprietary interest, e.g. hire purchase. Such contracts are outside the scope of this chapter.

On the other hand, there are agreements which are intended to provide no more than possession and use of the equipment essentially as a bailee in return for a hire fee. These agreements fall into two categories: 'finance leases' and 'operating leases'.

The two precedents accompanying this chapter (**Precedent 15A** for a finance lease and **Precedent 15B** for an operating lease) are both modelled as master agreements so that they will cover more than one leasing by the use of schedules. If a one-off lease is required either form will be easily adaptable.

15.2 Finance leases

It is usually envisaged in such agreements that the revenue earned from the equipment will virtually equate to the equipment's total value plus the profit the lessor wishes to make for itself. The lease will be long term. There are important fiscal consequences of such an arrangement. The equipment may be treated as capital owned by the lessor for which he can claim fiscal allowance for depreciation. The lessee on the other hand may be able to recover the total of his outgoings on hiring the equipment as a revenue cost. However, there are restraints on the fiscal effectiveness of such arrangements in some instances – see the Capital Allowances Act 2001, ss.221–228.

The lease reflects the fact that the lessor is not the supplier of the equipment. It is therefore important to ensure as much as possible that he is not liable for defects, misrepresentations, etc. which originate with the supplier.

15.3 Operating leases

These may be, but are not necessarily, shorter term hirings where the equipment may be re-hired to another hirer. These are essentially pure contracts of bailment for reward. More of the obligations of maintenance and repair of the equipment will sometimes but not always remain with the lessor.

Again, there are important fiscal ramifications from a leasing arrangement. They may be entered into where it is not possible for the lessor to reclaim 100 per cent of the capital allowances. It must, therefore, derive a greater profit from the hiring.

Tax advice is outside the scope of this work and so the above should be taken as no more than an indication of the issues that may need to be considered when deciding whether to use a leasing agreement as opposed to one in which ownership may pass.

PRECEDENT 15A   Equipment leasing master agreement finance based

EQUIPMENT LEASING MASTER AGREEMENT FINANCE BASED

THIS AGREEMENT dated [*date*] is made by and between:

1. [*Name*] a company incorporated in England and Wales under company number [*number*] and whose registered office is at [*address*] ('the Lessor'); and
2. [*Name*] a company incorporated in England and Wales under company number [*number*] and whose registered office is at [*address*] ('the Lessee').

RECITALS

1. Under this Agreement the Lessee wishes to lease equipment from the Lessor as set out in the Schedule[s] hereto as varied from time to time.
2. It is intended by the Parties hereto that each hiring of equipment shall be a separate transaction subject to the terms and conditions set out below.

DEFINITIONS

In this Agreement and the Schedules, the following words shall have the following meaning:

'Agreed Address'	The agreed address of each party as set out in Schedule 1.
'Equipment'	The equipment specified in the Schedules in respect of each particular Lease as varied from time to time.
'Fiscal Assumptions'	Assumptions that form the basis of the calculation of the Rental in each Schedule as follows:

1. The rate of corporation tax stated at the date set out in the Schedule will remain the same throughout the Minimum Period.
2. The law regarding the taxation of companies as it applies to this Agreement and as it is interpreted by the Inland Revenue, will remain unchanged during the Minimum Period.

3. Writing down allowances on the expenditure incurred by the Lessor in providing the Equipment will qualify, in accordance with the provisions of Section 220 of the Capital Allowances Act 2001 ('CAA'):

(a) at the rate of [...]% during the accounting period during which the Lessor incurred the expenditure and that period is proportionate to the part of the accounting period which occurs after the expenditure was incurred;

(b) at the same rate on the qualifying expenditure in each of the subsequent accounting periods.

'Lease' and 'Leases'	The leases under which the Equipment is leased to the Lessee as set out in the Schedules.
'Minimum Period'	The initial and minimum period for each Lease as set out in the relevant Schedule.
'Nett Rate of Return'	The nett rate of return on the Lessor's investment in the purchase, leasing and disposal of the Equipment as set out in each Schedule. Each Nett Rate of Return is based upon the Fiscal Assumptions and the assumptions:

1. that the Term continues for the Minimum Period;
2. the aggregate of the rentals payable during the Minimum Period are paid when due;
3. the Lessor does not record a pre-tax loss on the transaction.

'Nett Value'	The value of the Equipment after repossession by the Lessor under this Agreement which, if sold, will equate to the sale price. If the Equipment is not resold then the Nett Value will be that certified by an independent valuer appointed by the Parties in accordance with Clause 12.
'Party' and 'Parties'	The Lessor and the Lessee.
'Premises'	The premises specified in each Schedule.
'Rental' and 'Rentals'	The rental payable under each Lease as set out in the Schedules.
'Rental Day'	The day on which Rental is due as set out in the Schedules.
'Schedule' and 'Schedules'	The schedules to this Agreement as varied from time to time.
'Supplier'	The third party supplier of the Equipment as recorded in the relevant Schedule.
'Term'	The term of each Lease as set out in the Schedules.
'Total Loss'	Total loss, constructive total loss or arranged total loss of the Equipment.

INTERPRETATION

In this Agreement:

1. The singular includes the plural and one gender includes all.
2. References to Schedules and Clauses are to those in this Agreement.
3. Reference to a statutory provision includes any amendment or replacement provision relevant to the Agreement.

4.   Reference to a document includes that document as amended, altered or replaced subsequent to the date of this Agreement.
5.   Reference to writing includes facsimile transmission, e-mail, and similar media unless the context otherwise expressly provides.
6.   Time expressed in days excludes the first day but includes the last day. If the last day does not fall on a normal business day in both England and Wales then the last day will be deemed to be the first normal business day.
7.   The headings in this document do not form part of the Agreement.

OPERATIVE PROVISIONS

1. Status of this Agreement and the Schedules

1.1. This Agreement shall operate as a master agreement the terms and conditions of which will apply to all Leases. Each Schedule shall constitute a separate agreement for leasing of Equipment save that more than one item of Equipment may be included in each Schedule. A breach of any of the provisions of a Lease shall be deemed to be a breach of this Agreement and vice versa.

2. Uninterrupted use of the Equipment

2.1. Provided that the Lessee is not in breach of any of the terms of a Lease or of this Agreement it may enjoy uninterrupted possession and use of the Equipment during the Term.

3. Lessee's obligations

3.1. The Lessee will inspect the Equipment on delivery and notify the Lessor in writing of any defect. Failure to do so will result in the conclusive presumption that the Equipment is in good order and condition, free from defect and fit for its purpose.

3.2. The Lessee agrees to the following obligations during the Term:

3.2.1. to pay without the need for demand and without any deduction, counterclaim or set off the Rental by the Rental Day and all other sums due to the Lessor under this Agreement. Time shall be of the essence in respect of such payments. Failure to pay any sum due within 21 days of the due date shall constitute a repudiation of this Agreement

3.2.2. to permit the Lessor upon giving reasonable notice to inspect the Equipment and any logbook or record relating thereto during normal business hours

3.2.3. to keep the Equipment on the Premises at all times; in the case of moveable Equipment including motor vehicles to use and keep the Equipment only as set out in the relevant Schedule

3.2.4. to use the Equipment in accordance with any operating instructions and in a proper and workmanlike way

3.2.5. to maintain the Equipment at its own expense ensuring that it complies with all warranty requirements of the Supplier; in the case of Equipment subject to any licence or conditions of use to undertake to comply with all obligations and restrictions resulting therefrom including where appropriate entering into any required maintenance agreement with the Supplier

3.2.6. to ensure that where appropriate all licences required for the use or possession of the Equipment shall be maintained

3.2.7. to ensure that any taxes or duty due in relation to the Equipment is paid

3.2.8. to comply with any legal requirements arising from the possession or use of the Equipment including such safety or other modifications as may be from time to time required by any legislative or regulatory provision

3.2.9. to mark the Equipment clearly and visibly with a notice stating that it is the property of the Lessor

3.2.10. to ensure that the Equipment is kept free from any form of distraint, seizure, charge, mortgage, lien, pledge or other encumbrance

3.2.11. not to deal with the Equipment by way of sale, lease, hire, loan, gift or any parting or sharing of possession or control unless and only to the extent that any such dealing is permitted in the relevant Schedule

3.2.12. not to affix the Equipment permanently to or in any building or land unless and only to the extent that any such dealing is permitted in the relevant Schedule

3.2.13. if the Equipment is affixed to any land or building as is permitted by the relevant Schedule to ensure that it shall be capable of removal without material damage to the building or land

3.2.14. where Equipment is so affixed to take all reasonable steps to ensure that title in the Equipment does not pass to the landowner or landlord

3.2.15. to repair and make good any damage resulting from the removal of the Equipment from the building or land and to indemnify the Lessor against costs, liability or losses arising therefrom however caused

3.2.16. where the Equipment becomes a fixture as defined by Section 173 of the CAA to warrant that the circumstances are such that by virtue of Section 176 of the CAA they would have been treated for material purposes as being owned by the Lessee if the Lessee had bought the Equipment and incurred capital expenditure in doing so at the commencement of the Term and the Lessee is leasing the Equipment for the purposes of a qualifying activity carried on by it or for leasing otherwise than in the course of a qualifying activity

3.2.17. if the Equipment is or may become a fixture as defined by the CAA, Section 173 on demand and in such form as the Lessor or its inspector of taxes may prescribe to sign and deliver to the Lessor an election that the CAA, Section 177 shall apply or an election in any other form and under any other authority (statutory or otherwise) in response to which the Lessor's inspector of taxes will treat the Equipment to like effect for material purposes as being owned by the Lessor

3.2.18. in the event of damage to or destruction of the Equipment whilst in the Lessee's possession, to repair or replace it with like Equipment at its own expense

3.2.19. where, in the case of Equipment including computer programs, there are software updates to be installed to undertake to ensure that the software is kept up to date at its own expense

3.2.20. if the Equipment requires to be installed in specially prepared premises or location as specified in the appropriate Schedule then to ensure that it complies with all such requirements as set out in the Schedule

3.2.21. to maintain a complete and accurate record of maintenance and repairs in relation to the Equipment

3.2.22. not to modify the Equipment without the express prior written permission of the Lessor save where such modification is required by statute or regulation

3.2.23. [not to claim any capital allowance on the Equipment]

3.2.24. to keep the Equipment insured comprehensively against all risks in the joint names of the Parties for its full [market *or* replacement] value and to provide a copy of all such insurance documents to the Lessor

3.2.25. to maintain insurance in the Parties' joint names against all third party risks [in the minimum sum of £[...] *or* as required by the Road Traffic Act 1991] arising from the possession, control, ownership or use of the Equipment and to undertake to ensure that all moneys received from the insurer are paid directly to meet any claim to which the payment relates

3.2.26. to pay all insurance premiums timeously and to furnish the Lessor with copies thereof including certificates where appropriate

3.2.27. to ensure that the Lessee has complied with the obligations of utmost good faith when seeking and obtaining insurance under this Agreement and to comply with the conditions of any insurance obtained

3.2.28. to inform the Lessor forthwith upon any major damage to the Equipment and to provide full details of any claim being made under the insurance referred to in this Clause 3

3.2.29. in the event that the Lessee fails to obtain adequate or appropriate insurance for the Equipment to reimburse any premium the Lessor has paid, it being acknowledged hereby that the Lessor may (but is not obliged to) take out insurance under this Agreement in relation to the Equipment as set out in this Clause 3 if the Lessee defaults in doing so.

4. Return of the Equipment

4.1. The Lessee agrees to deliver up the Equipment to the Lessor at the expiry of the Term or upon earlier determination in accordance with this Agreement in good order and repair.

4.2. Delivery up of the Equipment shall be to the address or location set out in the relevant Schedule.

4.3. [The Lessee agrees to give reasonable access to the agents of the Lessor during the last [8] weeks of the Term in order for the Lessor to take such steps as are reasonably necessary for the removal, re-hiring or other disposal of the Equipment].

5. Total Loss of the Equipment

5.1. If there is a Total Loss of the Equipment during the Term the Lessee will:

5.1.1. immediately inform the Lessor in writing

5.1.2. pay the Lessor within [28] days of the occurrence of the Total Loss an amount equivalent to the Nett Value as calculated under Clause 12 less the insurance money received or receivable in relation thereto

5.1.3. pay the proceeds of the insurance policy or policies referred to in Clause 3 if paid to the Lessee.

5.2. Interest shall be payable on the amount receivable by the Lessor under this Clause from the date of the occurrence of the Total Loss at an annual rate of [8]%.

5.3. The Lease of the Equipment shall terminate on the occurrence of Total Loss though this Agreement shall continue in full force and effect.

6. Indemnity

6.1. The Lessee will indemnify the Lessor in respect of any losses, damage or liability not fully covered by insurance that the Lessor may incur as a result of:

6.1.1. the Lessee's acts or omissions, whether deliberate, accidental, negligent or reckless, in the course of the performance or purported performance of its obligations or rights under this Agreement whether such acts or omissions amount to a breach of an express or implied obligation under this Agreement or a breach of any other legal requirement or obligation, code of practice, licence, consent, forbearance, approval, permission or rule

6.1.2. the presence or use of the Equipment during the Term.

6.2. For the avoidance of doubt losses, damage and liability shall include but not be limited to damage to or loss of the Equipment, economic and commercial loss, loss of goodwill, legal and other costs associated with legal proceedings of any kind which the Lessor has to bring or to which it has to respond, fines, penalties, damages and any financial consequence whatever flowing directly or indirectly from the matters set out in this Clause 6.

7. Fiscal considerations

7.1. The Lessee will provide such documentation and information to the Inland Revenue as it may require regarding the Equipment and its use. The Lessee will also provide to the Lessor such information and documentation as it may require for the purpose of responding to any inquiry from or requirement of the Inland Revenue.

7.2. The Rental in respect of each piece of Equipment is fixed, as stated in the relevant Schedule, based upon the Fiscal Assumptions.

7.3. In the event that any of the Fiscal Assumptions no longer applies and as a result the total of Rentals to be paid during the Minimum Period would result in the Nett Rate of Return being reduced then the Lessor may notify the Lessee in writing that it requires to adjust the Rental so as to ensure that the total of rentals receivable by the Lessor shall equate to the Nett Rate of Return which would be achieved if the Fiscal Assumptions had been met.

8. Assignment of express warranties and guarantees in relation to the Equipment

8.1. The Lessor will assign at the Lessee's expense the benefit of all warranties and guarantees in its favour provided by the Supplier or the manufacturer in relation to the Equipment.

9. Exclusion of express and implied warranties by the Lessor

9.1. The Lessor leases the Equipment to the Lessee without the benefit of any warranty, representation or condition as to the quality, condition, performance, capability or fitness for purpose, whether express or implied by statute, common law or usage and all such warranties and representations are expressly excluded.

9.2. The Lessor gives no warranty either express or implied that the possession or use of the Equipment by the Lessee or those who have permission under the relevant Schedule to have possession or control will not constitute an infringement of any third party's patents, trademarks, registered designs, copyrights, confidential information or other intellectual property rights and the Lessor will not be liable to the Lessee for any losses or damage of whatever kind it may suffer in connection therewith.

10. Exclusion of liability

10.1. The Lessor shall not be liable to the Lessee:

10.1.1. for any loss, injury or damage resulting from any defect in the Equipment whether apparent or otherwise

10.1.2. for any misstatement, misrepresentation, warranty or inducement, made by any third party including but not limited to the Supplier or anyone acting on his behalf which induced the Lessee to lease the Equipment from the Lessor

10.1.3. if the Equipment is unusable for any period during the Term for any reason whatever

10.1.4. for any loss or damage sustained by the Lessee as a result of the Lessor lawfully re-taking possession of the Equipment.

10.2. Nothing in this Clause 10 shall limit the liability of the Lessor for personal injury or death caused by its negligence.

11. Lessor's right to terminate

11.1. The Lessor may terminate this Agreement forthwith in the event that the Lessee:

11.1.1. is in breach of the terms of the Lease or this Agreement

11.1.2. fails to pay any Rental punctually on a Rental Day or any other sum when due

11.1.3. does or allows to be done anything which puts at risk or endangers the Equipment

11.1.4. is [declared bankrupt *or* wound up due to insolvency]

11.1.5. makes or seeks a composition with its creditors

11.1.6. enters into or seeks an insolvent voluntary arrangement

11.1.7. becomes the subject of the appointment of a manager, receiver or liquidator

11.1.8. is the subject of an administration order

11.1.9. has its assets charged or seized for the satisfaction of a debt

11.1.10. divulges confidential business information in connection with this Agreement to an unauthorised third party

11.1.11. does not furnish any document or other information which the Lessee is obliged to provide within [...] days of its due date

11.1.12. abandons the Equipment.

11.2. In the event of termination the Lessor's consent to the Lessee's possession of the Equipment shall determine immediately and the Lessor may recover possession of the Equipment.

12. Effect of termination

12.1. Upon termination of the Lease for whatever reason by the Lessor the Lessee shall pay to the Lessor:

12.1.1. any arrears of Rental including Rental due for part of a Rental period

12.1.2. all remaining Rental that would have been payable until the end of the Minimum Period [less a discount at the rate of [...]% per year]

12.1.3. damages for breach of the Agreement or Lease together with such costs as have been incurred by the Lessor in regaining possession of the Equipment, selling or attempting to sell the Equipment and all other consequential costs and expenses.

12.2. The Lessor will give the Lessee credit for the Nett Value. In the absence of a sale of the Equipment the Nett Value of the Equipment shall be determined by an independent valuer appointed by agreement between the Parties and in default thereof by the Supplier, or if the Supplier is unable to carry out a valuation, by a manufacturer or supplier of similar standing. The valuer shall act as an expert not as an arbitrator.

13. Interest

13.1. Interest will be payable on late payments at the rate of [...]% calculated daily.

14. [Refund of Nett Value

14.1. Provided that the Lessee has complied with the terms of this Agreement and the Lease the Lessor shall refund at the end of the Term a sum equivalent to the Nett Value.

14.2. For the avoidance of doubt the refund under this Clause 14 shall not be payable if the Lease has been terminated in accordance with the provisions of Clause 11].

15. Waiver

15.1. No failure, neglect or delay in enforcing any of the terms of this Agreement may be construed as a waiver of any of the Lessor's rights in respect thereof nor such neglect, failure or delay a variation of the express terms of the Agreement.

15.2. The Lessor may at its absolute discretion in whole or in part release, compound or compromise, or grant time or indulgence to any party for, any liability under this Agreement without affecting its rights against that or any other party under the same or any other liability.

16. Time of the essence

16.1. Time shall be of the essence in this Agreement in respect of any time limit, date, period or term whether as originally set out herein or by any subsequent variation or agreement.

17. Whole agreement and previous agreements

17.1. This Agreement supersedes and replaces any previous agreement between the Lessor and the Lessee whether oral or in writing in relation to the Lease. The Parties hereby agree that in entering into this Agreement they have not relied upon any warranty or representation made by or on behalf of the other Party save where expressly stated in this Agreement. The Parties hereby agree that this Agreement constitutes the whole agreement between the Parties in respect of the Lease.

18. Notices

18.1. All notices under this Agreement shall be in writing and shall be delivered personally [or by first class, registered or recorded post] [or by facsimile transmission] in every case to the other Party's Agreed Address. [In the case of first class post notice will be deemed to be received [3] business days after the date of posting.]

19. Variation of this Agreement

19.1. Any variation of the terms of this Agreement must be in writing signed by the Lessor and the Lessee.

20. Third party rights

20.1. The Parties to this Agreement agree that it is not hereby intended that any rights should be conferred upon or enforceable by any third party as defined in the Contracts (Rights of Third Parties) Act 1999.

21. Law and jurisdiction

21.1. This Agreement is governed by the law of England and Wales and is subject to the [exclusive] jurisdiction of the courts of England and Wales.

22. Further action

22.1. The Parties agree that they will expeditiously carry out such further acts as may be necessary for the purpose of this Agreement including the execution and delivery of such instruments, deeds, licences, notifications as may be reasonably required by the other Party or by law.

23. Schedules

23.1. The Schedules form part of this Agreement including any subsequent amendments made thereto.

Signed, etc.

SCHEDULE 1
Parties' Agreed Addresses

[*Set out the Parties' Agreed Addresses*]

Signed, etc.

SCHEDULE 2 [*etc.*]

[*Set out details of: Equipment; Term of Lease including Minimum Period and Rental Day[s]; Rental; Fiscal Assumptions; Nett Rate of Return; Premises; Supplier*]

Signed, etc.

PRECEDENT 15B   Operating equipment leasing (master) agreement

OPERATING EQUIPMENT LEASING (MASTER) AGREEMENT

THIS AGREEMENT dated [*date*] is made by and between:

1. [*Name*] a company incorporated in England and Wales under company number [*number*] and whose registered office is at [*address*] ('the Lessor'); and
2. [*Name*] a company incorporated in England and Wales under company number [*number*] and whose registered office is at [*address*] ('the Lessee').

RECITALS

1. Under this Agreement the Lessee wishes to lease the Equipment from the Lessor as set out in the Schedule[s] hereto as varied from time to time.
2. It is intended by the Parties hereto that each hiring of Equipment shall be a separate transaction subject to the terms and conditions set out below.

DEFINITIONS

In this Agreement and the Schedules, the following words shall have the following meaning:

'Accounting Period'	'Accounting Period' means an accounting period as defined in Section 1119 of the Corporation Tax Act 2010 ('CTA'). The first Accounting Period is that in which the Cost was incurred by the Lessor and the last is that in which the Minimum Period expires or the lease ends if terminated earlier.
'Actual Market Value'	The market value of the Equipment taking into account its actual condition at the time of valuation assuming a willing seller and a willing buyer or the price realised on a bona fide sale at arm's length by the Lessor, whichever is the lesser.
'Agreed Address'	The agreed address of each party as set out in Schedule 1.
'Assumed Market Value'	The market value of the Equipment as determined by the Expert assuming a willing seller, a willing buyer and that the Equipment has been properly maintained throughout the Term.

'Cost Incurred'	The whole of the capital expenditure (excluding VAT) incurred by the Lessor in the provision of the Equipment.
'Equipment'	The equipment specified in the Schedules in respect of each particular Lease as varied from time to time.
'Expert'	The expert appointed by the Parties in accordance with this Agreement.
'Fiscal Assumptions'	Assumptions that form the basis of the calculation of the Rental in each Schedule as follows:

1. the rate of corporation tax stated at the date set out in the Schedule will remain the same throughout the Minimum Period;

2. the law regarding the taxation of companies as it applies to this Agreement and as it is interpreted by the Inland Revenue, will remain unchanged during the Minimum Period;

3. the whole of the Cost Incurred is incurred as set out in the Schedule, qualifies for Writing Down Allowances and continues to qualify throughout each Accounting Period occurring during the Minimum Period;

4. in each Accounting Period during the Minimum Period the applicable rate of Writing Down Allowances is [...]% of the Qualifying Expenditure;

5. no Writing Down Allowances are withdrawn and except for the sale of the Equipment at the expiry or earlier termination of the Lease no balancing charge arises;

6. [expenditure incurred by the Lessor on Equipment which amounts to a fixture is not excluded from the expression 'on the provision of Machinery or Plant' by virtue of Sections 21 and 22 of the Capital Allowances Act 2001 ('CAA') *or* all Rentals payable under this Agreement and any costs or expenses incurred by the Lessor in connection with it are deductible as trading expenses for the purpose of corporation tax in the Accounting Period in which such costs or expenses are incurred by the Lessor];

7. the Lessor is able to set off losses for tax purposes arising from this Agreement against profits pursuant to the CTA, Section 37 [and to surrender by way of group relief to any other member of the Lessor's group of companies pursuant to the CTA, Sections 97 to 188];

8. the liability of the Lessor for the payment of corporation tax shall be in accordance with the Corporation Tax (Instalment Payments) Regulations 1998;

9. the Lessor's expenditure is not expenditure met by contributions in the circumstances set out in the CAA, Section 532;

10. the accountancy rental earnings in respect of this Agreement for any Accounting Period shall not exceed the normal rent for that period as both of those expressions are defined in the CTA, Sections 896 and 897;

11. the Equipment is sold on the last day of the Minimum Period for an amount which equates to the Qualifying Expenditure.

'Lease' and 'Leases'	The leases under which the Equipment is leased to the Lessee as set out in the Schedules.
'Market Value'	The market value as determined by the Expert of the Equipment assuming a willing seller, a willing buyer and that the Equipment is properly maintained at all times prior to the valuation.
'Minimum Period'	The initial and minimum period for each Lease as set out in the relevant Schedule.
'Nett of Tax Rate of Return'	The nett of tax rate of return on the Lessor's investment in the purchase and leasing of the Equipment as set out in each Schedule during the Minimum Period. Each Nett of Tax Rate of Return is based upon the Fiscal Assumptions and the further assumptions:

1. that the Term continues for the Minimum Period;
2. the aggregate of the rentals payable during the Minimum Period are paid when due;
3. the Lessor does not record a pre-tax loss on the transaction.

'Party' and 'Parties'	The Lessor and the Lessee.
'Premises'	The premises specified in each Schedule.
'Qualifying Expenditure'	Expenditure as defined in Section 57 of the CAA.
'Rental' and 'Rentals'	The rental payable under each Lease as set out in the Schedules.
'Rental Day'	The day on which Rental is due as set out in the Schedules.
'Schedule' and 'Schedules'	The schedules to this Agreement as varied from time to time.
'Term'	The term of each Lease as set out in the Schedules.
'Total Loss'	Total loss, constructive total loss or arranged total loss of the Equipment.
'Writing Down Allowance'	Writing down allowances as defined in Sections 55 and 56 of the CAA.

INTERPRETATION

In this Agreement:

1. The singular includes the plural and one gender includes all.
2. References to Schedules and Clauses are to those in this Agreement.
3. Reference to a statutory provision includes any amendment or replacement provision relevant to the Agreement.
4. Reference to a document includes that document as amended, altered or replaced subsequent to the date of this Agreement.
5. Reference to writing includes facsimile transmission, e-mail, and similar media unless the context otherwise expressly provides.
6. Time expressed in days excludes the first day but includes the last day. If the last day does not fall on a normal business day in both England and Wales then the last day will be deemed to be the first normal business day.
7. The headings in this document do not form part of the Agreement.

OPERATIVE PROVISIONS

1. Status of this Agreement and the Schedules

1.1. This Agreement shall operate as a master agreement the terms and conditions of which will apply to all Leases. Each Schedule shall constitute a separate agreement for leasing of Equipment save that more than one item of Equipment may be included in each Schedule. A breach of any of the provisions of a Lease shall be deemed to be a breach of this Agreement and vice versa.

2. Uninterrupted use of the Equipment

2.1. Provided that the Lessee is not in breach of any of the terms of a Lease or of this Agreement it may enjoy uninterrupted possession and use of the Equipment during the Term.

3. Lessee's obligations

3.1. The Lessee will inspect the Equipment on delivery and notify the Lessor in writing of any defect. Failure to do so will result in the conclusive presumption that the Equipment is in good order and condition, free from defect and fit for its purpose.

3.2. The Lessee agrees to the following obligations during the Term:

3.2.1. to pay without the need for demand and without any deduction, counterclaim or set off the Rental by the Rental Day and all other sums due to the Lessor under this Agreement. Time shall be of the essence in respect of such payments. Failure to pay any sum due within 21 days of the due date shall constitute a repudiation of this Agreement

3.2.2. the Lessor will be permitted upon giving reasonable notice to inspect the Equipment and any logbook or record relating thereto during normal business hours

3.2.3. the Equipment will be kept on the Premises at all times; in the case of moveable Equipment including motor vehicles the Equipment will be used and kept only as set out in the relevant Schedule

3.2.4. to use the Equipment in accordance with any operating instructions and in a proper and workmanlike way

3.2.5. to maintain the Equipment at its own expense ensuring that it complies with all warranty requirements; in the case of Equipment subject to any licence or conditions of use to undertake to comply with all obligations and restrictions resulting therefrom including where appropriate entering into any required maintenance agreement; to ensure that where appropriate all licences required for the use or possession of the Equipment shall be maintained; to ensure that any tax or duty due in relation to the Equipment is paid

3.2.6. to comply with any legal requirements arising from the possession or use of the Equipment including such safety or other modifications as may be from time to time required by any legislative or regulatory provision

3.2.7. to mark the Equipment clearly and visibly with a notice stating that it is the property of the Lessor

3.2.8. to ensure that the Equipment is kept free from any form of distraint, seizure, charge, mortgage, lien, pledge or other encumbrance

3.2.9. not to deal with the Equipment by way of sale, lease, hire, loan, gift or any parting or sharing of possession or control unless and only to the extent that any such dealing is permitted in the relevant Schedule

3.2.10. not to affix the Equipment permanently to or in any building or land unless and only to the extent that any such dealing is permitted in the relevant Schedule

3.2.11. if the Equipment is affixed to any land or building as is permitted by the relevant Schedule to ensure that it shall be capable of removal without material damage to the building or land

3.2.12. where Equipment is so affixed to take all reasonable steps to ensure that title in the Equipment does not pass to the landowner or landlord

3.2.13. to repair and make good any damage resulting from the removal of the Equipment from the building or land and to indemnify the Lessor against costs, liability or losses arising therefrom however caused

3.2.14. where the Equipment becomes a fixture as defined by Section 173 of the CAA to warrant that the circumstances are such that by virtue of Section 176 of the CAA it would have been treated for material purposes as being owned by the Lessee if the Lessee had bought the Equipment and incurred capital expenditure in doing so at the commencement of the Term and the Lessee is leasing the Equipment for the purposes of a qualifying activity carried on by it or for leasing otherwise than in the course of a qualifying activity

3.2.15. if the Equipment is or may become a fixture as defined by the CAA, Section 173 to sign and deliver to the Lessor on demand and in such form as the Lessor or its inspector of taxes may prescribe an election that the CAA, Section 177 shall apply or an election in any other form and under any other authority (statutory or otherwise) in response to which the Lessor's inspector of taxes will treat the Equipment to like effect for material purposes as being owned by the Lessor

3.2.16. in the event of damage to or destruction of the Equipment whilst in the Lessee's possession, to repair or replace it with like Equipment at its own expense

3.2.17. where, in the case of Equipment including computer programs, there are software updates to be installed to undertake to ensure that the software is kept up to date at its own expense

3.2.18. if the Equipment requires to be installed in specially prepared premises or location as specified in the appropriate Schedule then to ensure that it complies with all such requirements as set out in the Schedule

3.2.19. to maintain a complete and accurate record of maintenance and repairs in relation to the Equipment

3.2.20. not to modify the Equipment without the express prior written permission of the Lessor save where such modification is required by statute or regulation

3.2.21. not to claim any capital allowance on the Equipment

3.2.22. to keep the Equipment insured comprehensively against all risks in the joint names of the Parties for its full [market *or* replacement] value and to provide a copy of all such insurance documents to the Lessor

3.2.23. to maintain insurance in the Parties' joint names against all third party risks [in the minimum sum of £[...] *or* as required by the Road Traffic Act 1991] arising from the possession, control, ownership or use of the Equipment and to undertake to ensure that all moneys received from the insurer are paid directly to meet any claim to which the payment relates

3.2.24. to pay all insurance premiums timeously and to furnish the Lessor with copies thereof including certificates where appropriate

3.2.25. to ensure that the Lessee has complied with the obligations of utmost good faith when seeking and obtaining insurance under this Agreement and to comply with the conditions of any insurance obtained

3.2.26. to inform the Lessor forthwith upon any major damage to the Equipment and to provide full details of any claim being made under the insurance referred to in this Clause 3

3.2.27. in the event that the Lessee fails to obtain adequate or appropriate insurance for the Equipment to reimburse any premium the Lessor has paid, it being acknowledged hereby that the Lessor may (but is not obliged to) take out insurance under this Agreement in relation to the Equipment as set out in this Clause 3 if the Lessee defaults in doing so.

4. Return of the Equipment

4.1. The Lessee agrees to deliver up the Equipment to the Lessor at the expiry of the Term or upon earlier determination in accordance with this Agreement in good order and repair.

4.2. Delivery up of the Equipment shall be to the address or location set out in the relevant Schedule.

4.3. [The Lessee agrees to give reasonable access to the agents of the Lessor during the last [8] weeks of the Term in order for the Lessor to take such steps as are reasonably necessary for the removal, re-hiring or other disposal of the Equipment].

5. Total Loss of the Equipment

5.1. If there is a Total Loss of the Equipment during the Term the Lessee will:

5.1.1. immediately inform the Lessor in writing

5.1.2. pay such amount as the Expert may determine as the amount (if any) by which the Assumed Market Value at the time of the Total Loss exceeds the sum recovered from the insurance policy referred to in Clause 3. The Expert will be appointed by agreement between the Parties or in default thereof upon joint application by the Parties to the President of the Law Society of England and Wales. The Expert shall act as an expert not as an arbitrator

5.1.3. pay the proceeds of the relevant insurance policy under Clause 3 if paid to the Lessee

5.1.4. pay such further or other sum as is necessary adequately to compensate the Lessor for the loss of the Equipment.

5.2. Interest shall be payable on the amount receivable by the Lessor under this Clause from the date of the occurrence of the Total Loss at an annual rate of [...]%.

5.3. The Lease of the Equipment shall terminate on the occurrence of Total Loss though this Agreement shall continue in full force and effect.

6. Indemnity

6.1. The Lessee will indemnify the Lessor in respect of any losses, damage or liability not fully covered by insurance that the Lessor may incur as a result of:

6.1.1. the Lessee's acts or omissions, whether deliberate, accidental, negligent or reckless, in the course of the performance or purported performance of its obligations or rights under this Agreement whether such acts or omissions amount to a breach of an express or implied obligation under this Agreement or a breach of any other legal requirement or obligation, code of practice, licence, consent, forbearance, approval, permission or rule

6.1.2. the presence or use of the Equipment during the Term.

6.2. For the avoidance of doubt losses, damage and liability shall include but not be limited to damage to or loss of the Equipment, economic and commercial loss, loss of goodwill, legal and other costs associated with legal proceedings of any kind which the Lessor has to bring or to which it has to respond, fines, penalties, damages and any financial consequence whatever flowing directly or indirectly from the matters set out in this Clause 6.

7. Fiscal considerations

7.1. The Lessee will provide such documentation and information to the Inland Revenue as it may require regarding the Equipment and its use. The Lessee will also provide to the Lessor such information and documentation as it may require for the purpose of responding to any inquiry from or requirement of the Inland Revenue.

7.2. The Rental in respect of each piece of Equipment is fixed, as stated in the relevant Schedule, based upon the Fiscal Assumptions.

7.3. In the event that any of the Fiscal Assumptions no longer applies and as a result the total of Rentals to be paid during the Minimum Period would result in the Nett of Tax Rate of Return being reduced then the Lessor may notify the Lessee in writing that it requires to adjust the Rental so as to ensure that the total of Rentals receivable by the Lessor shall equate to the Nett of Tax Rate of Return which would be achieved if the Fiscal Assumptions had been met. Such adjustment will be reflected by equal adjustments to each [monthly] Rental payment for the remainder of the Minimum Period. If the adjustment is made after the end of the Minimum Period or after all Rental payments have been made then the adjustment shall be by one single payment.

7.4. If the Lessor decides to adjust the Rental under the circumstances set out in this Clause 7 then it will notify the Lessee in writing not less than [4] weeks before the first adjusted Rental is due, or if all Rental payments have been made or the Minimum Period has ended then [4] weeks before the single payment is required.

8. Assignment of express warranties and guarantees in relation to the Equipment

8.1. The Lessor will assign to the Lessee at the Lessee's expense the benefit of all warranties and guarantees in its favour provided by the supplier or manufacturer of the Equipment for the duration of the Term.

8.2. The Lessee will re-assign the benefits to the Lessor at the end of the Term and hereby appoints the Lessor as its attorney for the purpose of effecting such re-assignment if necessary.

9. Exclusion of express and implied warranties by the Lessor

9.1. The Lessor leases the Equipment to the Lessee without the benefit of any warranty, representation or condition as to the quality, condition, performance, capability or fitness for purpose, whether express or implied by statute, common law or usage and all such warranties and representations are expressly excluded.

9.2. The Lessor gives no warranty either express or implied that the possession or use of the Equipment by the Lessee or those who have permission under the relevant Schedule to have possession or control will not constitute an infringement of any third party's patents, trademarks, registered designs, copyrights, confidential information or other intellectual property rights and the Lessor will not be liable to the Lessee for any losses or damage of whatever kind it may suffer in connection therewith.

10. Exclusion of liability

10.1. The Lessor shall not be liable to the Lessee:

10.1.1. for any loss, injury or damage resulting from any defect in the Equipment whether apparent or otherwise

10.1.2. for any misstatement, misrepresentation, warranty or inducement, made by any third party including but not limited to the supplier of the Equipment or anyone acting on his behalf which induced the Lessee to lease the Equipment from the Lessor

10.1.3. if the Equipment is unusable for any period during the Term for any reason whatever

10.1.4. for any loss or damage sustained by the Lessee as a result of the Lessor lawfully re-taking possession of the Equipment.

10.2. Nothing in this Clause 10 shall limit the liability of the Lessor for personal injury or death caused by its negligence.

11. Lessor's right to terminate

11.1. The Lessor may terminate this Agreement forthwith in the event that the Lessee:

11.1.1. is in breach of the terms of the Lease or this Agreement

11.1.2. fails to pay any Rental punctually on a Rental Day or any other sum when due

11.1.3. does or allows to be done anything which puts at risk or endangers the Equipment

11.1.4. is [declared bankrupt *or* wound up due to insolvency]

11.1.5. makes or seeks a composition with its creditors

11.1.6. enters into or seeks an insolvent voluntary arrangement

11.1.7. becomes the subject of the appointment of a manager, receiver or liquidator

11.1.8. is the subject of an administration order

11.1.9. has its assets charged or seized for the satisfaction of a debt

11.1.10. [divulges confidential business information in connection with this Agreement to an unauthorised third party]

11.1.11. does not furnish any document or other information which the Lessee is obliged to provide within [...] days of its due date

11.1.12. abandons the Equipment.

11.2. In the event of termination the Lessor's consent to the Lessee's possession of the Equipment shall determine immediately and the Lessor may recover possession of the Equipment.

12. Effect of termination

12.1. Upon termination of the Lease for whatever reason by the Lessor the Lessee shall pay to the Lessor:

12.1.1. any arrears of Rental including Rental due for part of a Rental period

12.1.2. the difference if any between the Assumed Market Value at the time of termination or delivery up, whichever is the later, and the Actual Market Value of the Equipment as determined by the Expert together with such costs as have been incurred by the Lessor in regaining possession of the Equipment, selling or attempting to sell the Equipment and all other consequential costs and expenses.

13. Interest

13.1. Interest will be payable on late payments at the rate of [...]% calculated daily.

14. Waiver

14.1. No failure, neglect or delay in enforcing any of the terms of this Agreement may be construed as a waiver of any of the Lessor's rights in respect thereof nor such neglect, failure or delay a variation of the express terms of the Agreement.

14.2. The Lessor may at its absolute discretion in whole or in part release, compound or compromise, or grant time or indulgence to any party for, any liability under this Agreement without affecting its rights against that or any other party under the same or any other liability.

15. Time of the essence

15.1. Time shall be of the essence in this Agreement in respect of any time limit, date, period or term whether as originally set out herein or by any subsequent variation or agreement.

16. Whole agreement and previous agreements

16.1. This Agreement supersedes and replaces any previous agreement between the Lessor and the Lessee whether oral or in writing in relation to the Lease. The Parties hereby agree that in entering into this Agreement they have not relied upon any warranty or representation made by or on behalf of the other Party save where expressly stated in this Agreement. The Parties hereby agree that this Agreement constitutes the whole agreement between the Parties in respect of the Lease.

17. Notices

17.1. All notices under this Agreement shall be in writing and shall be delivered personally [or by first class, registered or recorded post] [or by facsimile transmission] in every case to the other Party's Agreed Address. [In the case of first class post notice will be deemed to be received [3] business days after the date of posting.]

18. Variation of this Agreement

18.1. Any variation of the terms of this Agreement must be in writing signed by the Lessor and the Lessee.

19. Third party rights

19.1. The Parties to this Agreement agree that it is not hereby intended that any rights should be conferred upon or enforceable by any third party as defined in the Contracts (Rights of Third Parties) Act 1999.

20. Law and jurisdiction

20.1. This Agreement is governed by the law of England and Wales and is subject to the [exclusive] jurisdiction of the courts of England and Wales.

21. Further action

21.1. The Parties agree that they will expeditiously carry out such further acts as may be necessary for the purpose of this Agreement including the execution and delivery of such instruments, deeds, licences, notifications as may be reasonably required by the other Party or by law.

22. Schedules

22.1. The Schedules form part of this Agreement including any subsequent amendments made thereto.

SCHEDULE 1

Parties' Agreed Addresses

[*Set out the Parties' Agreed Addresses*]

Signed, etc.

SCHEDULE 2 [etc.]

[*Set out details of: Equipment; Term of Lease including Minimum Period and Rental Day [s], Rental; Fiscal Assumptions; Nett of Tax Rate of Return; Premises*]

Signed, etc.

16

Marketing and advertising agency

16.1 Introduction

Marketing and advertising is a complex business which leads to complicated legal arrangements. An agency is entrusted with very market-sensitive information by its clients. The relationship can often be an intensely personal one as well as corporate. A client places a considerable amount of trust in its marketing and advertising people.

On the other hand, the usual legal arrangement in the industry is for the agency to enter into contracts with third parties as principal in connection with the accounts it is managing. It is therefore exposed to a possibly high level of risk and for substantial sums of money. Many of the media used, e.g. national newspapers, television, radio, charge very large sums of money. Moreover, the agency may have to employ productions studios and the like, again all high value.

A further risk to the agency comes from the fact that it may itself be legally responsible for material it publishes on the basis of information provided by the client.

The contractual relationship with the client, therefore, must reflect this level of risk.

Whilst the marketing and advertising industry is not over-regulated it is subject to a degree of control especially regarding the accuracy of advertisements. Where the product is related to financial investment there is important statutory intervention in the form of the Financial Services and Markets Act 2000.

In this chapter the precedent is in the form of a full service advertising and marketing client contract (**Precedent 16A**). It is comprehensive and therefore may be adapted to a range of more limited services.

Copyright can often be an issue with material produced by an agency. The precedent includes a simple solution which may not, however, suit every situation. A specialist work on intellectual property should be consulted if an alternative solution is sought.

PRECEDENT 16A   Marketing and advertising agency contract

MARKETING AND ADVERTISING AGENCY CONTRACT

THIS AGREEMENT dated [*date*] is made by and between:

1. [*Name*] a company incorporated in England and Wales under company number [*number*] and whose registered office is at [*address*] ('the Agency'); and

2. [*Name*] a company incorporated in England and Wales under company number [*number*] and whose registered office is at [*address*] ('the Client').

RECITALS

1. The Agency provides advertising and marketing services.
2. The Client is a company engaged in the business of [...].
3. By this Agreement it is intended that the Agency shall be appointed to provide advertising and marketing services on [a non-exclusive *or* an exclusive basis] to the Client in the Territories and in respect of the Accounts.

DEFINITIONS

In this Agreement and the Schedules, the following words shall have the following meaning:

'Accounts'	Those accounts listed in Schedule 1 for which the Agency will provide the Services.
'Agreed Addresses'	The agreed addresses of the Parties set out in Schedule 2.
'Commencement Date'	The date this Agreement shall commence as set out in Schedule 3.
'Fee' and 'Fees'	The fees payable to the Agency as set out in Schedule 4.
'Initial Period'	The period between the Commencement Date and the first Renewal Date.
'Party' and 'Parties'	The Agency and the Client.
'Renewal Date'	The date on which this Agreement is renewed which shall be the anniversary of Commencement Date in each subsequent year.
'Renewal Period'	The period after a Renewal Date and before the next Renewal Date.
['RPI']	[The Retail Price Index maintained and published by the Office for National Statistics.]
'Schedule' and 'Schedules'	The Schedules to this Agreement.
'Sub-contractors'	Contractors engaged by the Agency to carry out services or functions that would otherwise be carried out by Agency staff.
'Services'	The services identified and set out in Schedule 1.
'Term'	The period during which the Agency will provide the Services.
'Territories'	The territories identified in Schedule 1 in respect of which the Agency will provide the Services.

INTERPRETATION

In this Agreement:

1. The singular includes the plural and one gender includes all.
2. References to Schedules and Clauses are to those in this Agreement.
3. Reference to a statutory provision includes any amendment or replacement provision relevant to the Agreement.
4. Reference to a document includes that document as amended, altered or replaced subsequent to the date of this Agreement.
5. Reference to writing includes facsimile transmission, e-mail, and similar media unless the context otherwise expressly provides.
6. Time expressed in days excludes the first day but includes the last day. If the last day does not fall on a normal business day in both England and Wales then the last day will be deemed to be the first normal business day.
7. The headings in this document do not form part of the Agreement.

OPERATIVE PROVISIONS

1. Client to appoint Agency

1.1. The Client hereby agrees to appoint the Agency to provide the Services [in the Territories].

2. Status of Agency

2.1. The Agency acts in all its contracts entered into with third parties arising from this Agreement as a principal and not as an agent of the Client.

3. The Term

3.1. The Term shall be the Initial Period and the subsequent Renewal Periods. The Term shall automatically continue until terminated under the provisions of this Agreement.

4. The Services

4.1. The Agency will provide the Services set out in Schedule 1 as varied from time to time.

4.2. [Where appropriate the Agency will allocate the specific employee or Sub-contractor requested by the Client to a particular Account as specified in Schedule 1 from time to time. Whilst the Agency will use its best endeavours to ensure that a specific employee or Sub-contractor is allocated it reserves the right to amend, change or substitute for that employee or Sub-contractor a suitable alternative and to do so will not constitute a breach of this Agreement].

5. Provision of information and briefings

5.1. The Client undertakes to provide clear and precise briefings as to its requirements and intentions in relation to work it wishes the Agency to undertake through the Services. It will provide such information or additional information as the Agency reasonably requires for this purpose when requested.

6. The Agency and other clients

6.1. During the Term the Agency will not provide services the same as or similar to the Services in the Territories without the Client's prior written permission:

> **6.1.1.** in respect of any product or service which is similar to any of the Accounts [or that of an associated or group company of the Client]

6.1.2. to a direct competitor of the Client [or of any associated or group company of the Client in respect of any of the Accounts].

7. Campaign plans

7.1. The Agency will first submit to the Client an outline campaign plan for its approval. When written approval of the outline campaign is given by the Client the Agency will:

7.1.1. submit for the Client's approval plans, storyboards, copy, images, scripts, layouts, artwork and such other materials as are appropriate

7.1.2. details of media, filming, recording and relevant schedules as are appropriate

7.1.3. wherever possible detailed estimates of costs, fees, third party charges and any other disbursements or outgoings in relation to the campaign. The Agency will thereafter inform the Client in writing of any anticipated material change in the cost.

8. Records of meetings, instructions, etc.

8.1. The Agency undertakes to provide within [72] hours written records of all material meetings between the Parties in relation to the Services and to record and provide to the Client within [72] hours a written record of any oral instructions received by it from the Client. Both records may be in note or bullet point form. Any material inaccuracy must be brought to the Agency's attention by the Client within [72] hours of the Client receiving the same.

9. Amendments

9.1. Amendments to a campaign (but not to this Agreement) by the Client may be requested by the Client after written approval has been given and the Agency will use its best endeavours to implement such changes subject to:

9.1.1. such changes not being precluded by contractual arrangements entered into by the Agency on the basis of the original written approval

9.1.2. the Client being prepared to accept any further or additional costs which may result therefrom which may include but not be limited to costs and charges incurred by the Agency to third parties.

10. Fees

10.1. The Fees payable to the Agency in relation to the Services provided under this Agreement shall be in accordance with those set out in Schedule 4 as varied from time to time.

10.2. A Fee shall be paid upon invoicing by the Agency. The Client and the Agency will agree a schedule of payments for ongoing work which shall be set out in Schedule 6 as varied from time to time.

10.3. If the Client does not make a payment by the date stated in an invoice or as otherwise provided for in this Agreement then the Agency shall be entitled:

10.3.1. to charge interest on the outstanding amount at the rate of [5]% a year above the base lending rate of [...] Bank plc, accruing daily

10.3.2. to require the Client to pay, in advance, for any Service which has not yet been performed

10.3.3. not to perform any further Service.

10.4. When making a payment the Client shall quote relevant reference numbers and the invoice number.

11. Determination of revised Fees

11.1. Where the Client has agreed to pay to the Agency an annual [or other periodic] Fee it shall be automatically reviewed on the following basis.

11.2. The Fee for any Renewal Period is to be determined by the Agency and notified in writing to the Client not less than [3] months prior to the relevant Renewal Date. [A Fee for any Renewal Period may not increase by a greater percentage than any percentage increase in the RPI between the beginning and end of the previous Renewal Period (or in the case of the first Renewal Period between the Commencement Date and the first Renewal Date)].

11.3. The Parties may agree a different figure from that set out in Clause 11.1, but in default of such agreement prior to the Renewal Date, the Fee payable shall be that set out in Clause 11.1.

12. Hourly or daily charge

12.1. Where an hourly or daily charge is payable by the Client the Fee shall be calculated by reference to the hourly charge-out rates as varied from time to time and set out in Schedule 4.

13. Commission

13.1. Where the Agency purchases any media, production or other service as part of a Service to the Client it shall be entitled to charge a commission of not more than [15]% to the buying in price paid by the Agency.

14. [Minimum Remuneration

14.1. The Client undertakes to pay the Agency a minimum [commission *or* total] Fee of £[...] during the Initial Period and each Renewal Period. If during the Initial Period and any Renewal Period the Fee payable [for commission *or* in total] is less than the minimum sum stated herein the Client shall make up the difference.

14.2. The minimum remuneration payable under this Clause 14 shall be varied for each Renewal Period by the percentage increase in the RPI between the beginning and end of the previous Renewal Period (or in the case of the first Renewal Period between the Commencement Date and the first Renewal Date)].

15. [Performance related payment

15.1. If the Agency achieves the results set out in Schedule 5 [by the end of the Initial or a Renewal Period] then the Client will make an additional payment in accordance with the table in Schedule 5].

16. Media space and time charges

16.1. The Agency will charge the Client for media costs at the providers' published rates from which it will deduct its commission. In the event that a discount, reduction or refund is made by a provider the Agency will pass on such discount, reduction or refund to the Client.

16.2. The Agency will utilise proof of appearance systems where available after consultation with the Client.

17. Cost of market research

17.1. Market research commissioned by the Client and carried out by the Agency (or Sub-contractor) will be discussed in advance with the Client and its scope and cost basis agreed.

18. Disbursements, materials and additional services

18.1. Materials, disbursements and additional services will be invoiced [at cost] [inclusive of commission where appropriate].

18.2. The following materials, disbursements and additional services will be invoiced in addition to the Fee:

18.2.1. [*Set out details of items to be charged for such as film production, artwork, legal clearance, hotels, travel, insurance, etc. It may be sensible to specify whether there is distinction between services provided inside and outside the Territory*].

19. Foreign currency

19.1. Where media space and time, market research, materials, disbursements and additional services have to be purchased in a foreign currency by the Agency the Client will be charged the sterling equivalent [at the rate prevailing at the time of payment of the invoice from the supplier by the Agency].

20. Payment for media space and time, market research, disbursements, materials and additional services

20.1. Charges for materials, disbursements and additional services will invoiced on a monthly basis and must be paid within [14] days. Where substantial outlay is required in advance by the Agency the Agency will invoice the Client in advance.

20.2. Where any surcharge, penalty or increased charge has been incurred because of the action or inaction of the Client, whether by delay, mistake or whatever reason or cause, the Client shall be liable to reimburse the Agency in full and the surcharge, penalty or increased charge will be invoiced to the Client.

20.3. If the Client does not make a payment by the date stated in an invoice or as otherwise provided for in this Agreement then the Agency shall be entitled:

20.3.1. to charge interest on the outstanding amount at the rate of [5]% a year above the base lending rate of [...] Bank plc, accruing daily

20.3.2. to require the Client to pay, in advance, for any disbursements, materials and services.

20.4. When making a payment the Client shall quote relevant reference numbers and the invoice number.

21. Keeping of records

21.1. The Agency will keep a full record of all charges and expenditure incurred by it which are reimbursable by the Client. [The Client may carry out (by itself or its agent) an audit of the Agency's records in respect thereof on giving not less than [14] days written notice to the Agency. The audit must be carried out during normal office hours and the Agency will afford the Client access to all relevant books and vouchers. In the event that there has been an overpayment by the Client the Agency shall reimburse it within [14] days].

21.2. As part of the Agency's remuneration is based upon results the Client will keep a full record of those matters upon which the relevant targets are based. Within [14] days of the end of the Initial Period and thereafter of each Renewal Period the Client will provide the Agency with the relevant information indicating which target[s] has been met. The Client will permit an audit of the relevant records within [14] days of receiving written notice from the Agency and will make up any underpayment within [14] days of receiving an invoice from the Agency.

22. Third party contracts

22.1. The Agency will provide the Client with copies of the terms and conditions and other contractual provisions relating to contracts into which it enters with third parties in connection with the Services if requested by the Client. In every case, unless expressly agreed to the contrary, the terms and conditions and other contractual obligations and benefits as between the Agency and the Client in relation thereto will correspond to those between the Agency and the third parties save in respect of the fee or charge payable.

22.2. Before appointing a third party supplier the Agency will consult the Client and if required obtain more than one quotation where appropriate. Where the Agency has a financial or other interest in a potential supplier it will so inform the Client.

23. Copyright

23.1. [The Agency will retain copyright in all advertising and other material it produces for and is paid for by the Client [subject to the right of the Client to use, modify or adapt it for its own purposes as it wishes]].

23.2. For the avoidance of doubt the Client will not obtain the copyright in:

23.2.1. stock photographs obtained from news or photographic agencies

23.2.2. photographic or film negatives.

24. Confidential information

24.1. The Parties agree not to disclose any confidential information provided by the other Party during the Term or at any time thereafter to any third party save where the law requires. The Parties also agree not to use any such confidential information for any purpose other than for the provision of the Services and will not use the information for any business or other purpose of their own. For the avoidance of doubt such information includes but is not limited either in type, *genus* or subject to:

24.1.1. all business information supplied to the Agency by the Client for the purpose of the Agency providing the Services

24.1.2. all marketing information and intelligence

24.1.3. all trade secrets, processes and formulae.

24.2. For the proper protection of the confidential information the Parties will ensure that:

24.2.1. any employee or member of their staff, whether temporary or permanent, will at the commencement of their employment and no later be provided with a contract of employment or engagement which will include a like obligation to that of the Party in respect of confidential information

24.2.2. any [director *or* partner] of the Parties or any associated [company *or* firm] will be required to provide an undertaking in regard to confidential information in like form to that set out before being given access to confidential information.

24.3. Where appropriate the Agency will obtain like assurances from any third party entrusted with confidential information prior to disclosing to that party.

25. Warranties

25.1. The Agency warrants that it will maintain:

25.1.1. professional indemnity insurance throughout the Term at a level of at least £[...] for any single claim

25.1.2. sufficient insurance adequately to cover any property belonging to the Client which is in its possession or care or placed by the Agency in the possession or care of a third party in connection with the Services

25.1.3. transmission and production insurance for all advertising undertaken for television.

25.2. [The Agency warrants that, having taken such legal and other professional advice as the Parties have agreed, the publication and any other use of the materials provided under this Agreement shall not infringe any civil or criminal law or regulation including copyright, design right, libel, trademark or constitute passing off [in the Territories]].

25.3. The Client warrants that to the best of its knowledge information and belief all Account information supplied to the Agency before and during the Term will be accurate and not in any way contrary to [English law *or* any law applicable in any part of the Territory].

26. Indemnities

26.1. The Client agrees to indemnify the Agency in respect of any losses, damage or liability the Agency may incur as a result of its acts or omissions, whether deliberate, accidental, negligent or reckless, in the course of the performance or purported performance of its obligations or rights under this Agreement whether such acts or omissions amount to a breach of an express or implied obligation under this Agreement or a breach of any other legal requirement or obligation, code of practice, licence, consent, forbearance, approval, permission or rule.

26.2. For the avoidance of doubt losses, damage and liability shall include but not be limited to economic and commercial loss, loss of goodwill, legal and other costs associated with legal proceedings of any kind which the Agency has to bring or to which it has to respond, fines, penalties, damages and any financial consequence whatever flowing directly or indirectly from the matters set out in this Clause 26.

27. Extent of Agency's liability

27.1. The liability of the Agency under or in connection with this Agreement for the provision of the Services whether arising in contract, tort, negligence, breach of statutory duty or otherwise howsoever shall not exceed [£[...] *or* a refund of that part of the Fee for the Initial or Renewal Period (as applicable) in which the claim arises already paid by the Client to the Agency under this Agreement. The relevant Fee for the purpose of this Clause 27 will be that which relates to the particular Service in respect of which a successful claim is brought by the Client].

27.2. The Agency shall not be liable to the Client for any indirect, consequential or economic loss including but not limited to damage, costs or expenses of any description, loss of profit, business, goodwill, turnover or any other loss arising from its performance or non-performance of its obligations in connection with this Agreement whether arising from breach of contract, tort, breach of duty, negligence or any other cause of action.

27.3. Nothing in this Agreement shall exclude or limit the Agency's liability for death or personal injury or in any other way which is contrary to law.

28. Termination

28.1. The Agency may terminate this Agreement forthwith in the event that the Client:

28.1.1. is [declared bankrupt *or* wound up due to insolvency]

28.1.2. makes or seeks a composition with its creditors

28.1.3. enters into or seeks an insolvent voluntary arrangement

28.1.4. becomes the subject of the appointment of a manager, receiver or liquidator

28.1.5. is the subject of an administration order

28.1.6. has its assets charged or seized for the satisfaction of a debt

28.1.7. divulges confidential business information to an unauthorised third party

28.1.8. fails to pay any sum due under this Agreement for more than [28 days] after its due date

28.1.9. fails to furnish any document or other information which the Client is obliged to provide within [28 days] of its due date.

29. Advertising standards and levies

29.1. The Parties will each use their best endeavours to ensure that they comply with all advertising regulations.

29.2. The Client will forthwith inform the Agency in the event that it considers that any proposed or actual advertising is misleading or false.

29.3. The Agency will include in its invoices to the Client if applicable a figure for the levies payable to the Advertising Standards Board of Finance and the Broadcast Advertising Standards Board of Finance (or any successors).

29.4. If the Client is paying commission to the Agency no commission will be payable on the levies.

30. [Promotion of financial products

30.1. It will be the responsibility of the Client to ensure that any promotion to which the Financial Services and Markets Act 2000 ('FSMA') is applicable complies with the FSMA and all relevant rules, regulations and guidance issued by the Financial Services Authority].

31. Data protection

31.1. Each Party shall ensure that it complies with all the requirements of the Data Protection Act 1998 and any other relevant legislation and regulations in matters related to the performance of this Agreement.

32. Waiver

32.1. No failure, neglect or delay in enforcing any of the terms of this Agreement may be construed as a waiver of any of the other Party's rights in respect thereof nor such neglect, failure or delay a variation of the express terms of the Agreement.

33. *Force majeure*

33.1. The Agency shall not have any liability to the Client for any delay, omission, failure or inadequate performance of this Agreement which is the result of circumstances beyond the reasonable control of the Agency. Where the Agency is so affected in its performance of this Agreement it will notify the Client in writing as soon as is reasonably possible.

33.2. Where the performance of this Agreement is affected by *force majeure* the Agency shall use its best endeavours to overcome the problem as soon as practically possible.

33.3. In the event that the *force majeure* renders or is likely to render materially full performance of a Service impossible for a period of more than [12] weeks then the Client may terminate the Agreement in respect [only] of that Service upon giving the Agency [4] weeks written notice.

33.4. For the avoidance of doubt any losses or costs that either Party incurs as a result of a *force majeure* shall be borne by that Party.

34. No solicitation

34.1. Each of the Parties shall not for a period of [12] months after the date of this Agreement seek to entice away or recruit any employee of the other who was so employed at the date of this Agreement.

35. Invalid clauses

35.1. In the event that any term of this Agreement is found to be invalid or otherwise unenforceable then such term shall be regarded and construed as severable from the Agreement so as not to affect the validity and enforceability of the remainder.

36. Assignment

36.1. Neither Party may assign, charge, mortgage, sub-contract, delegate or otherwise assign or transfer its rights or obligations under this Agreement save where express provision in made for the same in this Agreement, without the prior written consent of the other Party.

36.2. A Party may assign or transfer its rights under this Agreement if such assignment or transfer takes place in the context of the disposal of all of its business to which the Service is related provided that the proposed assignee or transferee undertakes to the other Party directly in a form reasonably required by that other Party to be bound by the obligations of the proposed assignor.

37. [Third party rights

37.1. The Parties to this Agreement agree that it is not hereby intended that any rights should be conferred upon or enforceable by any third party as defined in the Contracts (Rights of Third Parties) Act 1999].

38. Whole agreement

38.1. This Agreement supersedes and replaces any previous agreement between the Parties whether oral or in writing in relation to the Services. The Parties hereby agree that in entering into this Agreement they have not relied upon any warranty or representation made by or on behalf of the other Party save where expressly stated in this Agreement. The Parties hereby agree that this Agreement constitutes the whole agreement between the Parties in respect of the Services.

38.2. Nothing in this Clause 38 shall be construed as limiting or excluding either Party's liability to the other for fraud or deceit in inducing the making of this Agreement.

39. Notices

39.1. All notices under this Agreement shall be in writing and shall be delivered personally [or by first class, registered or recorded post] [or by facsimile transmission] in every case to the other Party's Agreed Address. [In the case of first class post notice will be deemed to be received [3] business days after the date of posting.]

40. Law and jurisdiction

40.1. This Agreement is governed by the law of England and Wales and is subject to the [exclusive] jurisdiction of the courts of England and Wales.

41. Schedules

41.1. The Schedules form part of this Agreement including any subsequent amendments made thereto.

Signed, etc.

SCHEDULE 1

The Accounts, the Services and the Territories

[*List the Accounts covered by this Agreement, the Services required for each and the Territories relevant to each*]

Signed, etc.

SCHEDULE 2

Parties' Agreed Addresses

[*List Agreed Addresses of the Parties*]

Signed, etc.

SCHEDULE 3

Commencement Date

The Commencement Date for this Agreement shall be [*date*]

Signed, etc.

SCHEDULE 4

Fees

[*Depending on the basis for Fee charges this Schedule should set out annual retainer/hourly rates/results-based Fee) but not third party charges, commission rates etc.*]

Signed, etc.

SCHEDULE 5

Targets for results-based Fee

[*The relevant targets or other measures should be set out here.*]

Signed, etc.

SCHEDULE 6

Agreed payments schedule

[*The agreed payments schedule should be set out here.*]

Signed, etc.

17

Sale of goods

17.1   Introduction

This chapter relates to contracts for the sale of goods in a commercial context and therefore does not include consumer contracts. It deals with both domestic and international contracts. It should be borne in mind that there is a substantial difference between domestic and international contracts for sale of goods in the matter of freedom of contract – see the Unfair Contract Terms Act (UCTA) 1977, s.26 – because in the case of international contracts the constraints on excluding or limiting liability by reference to a test of reasonableness are excluded.

A very necessary pre-consideration is the choice of law. This is now governed by Regulation 593/2008/EC (Rome I) which, at least in a commercial context, allows for considerable freedom as to choice of law. Enforceability will be governed by Regulation 44/2001/EC.

UCTA 1977, s.2(1) provides that no term which purports to exclude or limit liability for negligence causing death or personal injury can be effective. Any other limitation or exclusion clause is subject to a test of reasonableness (s.2(2) and see Schedule 2) as is one excluding liability for misrepresentation (s.8(1)). The exclusion or restriction of liability for breach of the terms implied by the Sale of Goods Act (SOGA) 1979, ss.13–15 is subject to the statutory test of reasonableness (s.6(2) and (3)).

Where one party deals on the written standard terms of business of the other, the latter can only restrict or exclude liability for breach, or claim to be entitled to render a performance substantially different from that which may be reasonably expected or to render no performance at all in respect of whole or part of the contract by reference to a contract term to the extent that such is reasonable (s.3). Terms authorised by statute or international treaty are excluded (s.29).

A distinction must be drawn between a contract for the sale of goods under which title passes (SOGA 1979, s.2(4)) and an agreement to sell goods (s.2(5)) under which transfer of title is postponed or is subject to the fulfilment of a condition (see, for example, *Shaw* v. *Metropolitan Police Commissioner* [1987] 1 WLR 1332, CA).

Under a sale of goods contract general ownership in the goods must pass, not some other lesser or different interest, e.g. the rights of a bailee to possession (SOGA 1979, s.61(1)). However a part owner can transfer his part ownership (s.2(2)).

This chapter includes two precedents. One is a set of standard terms and conditions for commercial sales (**Precedent 17A**). The other is a contract for the long-term sale of goods which is designed to provide that each sale is a separate transaction subject to the seller's standard terms and conditions (**Precedent 17B**).

PRECEDENT 17A   Standard conditions of sale

STANDARD TERMS AND CONDITIONS

1. In these standard conditions the following shall have the meaning set out in this clause unless the context otherwise requires:

'Purchaser'	The party which has agreed to buy the goods from the Seller.
'Seller'	[*X co Ltd.*]
'Conditions'	Those terms set out in these standard conditions and any special conditions which the Seller has agreed in writing with the Purchaser.
'Goods'	Those articles which the Purchaser has agreed to purchase.
'Delivery Date'	The date upon which the Seller undertakes to deliver the Goods to the Purchaser.
'Price'	The price at which the Seller has agreed to sell and the Purchaser to buy the Goods.

2. The headings in these Conditions do not form a part thereof.

3. These Conditions apply to all contracts of sale between the Seller and the Purchaser to the exclusion of all others, whether contained in a purchase invoice, Purchaser's terms and conditions or otherwise save where either:

3.1. the Seller agrees in writing that the Conditions may be so varied or

3.2. such of the Purchaser's or other terms are consistent with the Conditions and purport

3.2.1. neither to add to nor increase the obligations of the Seller nor

3.2.2. to reduce, restrict or limit the obligations of the Purchaser.

4. The placing of any order by the Purchaser shall be deemed to be an offer to purchase Goods subject to these Conditions. The acceptance by the Purchaser of any Goods purchased from the Seller shall be conclusive evidence of acceptance of these Conditions.

5. Acceptance of any Goods shall be conclusive proof of acceptance by the Buyer of these terms and conditions.

6. No variation of these terms shall be effective unless contained in a document signed by the Seller.

7. **Price**

7.1. The Price of the Goods shall be that set out in Schedule 1 of this Agreement or the Seller's quoted price, whichever is applicable.

7.2. The Price set out or quoted does not include VAT which shall be chargeable in addition at the applicable rate.

8. Payment

8.1. Payment on any invoice is due within [30] days of rendering. Time is of the essence in respect of this term.

8.2. Interest on amounts overdue including VAT will accrue at the rate of [2%] above the ordinary lending rate of [...] Bank from time to time and will continue to accrue both before and after any judgment unless the relevant judgment rate after judgment is higher.

9. [Retention of title by the Seller

9.1. The title to any consignment of the Goods will remain with the Seller until the Seller has received:

9.1.1. full payment for them

9.1.2. full payment for any other Goods or products supplied under any other contract between the Seller and the Purchaser.

9.2. Until full payment is received as specified in this Clause 9 the Purchaser hereby acknowledges that he has possession of the Goods solely as bailee and in a fiduciary capacity for the Seller.

9.3. The Purchaser shall keep the Goods separate and clearly identifiable as the property of the Seller until title has passed under the provisions of this Clause 9].

10. The Goods

10.1. The quantity and description of the Goods supplied under these Conditions shall be as set out or identified in the Seller's quotation.

11. Warranty as to conformity with description

11.1. The Seller warrants that the Goods supplied under these Conditions will correspond, at the time of delivery, with the description it has given to the Purchaser. All other warranties, terms or conditions relating to quality, fitness for purpose or condition, whether implied by common law or statute, or express are excluded save where to do so would be by law impermissible.

12. Delivery

12.1. Risk shall pass on delivery and delivery shall be effected when:

12.1.1. the Goods are collected by the Purchaser or its agent or carrier or

12.1.2. the Goods are delivered to the address agreed in the order confirmation or such other address as has been agreed by the Parties in writing prior thereto. Delivery shall be on the Delivery Date but in respect thereof time shall not be of the essence although the Seller will use its best endeavours to effect it at the date therein specified. No liability will accrue to the Seller for late delivery of the Goods and in respect of short or non-delivery its liability shall be limited to a refund of that part of the purchase price which reflects the non-delivery or shortfall or the making up of such short delivery at the Seller's discretion.

13. Liability for breach

13.1. Whilst the Seller will endeavour at all times to comply with its legal and contractual obligations to the Purchaser it does not accept liability for any loss suffered by the Purchaser as a result of any misrepresentation, misdescription, breach of contract, breach of duty or other act or omission (unless fraudulent) however made or caused which constitutes more than a refund of any sum paid or the waiver of any sum contractually payable by the Purchaser for the Goods.

13.2. The Purchaser does not accept liability for any consequential economic or other losses suffered by the customer whether resulting from misrepresentation, misdescription, breach of contract, breach of duty or other act or omission (unless fraudulent) however caused.

13.3. Nothing in these Conditions shall limit the right of either Party to seek to recover damages for personal injury or death occasioned by breach of contract or breach of duty by the other Party, its employees or agents.

14. Acceptance

14.1. The Purchaser shall be deemed to have accepted the Goods [24] hours after delivery. Thereafter the Purchaser will not be entitled to reject the Goods on the basis that they do not conform to those to be supplied under these Conditions.

15. Liability after acceptance of the Goods

15.1. The Seller shall have no liability to the Purchaser in respect of the Goods after they have been accepted by it.

16. Liability after rejection of the Goods

16.1. If the Purchaser is entitled to and does reject the Goods the Seller shall have no further obligation to supply goods which conform to those the subject matter of these Conditions.

17. Law and jurisdiction

17.1. This Agreement is governed by the laws of England and Wales and is subject to the [exclusive] jurisdiction of the courts of England and Wales.

18. Invalid clauses

18.1. In the event that any term of these Conditions is found to be invalid or otherwise unenforceable then such term shall be regarded and construed as severable from the Conditions so as not to affect the validity and enforceability of the remainder.

19. [Schedules

19.1. The Schedules form part of this Agreement including any subsequent amendments made thereto.]

Signed, etc.

[SCHEDULE 1

Price list

[*Set out price list*]

Signed, etc.]

PRECEDENT 17B   Long-term sale agreement

SALE AGREEMENT

THIS AGREEMENT is dated [...] and is made BETWEEN:

1.   [*Name of purchaser*] [of [*address*] *or* whose registered office is at [*address*]], [*company registration number*] ('the Purchaser'); and
2.   [*Name of seller*] [of [*address*] *or* whose registered office is at [*address*]], [*company registration number*] ('the Seller').

RECITALS

1. The Seller [manufactures *or* deals in *or* imports *etc.*] the Goods as defined below.
2. The Purchaser requires the Goods [for resale *or* manufacturing *or* export *or* use in its [*construction*] business *etc.*].

DEFINITIONS

'Commencement Date'	The date upon which the supply of the Goods will begin under this Agreement.
'Confirmation of Receipt'	Written confirmation of receipt of a Purchase Order.
'Delivery Date'	The date upon which a purchase order will stipulate the time of delivery in accordance with the terms of this Agreement.
'Goods'	Those goods which are identified in Schedule 1 to this Agreement as may be amended from time to time by agreement.
'Minimum Value'	Minimum value of Goods to be purchased under this Agreement in each year of the Term as set out in Schedule 2 to this Agreement as may be amended from time to time by agreement.
'Parties'	The Seller and the Purchaser.
'Party's Agreed Address'	Each Party's agreed address for service of notices under this Agreement as set out in Schedule 3.
'Price'	The price of the Goods as set out Schedule 4 to this Agreement as may be amended from time to time by agreement.
'Purchase Order'	Orders in writing provided to the Seller by the Purchaser under the terms of this Agreement.
'Seller's Usual Terms and Conditions'	The Seller's usual terms and conditions as set out in Schedule 5 or as subsequently notified to the Purchaser from time to time during the Term.
'Specification'	Any description or details of or relating to the Goods as set out in Schedule 6 to this Agreement or as agreed from time to time by the Parties.
'Term'	The period of currency of this Agreement as agreed herein or as subsequently agreed, varied or extended by the Parties as set out in Schedule 7.

INTERPRETATION

In this Agreement:

1. The singular includes the plural and one gender includes all.
2. References to Schedules and Clauses are to those in this Agreement.
3. Reference to a statutory provision includes any amendment or replacement provision relevant to the Agreement.
4. Reference to a document includes that document as amended, altered or replaced subsequent to the date of this Agreement.
5. Reference to writing includes facsimile transmission, e-mail, and similar media unless the context otherwise expressly provides.

6.   Time expressed in days excludes the first day but includes the last day. If the last day does not fall on a normal business day in both England and Wales then the last day will be deemed to be the first normal business day.

7.   The headings in this document do not form part of the Agreement.

OPERATIVE PROVISIONS

1. Supply of Goods

1.1. The Commencement Date of this Agreement shall be [...].

1.2. The Purchaser may place and the Seller will accept Purchase Orders for Goods from the Commencement Date.

1.3. Each Purchase Order must be in writing and must state:

1.3.1. the Delivery Date [which unless agreed otherwise in writing will not be less than [10 days]]

1.3.2. the quantity and Specification of the Goods required. [The Seller will not be bound to accept a Purchase Order for [more] [less] than [a thousand] items of Goods for delivery within [1 month]].

1.4. Upon receipt of a Purchase Order the Seller shall send to the Purchaser within [7 days] a Confirmation of Receipt of the Order which shall specify the Price.

1.5. [The Purchaser will purchase Goods to at least the Minimum Value during each calendar year during the Term beginning with the Commencement Date].

1.6. In order to assist the Seller in providing the best service to the Purchaser the Purchaser will use its best endeavours not less than [8 weeks] before the commencement of each new year of the Term to provide an estimate of the likely volume of purchasing of Goods it anticipates making during that year. If that estimate should change thereafter the Purchaser will notify the Seller at the first opportunity.

1.7. The Seller will use its best endeavours to maintain sufficient stocks to meet the anticipated sales to the Purchaser based upon the Purchaser's estimates.

1.8. The Seller reserves the right to change the Specification of the Goods. If it does so it will notify the Purchaser in writing as soon as reasonably practical of the change in Specification.

2. Individual contracts of sale

2.1. Each Confirmation of Receipt of a Purchase Order shall constitute the acceptance of a separate contract to sell Goods to the Purchaser under the terms of this Agreement and subject to the Seller's Usual Terms and Conditions provided that the Confirmation of Receipt does not expressly state that the order is not accepted. In the event that the order is not accepted the Seller will specify in the Confirmation of Receipt the reason or reasons for its non-acceptance. For the avoidance of doubt the Seller may subsequently rely, in resisting any claim for breach of contract or other legal action by the Purchaser, upon any further or other ground for being entitled to reject the order even if such was not specified in the Confirmation of Receipt.

2.2. In the event that there is any inconsistency between the terms of this Agreement and the Seller's Usual Terms and Conditions the terms of this Agreement shall prevail.

3. Duration and termination of this Agreement

3.1. The Term of this Agreement is [... years] from the Commencement Date.

3.2. Non-payment, remediable and irremediable breaches

3.2.1. In the event that either Party:

3.2.1.1. fails to remedy any remediable breach of this Agreement or the Seller's Usual Terms and Conditions of which it has been notified in writing by the other Party within [28] days

3.2.1.2. commits any irremediable material breach or persistently commits any remediable breach of this Agreement or the Seller's Usual Terms and Conditions

then the other Party may terminate this Agreement forthwith by serving notice of termination.

3.2.2. In the event that the Purchaser fails to make any payment on time as required by this Agreement or the Seller's Usual Term and Conditions the Seller may terminate this Agreement forthwith by serving notice of termination.

3.3. Failure to purchase Goods to Minimum Value

3.3.1. If the Purchaser fails to purchase Goods to the Minimum Value during a year of the Term the Seller may terminate this Agreement on giving [21 *days*] written notice. Such notice must be given within [28 *days*] of the end of the relevant year calculated from the day after the anniversary of the Commencement Date.

3.4. Insolvency

3.4.1. Either Party may terminate this Agreement forthwith in the event that the other Party:

3.4.1.1. is [declared bankrupt *or* wound up due to insolvency]

3.4.1.2. makes or seeks a composition with its creditors

3.4.1.3. enters into or seeks an insolvent voluntary arrangement

3.4.1.4. becomes the subject of the appointment of a manager, receiver or liquidator

3.4.1.5. is the subject of an administration order

3.4.1.6. has its assets charged or seized for the satisfaction of a debt

3.4.1.7. fails to pay any sum due under this Agreement for more than [28 *days*].

3.5. [Re-organisation of business structure or ownership

3.5.1. Either Party may terminate this Agreement if there is any material re-organisation of the other Party's business structure unless:

3.5.1.1. such re-organisation is not the result of insolvency;

3.5.1.2. the resultant company or organisation is bound by the provisions of this Agreement

3.5.1.3. the beneficial ownership of the resultant entity is not in the hands of a competitor of the first Party mentioned herein except to the extent that such ownership does not exceed [10%] of the total].

4. Whole agreement and previous agreements

4.1. This Agreement supersedes and replaces any previous agreement between the Seller and the Purchaser whether oral or in writing in relation to its subject matter. The Parties hereby agree that in entering into this Agreement they have not relied upon any warranty or representation made by or on behalf of the other Party save where expressly stated in this Agreement. The Parties hereby agree that this Agreement constitutes the whole agreement between the Parties in respect of the subject matter.

4.2. Nothing in this Clause 4 shall be construed as limiting or excluding either Party's liability to the other for fraud or deceit in inducing the making of this Agreement.

5. Waiver

5.1. No failure, neglect or delay in enforcing any of the terms of this Agreement may be construed as a waiver of either Party's rights in respect thereof nor such neglect, failure or delay a variation of the express terms of the Agreement.

6. Variation

6.1. Any variation of the terms of this Agreement must be in writing signed by the Parties.

7. Agreement personal to the Parties

7.1. This Agreement is personal to the Parties. The Parties may not assign their rights or liabilities under this Agreement without the express prior written permission of the other Party.

8. Notices

8.1. All notices under this Agreement shall be in writing and shall be delivered personally [or by first class, registered or recorded post] [or by facsimile transmission] in every case to the other Party's Agreed Address. [In the case of first class post notice will be deemed to be received [3] business days after the date of posting.]

8.2. Any variation of the terms of this Agreement must be in writing signed by the Parties.

9. Law and jurisdiction

9.1. This Agreement is governed by the laws of England and Wales and is subject to the [exclusive] jurisdiction of the courts of England and Wales.

10. Schedules

10.1. The Schedules form part of this Agreement including any subsequent amendments made thereto.

Signed, etc.

SCHEDULE 1

The Goods

[*Describe Goods to be supplied by the Seller*]

Signed, etc.

SCHEDULE 2

Minimum Value

[*Set out details of Minimum Value of sales required*]

Signed, etc.

SCHEDULE 3
Agreed Addresses

[*Set out details of Agreed Addresses*]

Signed, etc.

SCHEDULE 4
Prices

[*Set out details of Prices*]

Signed, etc.

SCHEDULE 5
Seller's Usual Terms and Conditions

[*Copy of Terms and Conditions*]

Signed, etc.

SCHEDULE 6
Specification of the Goods

[*Set out Specification of the Goods*]

Signed, etc.

SCHEDULE 7
The Term

[*Term of the Agreement*]

Signed, etc.

18

Sponsorship

18.1 Introduction

The principal area for commercial sponsorship is sport. It is important always to distinguish between sponsorship and investment. The latter may give the investor some proprietary or direct commercial interest in the spondee whereas a characteristic of true sponsorship is that the 'interest' of the sponsor is entirely indirect.

The principal benefits to a sponsor will be:

(a) the promotion of its corporate image;
(b) promoting the image of the sponsor in the community connected with the sport;
(c) in some cases promoting a particular product or service where it is relevant to the sport.

Sponsorship can take many forms. It can relate to a particular event, to equipment or to sports clothes or to a venue such as a stadium. In some cases, especially where the object of the sponsorship is a particular event, there is a possibility of the sponsor incurring some degree of third party liability, or at the very least, potential damage to its reputation.

There are four broad types or levels of sponsorship:

1. **Sole sponsorship**
   This is where the sponsor has the exclusive rights to an event, promotion, etc. It alone will have its brand and name displayed. Sole sponsorship is often used in relation to a sporting venue and may involve the venue being renamed after the sponsor for the duration of the sponsorship. The benefit to the spondee is that there is only one sponsor to manage and the duration can be clear-cut and simple. With the benefits come disadvantages as well. Sole sponsorship may involve a substantial financial burden and the spondee is entirely reliant upon the one source.

2. **Primary sponsorship**
   A primary sponsor will be the principal sponsor for an event, etc. but there will be other secondary sponsors. This enables the financial benefit and burden to be spread.

3. **Secondary sponsorship**

   Very often secondary sponsors will support a particular aspect of an event, e.g. food, clothing, programmes, transport. This will often be relevant to their business.

4. **Equal sponsorship**

   The concept here is usually that the spondee will design a sponsorship package or packages which will cost a finite amount, be limited in number and provide comparable benefits to all sponsors of a particular package. The problem with this can be that if some packages remain unsold there is a temptation to lower the price as an alternative to running short of funding, which may cause a problem with the earlier tranche. Sponsors will almost always want to know how many packages will be available and whether they will be available to rival rather than complementary businesses.

The agreement need not necessarily be in the form of a signed agreement. In many cases a letter or even a terms and conditions of accepting sponsorship may suffice.

   The key elements from experience which have to be addressed are:

1. What precisely is the spondee offering in benefits to the sponsor?
2. What precisely must the sponsor do, for example, providing logos, copy or kit by a specific date or in a specific way?

The precedent in this chapter is intended to be indicative and includes example clauses and schedules (**Precedent 18A**). It is written from the point of view of the spondee. There may be tax implications for the sponsor but those are outside the scope of this chapter and are really for the potential sponsor to raise.

PRECEDENT 18A   Sponsorship agreement

SPONSORSHIP AGREEMENT

THIS AGREEMENT is made the [... day of ...]

BETWEEN:

1. [*Name of company*] a company incorporated in England under number [*registration number*] whose registered office is at [*address*] ('the Club'); and
2. [*Name of company*] a company incorporated in England under number [*registration number*] whose registered office is at [*address*] ('the Sponsor').

RECITALS

1. The Club wishes to help finance and support its activities by providing opportunities for the sponsorship of its [Events] [and] [Activities].
2. The Sponsor wishes to support the Club in its [Events] [and] [Activities] by sponsorship [which may include both financial and provision of goods and services in kind] under the terms of this Agreement.

DEFINITIONS

In this Agreement and the Schedules, the following words shall have the following meaning:

['Activities']	[The activities carried on by the Club as set out in Schedule 1].
'Commencement Date'	The commencement date of this Agreement is [*date*].
['Events']	[The events specified in Schedule 2].
'IPR'	All intellectual property rights relating to the protection by law of any design, invention, drawing, specification, mark, trade mark, get-up or other work including but not limited to those rights which may be protected by any form of registration including where applicable the right to seek such registration available for the protection of any discovery, invention, name, design, process or works in which copyright or any rights in the nature of copyright subsist and all patents, copyrights, registered designs, design rights, trade marks, service marks and other forms of protection from time to time subsisting in relation to the same, including the right to apply for any such registration.
'Party' and 'Parties'	The Club and the Sponsor.
['Platinum', 'Gold', 'Silver' and 'Bronze']	[Categories of sponsors and sponsorships as set out in Schedule 3].
'Protected Products'	Those classes of products and services which are listed in Schedule 5.
'[Sponsored Kit']	[Playing kit worn by the Club's members and representatives and paid for or provided by the Sponsor].
'Sponsor's Benefits'	The benefits to the Sponsor provided under this Agreement as set out in Schedule 3 and as varied from time to time by agreement.
'Sponsor's Obligations'	The obligations of the Sponsor as set out in Schedule 4.
'Term'	The term of this Agreement is [[…] months *or* […] years] from the Commencement Date.
['Venues']	[Venues where the Club organises Events from time to time [and as set out in Schedule 3]].

INTERPRETATION

In this Agreement:

1. The singular includes the plural and one gender includes all.
2. References to Schedules and Clauses are to those in this Agreement.
3. Reference to a statutory provision includes any amendment or replacement provision relevant to the Agreement.
4. Reference to a document includes that document as amended, altered or replaced subsequent to the date of this Agreement.
5. Reference to writing includes facsimile transmission, e-mail, and similar media unless the context otherwise expressly provides.
6. Time expressed in days excludes the first day but includes the last day. If the last day does not fall on a normal business day in both England and Wales then the last day will be deemed to be the first normal business day.
7. The headings in this document do not form part of the Agreement.

OPERATIVE PROVISIONS

1. Term

1.1. This Agreement shall take effect from the Commencement Date and continue until the end of the Term unless terminated earlier in accordance with the provisions below.

1.2. [The Term may be extended at the option of the Sponsor for a further period equating to the original Term provided that the Sponsor notifies the Club in writing of its intention to do so not less than [4] weeks before the expiry of the Term in which case the extended Term shall be on the same terms as in this Agreement save that it shall not have any provision for further extension].

2. Sponsor's Benefits and Obligations

2.1. The Club will provide the Sponsor with the Sponsor's Benefits in consideration for the Sponsor performing the Sponsor's Obligations.

3. Organisation of Events

3.1. The Events will be organised by the Club or its appointees and the Sponsor shall not be responsible for their organisation.

4. Obligations of the Club to the Sponsor

4.1. During the Term and on condition that the Sponsor has timeously complied with the Sponsor's Obligations in full the Club undertakes the following obligations to the Sponsor:

4.1.1. [the organisation and promotion of the Events to good and proper standard and in accordance with Schedule 2 including the design and use of appropriate logos and other marks]

4.1.2. [the inclusion of a sponsor's credit on [all] [programmes *or* advertising and promotional material]

4.1.3. [the carrying out of the Activities as set out in Schedule 1 in a proper and efficient way]

4.1.4. [the incorporation of the Sponsor's logo or mark in a manner acceptable to the Sponsor in the promotional material connected with the Events]

4.1.5. [not permitting the advertisement, sale or promotion of any of the Protected Products at any Event other than those of the Sponsor, though for the avoidance of doubt, it shall not be a breach of this obligation if the products or services of another sponsor or other third party are advertised, sold or promoted which sponsor or other third party is also in any way associated with the Protected Products but which Protected Products are not themselves advertised, sold or promoted at an Event by the other sponsor or third party]

4.1.6. [providing as much notice as reasonably possible and in any case not less than [4] weeks written notice of each Event]

4.1.7. [liaising with the Sponsor with a view to obtaining maximum publicity for the Sponsor at each Event]

4.1.8. [taking all reasonable steps to ensure that each Event is [televised *or* reported in the [national *or* local] press *or* advertised on [local] radio]

4.1.9. [obtaining all necessary licences, consents and permissions for each Event as required by law and consistent with best practice]

4.1.10. [providing appropriate VIP facilities for the Sponsor and its [number] nominated guests at any Event]

4.1.11. [in the event of any occurrence in connection with an Event which may have the effect of damaging the reputation and standing of the Sponsor but which is not caused or contributed to by the Sponsor by any act or omission on its part, using its best endeavours to minimise the impact thereon in liaison with the Sponsor]

4.1.12. [ensuring that all playing members or representatives of the Club wear the Sponsored Kit in all competitive matches displaying the Sponsor's logo]

4.1.13. [assisting in or facilitating the distribution of the Sponsor's products to attenders at Events].

4.2. The Club will appoint a named officer to provide contact and liaison with the Sponsor during the Term for the purpose of giving full effect to this Agreement.

4.3. The Club will fulfil the additional obligations set out in Schedule 6.

5. Indemnities

5.1. The Club shall indemnify the Sponsor against all public liability in connection with any Event (other than that incurred personally by the Sponsor due to its own acts or omissions) and shall undertake to arrange and hold public liability insurance against all risks with an insurer of good standing in a sum of not less than £[...]. The Club undertakes to ensure that the interest on the Sponsor is noted on such policy and to provide a copy thereof forthwith upon request.

5.2. The Sponsor will indemnify the Club in respect of any losses, damage or liability the Club may incur as a result of the Sponsor's acts or omissions, whether deliberate, accidental, negligent or reckless, in the course of the performance or purported performance of the Sponsor's Obligations under this Agreement whether such acts or omissions amount to a breach of an express or implied obligation under this Agreement or a breach of any other legal requirement or obligation, code of practice, licence, consent, forbearance, approval, permission or rule.

5.3. For the avoidance of doubt losses, damage and liability shall include but not be limited to legal and other costs associated with legal proceedings of any kind which the Club has to bring or to which it has to respond, fines, penalties, damages and any financial consequence whatever flowing directly or indirectly from the matters set out in this Clause 5.

6. Cancellation of an Event

6.1. The Club undertakes to obtain insurance cover with an insurer of good standing in a sum of not less than £[...] against unforeseen cancellation of any Event or part thereof and to ensure that such cover includes indemnification in full for any liability the Club may have to the Sponsor in connection therewith. The Club undertakes to ensure that the interest of the Sponsor is noted on such policy and to provide a copy thereof forthwith upon request.

7. [Other Sponsors

7.1. The Club hereby agrees not to appoint or accept other sponsors who will advertise, sell or promote the Protected Products at any Event or in connection with the Activities. For the avoidance of doubt, it shall not be a breach of this obligation if the products or services of another sponsor are advertised, sold or promoted which sponsor is also associated with the Protected Products but which Protected Products are not themselves advertised, sold or promoted at an Event or in connection with the Activities by the other sponsor].

8. Termination

8.1. Either Party may terminate this Agreement upon giving [28] days written notice to the other in the event that the other Party is in material breach of any term or condition of this Agreement or, if it is remediable, within [28] days of being given written notice of such breach and it has failed to remedy it.

9. [Re-organisation of business structure or ownership of the Club

9.1. The Sponsor may terminate this Agreement if there is any material re-organisation of the Club's business structure unless:

9.1.1. such reorganisation is not the result of insolvency

9.1.2. the resultant company or organisation is bound by the provisions of this Agreement

9.1.3. the beneficial ownership of the resultant entity is not in the hands of competitors of the Sponsor [except to the extent that such ownership does not exceed [10%] of the total]].

10. Effects of termination

10.1. In the event that this Agreement is terminated by the Sponsor due to material breach by the Club:

10.1.1. the Sponsor will be released from all further Sponsor's Obligations

10.1.2. the Club shall repay to the Sponsor any sum or appropriate apportionment of any sum which may have been paid by the Sponsor for any part of the Term which postdates the termination

10.1.3. the Club shall return to the Sponsor any products provided by the Sponsor still in its possession, care or control

10.1.4. [the Club shall cease to use any Sponsored Kit forthwith].

10.2. The Club shall reimburse the Sponsor in full for any expenditure it has reasonably incurred in expectation that the Agreement would continue until the end of the Term (or the extended Term if the original Term has expired at the time of breach and the Sponsor had elected to extend the Agreement under the provisions of this Agreement) but subject to the provisions of this Clause 10 and after deduction by the Club of the reasonable costs and expenses properly incurred by it in the performance of its obligations arising under this Agreement up to the date of termination.

10.3. In the event that this Agreement is terminated by either Party such termination shall not affect any accrued rights or remedies one Party may have against the other at the time of termination.

11. Insolvency

11.1. Either Party may terminate this Agreement if the other Party:

11.1.1. is wound up due to insolvency

11.1.2. makes or seeks a composition with its creditors

11.1.3. enters into or seeks an insolvent voluntary arrangement

11.1.4. becomes the subject of the appointment of a manager, receiver or liquidator

11.1.5. is the subject of an administration order

11.1.6. has its assets charged or seized for the satisfaction of a debt

11.1.7. behaves in a way which is likely to bring the other party into disrepute including but not limited to conviction for an indictable criminal offence.

12. Limitation of liability and loss

12.1. The Club shall not be liable to the Sponsor for any loss or damage it suffers in an amount greater than:

12.1.1. the return of the total of the monetary value of the sponsorship it has received from the Sponsor

12.1.2. the cost of any physical damage to the Sponsor's property in connection with an Event.

12.2. Neither Party shall be liable to the other for any economic, consequential or other losses including loss of reputation, profit or goodwill whether resulting from misrepresentation, misdescription, breach of contract, breach of duty or other act or omission (unless fraudulent) however caused.

12.3. Nothing in this Agreement shall limit the right of either Party to seek to recover damages for personal injury or death occasioned by breach of contract or breach of duty by the other Party, its employees or agents.

13. Time of the essence

13.1. Time shall be of the essence in respect of the provision of any sums, products or services due from the Sponsor under the terms of this Agreement and of any obligations set out in Schedule 4 which require action by the Sponsor by a particular time or date or within a specific period prior to an Event or other happening or deadline.

14. Warranties

14.1. The Club warrants that it has the exclusive right to put on the Events and undertake the Activities in the name of the Club.

14.2. The Sponsor warrants that it has the IPR and all other necessary rights in the logo[s], marks, designs, products and services provided by it under this Agreement so as to ensure that the Club will not be liable for any infringement of any third party's rights in connection therewith.

14.3. [The Club warrants that it shall not appoint more than [...] sponsors *or* The Club warrants that it shall appoint no other [Platinum] sponsor *or* The Club warrants that it shall not appoint more than [...] [Gold *or* Silver *or* Bronze] sponsors].

15. Assignment

15.1. This Agreement is personal to the Parties and neither Party may assign the rights or benefits of this Agreement to a third party.

16. No agency

16.1. Neither Party is for any purpose the agent of the other as a result of anything arising from this Agreement and each Party hereby undertakes not to represent to any third party that it has any authority to act on that other Party's behalf.

17. Invalid clauses

17.1. In the event that any term of this Agreement is found to be invalid or otherwise unenforceable then such term shall be regarded and construed as severable from the Agreement so as not to affect the validity and enforceability of the remainder.

18. Whole agreement

18.1. This Agreement supersedes and replaces any previous agreement between the Parties whether oral or in writing in relation to sponsorship. The Parties hereby agree that in entering into this Agreement neither has relied upon any warranty or representation made by or on behalf of the other Party save where expressly stated in this Agreement. The Parties hereby agree that this Agreement constitutes the whole agreement between the Parties in respect of sponsorship. The Parties agree that no variation may be made to it unless such variation is in writing and signed by both Parties.

19. Further action

19.1. The Parties agree that they will expeditiously carry out such further acts as may be necessary for the purpose of this Agreement including the execution and delivery of such instruments, deeds, licences, notifications as may be reasonably required by the other Party or by law.

20. Third party rights

20.1. The Parties to this Agreement agree that it is not hereby intended that any rights should be conferred upon or enforceable by any third party as defined in the Contracts (Rights of Third Parties) Act 1999.

21. Law and jurisdiction

21.1. This Agreement is governed by the law of England and Wales and is subject to the [*exclusive*] jurisdiction of the courts of England and Wales.

22. Schedules

22.1. The Schedules form part of this Agreement including any subsequent amendments made thereto.

Signed, etc.

SCHEDULE 1

The Activities of the Club

[*Set out main Activities, etc.*]

Signed, etc.

SCHEDULE 2

The Events

[*List Events and Venues*]

Signed, etc.

SCHEDULE 3

The Sponsor's Benefits

[The Sponsor's benefits for each category of sponsorship are as follows:

Platinum Sponsorship

- 'A Year-round package' – including inclusion on the Club website with link to the Sponsor's website.
- A round of golf for 4 players including lunch at a Championship golf course (subject to date availability).
- Complementary advert and article in each issue of Club Magazine.
- Dedicated mail-shot to club members 4 times a year.
- Guaranteed sales meeting with 25 leading club members.
- Display of your marketing material at all Events.

- Company logo on all Club literature, Club Kit, and advertisement hoardings at all Events.
- 20 VIP packages to Club Player of the Year Ceremony and Dinner.
- 10 complementary hotel rooms in close proximity to the venue for the Club Player of the Year Ceremony and Dinner.
- Video feature on the Sponsor's company played at Club Player of the Year Awards Ceremony and Dinner.
- Complementary full-page advert in Club Player of the Year Souvenir Programme and post-event publication.
- Opportunity to join chairman of Club presenting Grand Finale Award.
- Recognition in all Club Player of the Year related public relations.

Gold Sponsorship

- Inclusion on Club Player of the Year website for 1 year.
- Sponsor's logo on all relevant Club literature.
- 10 VIP packages to Club Player of the Year Ceremony and Dinner.
- The opportunity to purchase at very attractive rates up to 5 hotel rooms in close proximity to the venue for the Club Player of the Year Ceremony and Dinner.
- Video feature on the Sponsor played at Club Player of the Year Awards Ceremony and Dinner.
- Complementary ½ page advert in Club Player of the Year Souvenir Programme and post-event publication.
- Opportunity to announce Category Competition Winners and present Prize at Club Player of the Year Awards Ceremony and Dinner.

Silver Sponsorship

- Inclusion of Sponsor's logo on Club Awards website from [date to date].
- 8 VIP packages to Club Player of the Year Awards Ceremony and Dinner.
- The opportunity to purchase at very attractive rates up to 4 hotel rooms in close proximity to the venue for the Club Player of the Year Ceremony and Dinner.
- Video feature on the Sponsor played at Club Player of the Year Awards Ceremony and Dinner.
- Complementary ¼ page advert in Club Player of the Year Souvenir Programme and post-event publication.

Bronze Sponsorship

- 4 VIP packages to Club Player of the Year Awards Ceremony and Dinner.
- Complementary advert in Club Player of the Year Souvenir Programme and post-event publication.
- PowerPoint show featuring your Company played during the Club Player of the Year Awards Ceremony and Dinner.]

SCHEDULE 4

The Sponsor's Obligations

Platinum Sponsorship

[*These will be negotiated and agreed between the Sponsor and the Club and set out below*].

Gold Sponsorship

1. [[Payment of a fee of £[...] by [*date*] *or* Payment of the fee in instalments as follows: [*insert dates*]]
2. Provision of logo/company marks in form suitable for reproduction by [*insert date*]
3. Appointment of liaison officer by [*insert date*]]

[Etc.]

Signed, etc.

SCHEDULE 5

Protected Products and Services

1. [*Footballs*]
2. [*Rugby balls.*]

Signed, etc.

SCHEDULE 6

The Club's Additional Obligations

1. [In respect of each Event:

1.1. the erection and/or maintenance of advertising hoardings of [*insert dimensions*] at the north and east end of the pitch boundary at each Venue suitable for posters to be provided by the Sponsor

1.2. a public announcement referring to the Sponsor to be of not less that [*insert minutes*] duration].

Signed, etc.

Index